CONTENTS

1

PAINTS AND FINISHES — 1

2

CARPETING — 11

3

FLOORS
29

4

WALLS
63

A

Manufacturers and Associations

B

Resources

Index

Foreword

Interior Design is a complex business, no matter how you approach it. It is complex because it concentrates on the health, safety, and welfare of the people that will be using the spaces created. It is complex because it balances both the "real" and the "abstract" elements of space. It is complex because it confronts simultaneously both the "functional" and the "aesthetic." It is complex because it concerns money, in some cases, a great amount of money. It is complex because it juggles a myriad of details from construction documents to client's eccentricities. And it is complex because it combines so many different possibilities in materials and finishes.

Unfortunately, too often designers fail to take full advantage of the many materials and finishes available. Why, you might ask? Probably because it is simply easier to rework what has been done before, or they have not taken the time to investigate newer and exciting possibilities. Their exposure is limited. This is a fact that needs to be changed and improved.

If one reviews the history books and researches the work of the leading masters of Interior Design, in almost every case, you notice that the success of these individuals rests in part on their innovative and exciting use of a new material or their adaptation of a known material in an intriguing new way. The examples are endless. For instance, Marcel Breuer used the tubular steel from the handlebars of his bicycle as inspiration to form the frame of his famous Wassily Chair. Likewise, Charles Eames observed the fiberglass nose cones of World War II fighter bombers and eventually designed his famous fiberglass chair using this new and innovative material. Yet another example is Eileen Grays' innovative use of perforated metal for the drawers and shelving of one of her ingenious cabinets. The list is endless, but there is no doubt that each had an acute, almost passionate, affinity for materials.

It stands to reason, therefore, that with Rosemary Riggs' book, *Materials and Components of Interior Design,* the design student or the seasoned professional is exposed to valued information regarding hundreds of materials and finishes, and thus will have an advantage over their colleagues. With the numerous charts, illustrations, and biographical information, not to mention the glossaries and indexes, boundless information is readily available for new-found knowledge or confirmation of previous convictions. By informing in a clear and concise manner, this volume takes the edge off of the unknown and thus allows the designer a new-found freedom to expand his or her design horizons and accept the challenge to go beyond what has been done before and to create new and innovative applications. Read it with pleasure and excitement and relish in the possibilities.

Charles D. Gandy, FASID

*Charles D. Gandy, FASID, is president of Gandy/Peace Inc., based in Atlanta, Georgia and was National President of ASID in 1988.

Preface

While teaching an introductory class in interior design, I noticed that the students usually chose paint or wallpaper for the walls and always used carpeting on the floor, as though these were the only suitable treatments for walls and floors. I felt a need to break the cycle by exposing students to the fascinating world of materials—and so this book started to take shape.

I was unable to find a book that fully covered the exciting non-structural materials available to the interior designer. Some authors concentrated on historical aspects of the home, both in architecture and furniture. Some emphasized upholstered furniture, draperies, and carpets, while still others stressed the principles and elements of design and color and the aesthetic values that make up a home. However, no one concentrated on the "nuts and bolts" of interior design. Some books purporting to cover all types of flooring did not even mention wood floors, while others had only one or two paragraphs on the subject. This third edition has a new chapter on carpeting. Although this subject was not covered in my particular class, I received many requests to include carpet and have done so from the contract designers' point of view.

In the past, the interior design profession has dealt mainly with the more decorative aspects of design. Today it has become increasingly necessary for interior designers to be knowledgeable not only about the finishing materials used in the design field, but some of the structural materials as well. Many interior designers are working for, or with, architects, so it is important that they understand the properties and uses of all materials. Thus the *raison d'etre* of this textbook.

Most sales representatives realize that the interior design student of today is the customer of tomorrow, but there are still some who do not understand the scope of the interior design field. Many interior designers are women and I have found that the ability to talk knowledgeably about materials earns the respect of a man in the profession more than any other.

The installation methods have been included because, unfortunately, there are some contractors (luckily only a few) who will use the cheapest method of installation, one which may not be the best for that particular job. Installation methods have been taken from information provided by manufacturers, associations, and institutions involved in producing that product. Knowledge of the correct installation procedures will ensure a properly installed project. The teachers manual has many stories of problems with products that have been improperly installed, all of which have actually occurred.

In doing my research and talking to many manufacturers, I have found a growing awareness of attention being paid to what are the customers needs and wishes. Dependability is one of the things consumers require. This is reflected in the many warranties provided by manufacturers, in one case, a lifetime structural guarantee on a wood floor.

All disciplines have their own jargon, and in order to communicate properly with contractors and architects, it is necessary to be able to understand their language. When designers or prospective builders have read and studied *Materials and Components of Interior Design*, they will be able to talk knowledgeably with architects and contractors about the uses of materials and their methods of installation. This understanding will also enable them to decide for themselves which materials and methods are best, without being unduly influenced by personal bias or ease of installation.

This book can also serve as a reference for designers who are already practicing, because it brings to their attention new materials on the market and improvements in current ones. The appendices are a useful reminder of manufacturers and their products. When products are unique to one manufacturer, their name and product have been mentioned. Wherever possible, generic information has been used. A contractor who read the book said that from his point of view, contractors would also benefit from using this book as a reference tool.

In arranging the subject matter, I placed the chapter on paint first, since all types of surfaces—floors, walls, and ceilings—may be painted. Then, starting from the bottom up, the logical progression was chapters on carpets (the most used covering for floors), other floor materials, walls, and ceilings. Chapter 6 covers all the other components that make up a well-designed room, including mouldings, doors, hardware, and hinges. With the assistance of the Architectural Woodwork Institute, Chapter 7 is an explanation of what goes into the structure and design of fine cabinetry. This chapter will enable designers to provide rough drawings of cabinetry that are as economical as possible to construct. Chapter 8 covers kitchens. With the background of the previous chapter, it enables a designer to make an intelligent selection. This chapter also covers the various appliances and the newest innovations in kitchen design. Chapter 9 covers bathrooms, both residential and institutional. The last two chapters were included because designers will be called on more and more to assist in the renovation of homes—including the very expensive areas of kitchens and bathroom. These remodeling jobs will probably cost about 10 to 15 percent of the house value. A full bath added to the older three bedroom, one bath house will not only

guarantee recouping the cost but even increase resale value.

A glossary of words boldfaced in the text is placed at the end of each chapter to make it easier to relate to other words from the same subject matter. Appendix A is a listing of manufacturers and associations who sell or represent the products mentioned in the chapters. Appendix B lists the names and addresses of the manufacturers named previously. Every effort has been made to make this list as up to date as possible but businesses do change names and locations.

If one manufacturer seems to be given more emphasis than another at times, it is not because that product is better than others on the market, but merely that they have been extremely helpful in providing information, brochures, checking sections for accuracies, and, most important, providing photographs with which to illustrate the various sections.

I am indebted to the many, many manufacturers and trade organization who have so willingly provided me with technical information and brochures from which I have been able to compile an up-to-date summary. I am deeply indebted to the Carpet and Rug Institute for granting permission to quote the material found in their extremely informative book *Carpet Specifier's Handbook*. This handbook has been the basis for much of the information contained in the carpet chapter. I particularly would like to thank R. Carroll Turner of the Carpet and Rug Institute who made the latest changes in this handbook available. I have found the trade organizations to be very helpful and particularly wish to thank Architectural Woodwork Institute for many drawings as well as information. Other trade organizations that have assisted me with preparation of the text were the Marble Institute of America, the Brick Institute of America, the Door and Hardware Institute, and the Hardwood Plywood Manufacturers Association.

In order to be as accurate and current as possible with the information contained in the text, I was assisted by many professionals. Four individuals deserve my special thanks: Max Smith, AIA; Lee Last, ASID who checked the new carpet chapter to make sure it contained the information that designers will require; and Robert Hanks of Bridgepoint Corporation, who realized that proper maintenance is vital to the durability of carpeting. Most of all, I wish to thank my husband, sculptor Frank Riggs, for his support and encouragement, and for many of the line drawings in the text. I am also grateful to him for not complaining about meals served at odd times during the writing of this book.

Introduction

For too many years, the fields of architecture and interior design have been treated as two separate areas involved in creating a pleasant living environment. The architect planned the exterior and interior of the home, often with little attention to where the furniture was to be placed. The interior designer had to contend with such things as walls which were not long enough to allow placement of furniture, or heating vents being placed directly under the bed or some other piece of furniture.

On the other hand, designers would ruin the architect's designs by using the incorrect style furniture, thereby spoiling the whole concept of the building.

Today, these problems are gradually being resolved with many architects having interior designers on their staffs. The result is that both disciplines cooperate from the very beginning of the project.

From the interior designer's point of view, this cooperation involved learning and appreciating the language and problems associated with architecture. The American Institute of Architects (AIA) is the professional organization for architects. The American Society of Interior Designers (ASID) and the Institute of Business Designers (IBD) are the professional organizations for interior designers. It is because of the professionalism of these organizations that the fields of architecture and interior design have gradually become aware of the necessity for closer cooperation.

This book is dedicated to fostering that cooperation.

List of Trademarks

Antron is a registered trademark of E. I. Du Pont de Nemours & Co. Inc.

Scotchgard is a registered trademark of the 3M Company

Teflon is a registered trademark of E. I. Du Pont de Nemours Co. Inc.

Weardated is a registered trademark of Monsanto Co.

Traffic Control is a trademark of Monsanto Co.

Pattern Plus is a registered trademark of Hartco

Permgrain, and Permetage are registered trademarks of Permagrain Products, Inc.

Timeless is a trademark of Permagrain Products, Inc.

Oakweld is a trademark of Tarkett, Hardwood Division, North America

Gammapar is a registered trademark of The Applied Radiant Energy Corp.

HARDIBACKER is a registered trademark of James Hardie Building Products Inc.

Durock is a registered trademark of Durabond Div. of USG Industries Inc.

UTIL-A-CRETE is a registered trademark of American Olean.

Wonderboard is a registered trademark of Glascrete

Triad is a trademark of American Olean

Armstar is a registered trademark of Armstone

Latapoxy is a registered trademark of Laticrete International Inc.

VISTABRIK is a registered trademark of Pittsburgh Corning Corp.

Clorox is a registered trademark of The Clorox Company

Ipocork is a registered trademark of Ipocork Inc.

Masonite is a registered trademark of Masonite Corp.

WILSONART and Perma-Kleen are registered trademarks of Ralph Wilson Plastics Co.

Thin line series PC Glassblock, Vue, Essex, Argus, and Hedron are registered trademarks of Pittsburgh Corning Corp.

Pearl Gray is a registered trademark of The Georgia Marble Company

SHEETROCK is a registered trademark of U.S. Gypsum Company.

Eternawall is a registered trademark of Georgia-Pacific.

Softforms is a registered trademark of Pittcon Industries

FRESCO is a trademark of Pittcon Industries

Anaglypta and Lincrusta are registered trademarks of Mile Hi Crown.

NEOCON is a registered trademark of National Exposition of Contract Interior Furnishings

WILLIAMSBURG is a trademark of The Colonial Williamsburg Foundation

Quantum is a trademark of MDC Wallcoverings

Koroseal is a registered trademark of The B. F. Goodrich Co.

Kydex is a registered trademark of Kleerdex Company, a Rohn & Haas Co.

Flexwood and Flexwood + Plus are registered trademarks of Flexwood

Craftwood is a trademark of Ralph Wilson Plastics

Velcro is a registered trademark of Velcro USA Inc.

Tedlar and Corian are registered trademarks of E. I. DuPont de Nemours & Co. Inc.

Prefixx is a trademark of DiversTech General, Wallcovering Division

Vicrtex is a registered trademark of Vicrtex Wallcoverings

Peg-Board is a registered trademark of The Masonite Corp.

SOLICOR, Perma-Kleen and Primeline are registered trademarks of Ralph Wilson Plastics Co.

FORMICA and COLOR CORE are reigstered trademarks of Formica Corporation

Fill 'n Glaze is a trademark of the 3M Company.

Scotch-Brite is a registered trademark of the 3M Company.

Restoration Glass is a trademark of Bendheim Corp.

Varalite and Duroplex are trademarks of Taliq

Kaleidostrips and Damask are trademarks of American Olean Company

Duraplex is a registered trademark of Triarch Industries.

Paleo is a trademark of Forms + Surfaces Inc, a division of Armstrong World Industries Inc.

VITRICOR is a registered trademark of Nevamar

Avonite is a registered trademark of Avonite Corp.

Classique is a trademark of Chicago Metallic Corp.

A-Look is a registered trademark of Mitsubishi Kasei America Inc.

Barrisol is a registered trademark of Barrisol North America Inc.

INTERSECTIONS, Integrated Ceilings, Pipe and Junction and Transparencies are trademarks of USG Interiors, Inc.

Dome It is a registered trademark of The Original Dome Ceiling Inc.

Focal Point is a registered trademark of Focal Point Inc.

Forms + Surfaces is a registered trademark of Forms + Surfaces Inc, a division of Armstrong World Industries Inc.

Key 'n Keyless is a trademark of Schlage

Monogram is a trademark of GE Company

Ultra and Digitraul are registered trademarks of Traulsen

Kohler Color Coordinates is trademark of Kohler Co.

Broan-Nautilus is a registered trademark of Broan, a Nortek Co.

Village is a registered trademark of Foremost Wallcoverings

Ceran is a registered trademark of Schotle Corp.

Excalibur is a registered trademark of Whitford Corp.

Expressions, Savorizer, Haloring, Quick-Start and PerimaVent are trademarks of Jenn-Air Corp.

Spacemaker plus is a trademark of GE Company

Black Black is a trademark of Kohler Co.

Sculptura is a registered trademark of Elkay

Arabesque, Cactus Cutter, Cygnet, Epicure, Finesse, Multi-Swivel, San Raphael and San Tropez are trademarks of the Kohler Co.

Riser is a registered trademark of Moen

Perma-Edge and Perma-Tiers are registered trademarks of Ralph Wilson Plastics

GIBRALTAR is a registered trademark of Ralph Wilson Plastics

Fountainhead is a registered trademark of Nevamar Corp.

Novastone is a registered trademark of Johnstone Industries

Surrell is a registered trademark of Formica Corp.

Jacuzzi is a registered trademark of Jacuzzi Whirlpool Bath Inc.

Chablis, Environment, Freewill, Garland, Habitat, Tapestries, Terragon and Wellesley are trademarks of Kohler Co.

Sensorflo is a trademark of Speakman Co.

Marblstal is a registered trademark of Georgia Marble Co.

Paints and Finishes

It is only since 1867 that prepared paints have been available on the American market. Originally, paint was used to decorate a home, as in the frescoes at Pompeii, and it is still used for that purpose today. However, modern technology has now made paint both a decorative and a protective finish.

The colors used are also of great psychological importance. A study made by Johns Hopkins University showed that planned color environments greatly improved scholastic achievement. Many major paint companies now have color consultants who can work with customers on selection of colors for schools, hospitals, and other commercial and industrial buildings. Today, paint is the most inexpensive method of changing the environment.

Paint is commonly defined as a substance that can be put on a surface to make a film, whether white, black, or colored. This definition has now been expanded to include clear films.

CLASSIFICATION OF PAINTS

Most paints are classified according to their **vehicles** or **binders**—in other words, whether the contents of the vehicle or liquid portion is water, oil, varnish, or dissolved synthetic **resins**.

Oil Paints

Oil-based paints consist of a pigment suspended in linseed oil, a drier, and mineral spirits or other types of thinners. Until the development of alkyds, oil paints were considered the traditional house paint. Today, however, most oil-based paints are alkyds. Because oil-based paints are less durable and have a strong odor, alkyds have now replaced oil-based paints.

Alkyds

Alkyds are oil-modified resins that dry faster and are much harder than ordinary oils. Drying results both from evaporation of the **solvent** and **oxidation** of the oil. The more oil there is in the formula, the longer it takes to dry, the better the wetting properties, and the better the elasticity. Alkyds dry quickly and evenly, are durable for both interior and exterior applications, are easy to apply, and are moderately priced. However, alkyd-based exterior paints, when compared to latex exterior paints, do show poorer gloss and color rentention and tend to yellow over time.

Freshly made alkaline surfaces such as concrete, masonry, or plaster must be treated with an alkali-resistant primer before an alkyd is applied. Fumes of some alkyd paints are odorless but are toxic and flammable until the surface has dried. Therefore, the area should be very thoroughly ventilated. Alkyd paint is the most durable of the common finishing products. In some areas of the country, the amount of *volatile organic compounds* (VOC), expressed in pounds of VOC per gallon, is restricted. Solvent-containing coatings can be used safely if overexposure is avoided and proper protective equipment is used. The disposal of all types of coating materials is controlled by government regulations.

To comply with the VOC emissions, more soilds are being added which makes the paint heavier bodied and, therefore, they take longer to dry.

Latex Emulsion

Latex binders are synthetic materials that may vary in hardness, **flexibility, gloss** retention. There are several types of latex binders including styrene butadiene, poly-vinyl acetate, acrylics and vinyl acetate-acrylics with the pure acrylics being the preferable choice. Drying results from **coalescence** of latex particles as the water evaporates from the film. Advantages of latex paint over oils or alkyds include the ease of application, freedom from solvent odor, fast drying and recoating, minimal fire hazard, blister and peel resistance, and ease of cleanup (requires soap and water only). In exterior applications, latex paints are durable, chalk resistant, and have good color and gloss retention.

Latex exterior paint films tend to "breathe" allowing moisture, which accumulates behind the paint film, to escape without causing blistering and peeling. The main disadvantage is that they must be protected from freezing and applied at above-freezing temperatures—usually 50°F is recommended. Because of ease of application, the temptation may be to make the paint go further, thus, coverage may not be as heavy as needed for a good job.

There are several finishes or **lusters** available in both alkyds and latex:

Flat. Velvety, with a rich, soft-looking surface for walls requiring little washing.
Eggshell or Satin. Slightly higher light reflectance for walls in residential areas where finger marks need removing.
Flat or Eggshell enamel. Dull luster for washable surfaces.
Semi-gloss. Just enough sheen for contrast with flat-finished surfaces. Used in kitchens, bathrooms, nurseries, and school rooms in order to give greater resistance to wear and washing.

Gloss or High Gloss Enamel. Very shiny surface giving easy washability. However, the higher the gloss, the more likely it is to show surface discrepancies. This is true with both walls and woodwork, and demonstrates the importance of proper surface preparation.

The classification of paints according to gloss ratings depends on the ability of the surface to bounce back varying amounts of light beamed on it, and these readings show the relative reflectability of the coated surface as compared with a smooth flat mirror (see Table 1–1). The ratings in Table 1–1 measure the light reflectance of the surface only. Table 1–2 shows the percentage of light reflected by different hues and their different values.

Table 1-1
Standard gloss range for architectural and special coatings

Name	Gloss Range	Test Method (ASTM D-523)
Flat	Below 15	85° meter*
Eggshell	5–20	60° meter
Satin	15–35	60° meter
Semigloss	30–65	60° meter
Gloss	Over 65	60° meter

Source. Consumerism Subcommittee of the N.P.C.A. Scientific Committee acting with the Subcommittee D01.13 of the American Society for Testing and Materials (ASTM).

* Angle at which light is reflected.

Table 1-2
Percentage of light reflected by colors

Color	Percentage of Light Reflected
White	89%
Ivory	77
Canary yellow	77
Cream	77
Orchid	67
Cream gray	66
Sky blue	65
Buff	63
Pale green	59
Shell pink	55
Olive tan	43
Forest green	22
Coconut brown	16
Black	2

Enamels

Enamels are pigmented paints that produce a hard, glossy, durable surface. In the standard architectural coatings, the highest sheen is produced by an alkyd enamel, but many lacquers and urethanes can achieve higher sheens. Enamels come in semi-gloss and gloss, but a flat appearance can be produced by adding a **flatting** agent, though this addition can affect some performance properties.

Enamels and other paints should be applied to a properly prepared surface. A glossy surface will not have **tooth** and should be sanded with sandpaper or a liquid sanding material before application of another coat of paint.

Due to the VOC laws, latex enamels have been greatly improved and one advantage is that latex enamels do not yellow.

Pigments

Pigments confer the following properties: color, **hiding power** or opacity, protection and corrosion repression on iron and steel. Pigments are the minute solid coloring parts of paints, and different pigments have different purposes. **Titanium dioxide** is the best white pigment for hiding power. Other pigments, whether organic or inorganic, merely add color to the paint. The third type, such as **calcium carbonate** is inert, acts mainly as a filler, and is used in masonry paints.

Stains

Stains are pigments applied to bare or sealed wood and may be transparent or opaque, depending upon requirements. Medium to light hues enhance the wood surface. There are several different types of stains. Probably the most common for interior use is the oil-base type where the oil penetrates to a measurable depth, thereby giving a more durable colored base. The oil-based stains should be covered with a urethane varnish on doors and window sills in order to provide a protective, durable surface for the wood. Due to the higher cost of urethane varnish, other wood surfaces not subject to heavy traffic or abuse may be coated with an oil or alkyd varnish.

Water-based stains have a water vehicle and have a tendency to penetrate the surface rapidly but not always evenly. Because water raises the grain of the wood, sanding is necessary, whereas it is not needed with oil-base stains. Alcohol stains have an alcohol base, and dry extremely quickly due to the rapid evaporation of the solvent. They are mainly used under lacquer and are applied by spraying.

Non-grain raising (NGR) stains are more of a surface type of stain, rather than a penetrating one, but do not require sanding before application of the final coat. Both alcohol stains and NGR's are used industrially due to ease of application and fast drying qualities.

Varnish stains are pigmented and give a very superficial-colored protective surface to the wood. These are used when a cheap, fast finish is desired, but they never have the depth of color obtained with other stains. When the surface of a varnish stain is scratched, the natural wood color may show through.

Stain waxes do the staining and waxing in one process, penetrating the pores of the wood and allowing the natural grain to show, while providing the protective finish of a wax. Real wood paneling may be finished with a stain wax provided the surface of the wood will not be soiled.

Danish oil finish is used on wood; there are two types-clear and stain. The clear gives a natural finish while the stained contains a wood stain to achieve the stained effect. Danish oil finish has as its main components tung oil and boiled linseed oil, and gives the wood a rich, penetrating oil surface, while sealing the pores.

Primer

A primer is the first coat applied to the **substrate** to prepare for subsequent finishing coats and may have an oil, alkyd, or latex base. Some primers also serve as sealers and function on porous substrates such as some woods, but more especially on the paper used on **gypsum wallboard**. These non-penetrating sealers prevent the waste of paint caused by absorption of the porous materials and provide a good base for the final coats. Other primers are specially formulated for use on wood surfaces where the natural dyes might cause unsightly stains. Some finish coats are self-priming, while others require a separate primer. The manufacturers' specifications will give this information.

Varnish

Varnish is a transparent or pigmentless film applied to stained or unstained wood. Varnish dries and hardens by evaporation of the volatile solvents, oxidation of the oil, or both.

Where a hard, glossy finish that is impervious to moisture is desired, spar varnish is recommended for both outdoor and indoor use. In areas where moisture is not present, an alkyd varnish provides a slightly longer-lasting finish. Polyurethane is a synthetic resin used to make varnish resistant to water and alcohol, thus making it usable as a finish on wood floors and tabletops. This type of varnish does not yellow or change color as much as conventional varnishes. The moisture-cured urethane varnishes are more durable but are also more expensive. **Humidity** must be rigidly controlled because less than 30 percent humidity will cause too slow a curing time and too high humidity will cause too fast a curing time, resulting in a bubbly surface.

Where a satin finish is desired, the gloss varnish surface may be rubbd down with steel wool, or a "satin" varnish may be used. Names of finishes do not seem to vary as much in opaque paints as they do in varnishes. One manufacturer will label varnish "dull" and another will call it "flat." Semi-gloss may also be called "satin" or "medium-rubbed effect," and high gloss may simply be called "gloss." It should be remembered that the paired names are synonymous.

Shellac

Shellac is a resinous substance secreted by the lac bug and dissolved in alcohol. It is available in clear, orange, and pigmented white. Shellac was the original glossy, transparent surface finish for furniture and is the finish on most antiques. The urethane and oil varnishes have replaced shellac because they are not as quickly affected by heat and water. On a piece of furniture, shellac will turn white when exposed to water and/or heat. Shellac is an inexpensive finish. Old shellac should never be used, as the surface will not dry thoroughly. If there is any doubt about the age of a particular shellac, it should be tested before it is used on a project. If the surface remains tacky, the shellac should be thrown away as it will never harden.

Lacquer

Lacquer is a paint that dries by solvent evaporation only and is applied by a spray gun. Lacquer may or may not contain pigments and is used commercially in the finishing of wood furniture and cabinets. A fine built-up finish may be achieved by many coats of lacquer, each of which is finely sanded before the subsequent coats.

Flame-retardant Paints

Flame-retardant paints differ from conventional paints in that they are able to slow down the rate of combustion. Some of these fire-retardant paints are *intumescent*, which means that they form blisters and bubbles—thus forming an insulating layer—while others give off a gas that excludes air from the surface, thereby extinguishing the flames.

Flame-retardant paints are specified for public buildings, especially offices and hotels. After the tragic hotel fires of the early 1980s, it may become necessary to seriously consider these paints which, while not fireproof, do reduce the flammability of the substrate.

For many commercial painting contracts, a Class A fire rating is required by law, which means a **0–25 flame spread**. Included in some technical data are the amounts of smoke developed and fuel contributed. As more people die in fires due to smoke inhalation, perhaps the smoke development figure is more important than the flame spread figure. All major paint companies have flame-retardant paints and these manufacturers should be contacted for more specific information.

There is a great deal of misunderstanding about flame ratings and flame-retardant paints. The flame ratings are based on paints applied to a wood surface (fir) or a non-combustible surface (cement-asbestos board). A paint applied to a cement-asbestos board will have a lower flame rating than the same one applied in the same manner to the wood surface because of the difference in combustibility of the substrate materials.

Solvents

Solvents, when used in paints, are liquids that dissolve the resins or **gums** or other binder constituents. These liquids are mineral spirits in the case of alkyds and oil paints, water for latex emulsions, alcohol for shellac, and lacquer thinner for lacquers. These solvents are used as thinners and to clean the products in which they are used. Turpentine was used as a solvent before mineral spirits came on the market, but is not used so much today due to toxicity, high cost, and strong odor.

APPLICATION METHODS

There are four methods of applying paints—brush, roller, pad, and spray, either airless or conventional.

The pad and roller are do-it-yourself tools, although the roller may be used in remodeling where removal of furniture is impossible. The best available equipment should be used, as poor quality tools will result in a poor quality paint job.

Regardless of the material used for the bristles (hog hair or synthetic), brushes should have **flagged bristles** (which help load the brush with more paint) while assisting the paint to flow more smoothly. Cheap brushes have little or no flagging, which causes the paint to flow unevenly. Brushes are used for woodwork and for uneven surfaces, while rollers are used for walls and flat areas. Spray guns are used to cover large areas, especially in commercial interiors. Airless spraying uses fluid pressure and conventional spraying uses air pressure. Most airless spraying uses undiluted paint, thus providing better coverage but also using more paint. The operation of a conventional spray gun requires a solvent-reduced paint.

All surrounding areas must be covered or masked off to avoid overspray, and this masking time is always included in the painting contractor's estimates.

Spraying is eight to ten times faster than other methods of application. These figures refer to flat walls, but spraying is an easier and more economical method of coating uneven or irregular surfaces than brushing, since it enables the paint to penetrate into the crevices. When spraying walls, the use of a roller immediately after spraying does even out the coat of paint.

Spraying is also the method used for finishing furniture and kitchen cabinets. For a clear finish on furniture and cabinets, a heated lacquer is used, which dries quickly, cures to a very hard film with heat, and produces fewer toxic emissions. Heated lacquer is formulated to be used without **reduction**, thus giving a better finished surface. The **faux** finishes are obtained by using paints, but applying them by different methods other than those described previously—including stippling with a sponge, swirling which imitates marble, and other methods that will achieve the desired effect. Some even add sand to the paint to give a stucco finish.

SURFACE PREPARATION

Mildew is a major cause of paint failure. It is not produced by the paint itself, but is a fungus whose spores will thrive in any damp, warm place—exterior or interior. There are several mildew cleaning solutions available, the simplest of which is bleach and water. Other remedies have additional ingredients and may be purchased premixed, but caution should be used with these products as they are extremely irritating to the eyes and skin. Instructions should be read and followed very carefully.

Wood

Moisture is the major problem when painting wood. Five to 10 percent moisture content is the proper range. Today, most wood is **kiln-dried**, but exposure to high humidity may change that moisture content. While knots in the wood are not technically a moisture problem, they also cause difficulties when the surface is to be painted, as the resin in the knots may bleed through the surface of the paint; therefore, a special knot sealer or shellac must be used. The shellac should be sanded to give tooth and to prevent a shiny surface from showing when covered by a flat paint.

All cracks and nail holes must be filled with a suitable wood putty or filler. This may be applied before or after priming according to instructions on the can or in the paint guides. Some woods with open pores require the use of a paste wood filler (see Table 1–3). If a natural or painted finish is desired, the filler is diluted with a thinner; if the surface is to be stained the filler is diluted with the stain.

If coarse sanding is required, it may be done at an angle to the grain; medium or fine sanding grits should always be used with the grain. Awkward places should never be sanded across the grain because the sanding marks will show up when the surface is stained.

Plaster

When preparing a plaster wall for painting, it is necessary to be sure that the plaster is solid, has no cracks, and is smooth and level, as paint will only emphasize any problems. Badly cracked or loose plaster should be removed. If there are any large holes, a piece of wire mesh, expanded metal or heavy hardware cloth is used as a backing for the patching plaster. The edges of the hole should be dampened to give better adherence for the patching plaster. Small cracks should be enlarged to about 1/8 of an inch wide in a V-shaped manner. Again, the edges are moistened to provide a good bond with the patching compound. All cracks, even if hairline, must be repaired, as they will only enlarge with time. To achieve a smooth and level wall, the surface must be sanded with a fine sandpaper and, before the paint

Table 1-3
Wood classification according to openness of pores

Name	Soft	Hard	Open Pore	Closed Pore	Notes
Ash		X	X		Needs filler
Alder	X			X	Stains well
Aspen		X		X	Paints well
Basswood		X		X	Paints well
Beech		X		X	Varnishes well, paints poorly
Birch		X		X	Paints and varnishes well
Cedar	X			X	Paints and varnishes well
Cherry		X		X	Varnishes well
Chestnut		X	X		Requires filler, paints poorly
Cottonwood		X		X	Paints well
Cypress		X		X	Paints and varnishes well
Elm		X	X		Requires filler, paints poorly
Fir	X			X	Paints poorly
Gum		X		X	Varnishes well
Hemlock	X			X	Paints fairly well
Hickory		X	X		Needs filler
Mahogany		X	X		Needs filler
Maple		X		X	Varnishes well
Oak		X	X		Needs filler
Pine	X			X	Variable
Redwood	X			X	Paints well
Teak		X	X		Needs filler
Walnut		X	X		Needs filler

Source. Abel Banov, *Paintings & Coatings Handbook.* Torstar Corporation, 1973, p. 127.

is applied, the fine dust must be brushed from the wall surface. Plaster is extremely porous, so a primer-sealer is required, which may be latex, alkyd, or oil-based.

Gypsum Wallboard

On gypsum board, all seams must be taped and nail or screw holes filled with spackling compound or joint cement; these filled areas should then be sanded. Care should be taken not to sand the paper areas too much as this causes a slight roughness that may still be visible after the final coat has dried, particularly if the final coat has any gloss. Gypsum board may also have a texture applied, as described in Chapter 4, page 72, and the luster selected will be governed by the type of texture.

Gypsum board must also be brushed clean of all fine dust particles before the primer is applied.

Metals

Metals must have all loose rust, **mill scale**, and loose paint removed before a primer is applied. There are many methods of accomplishing this removal. One of the most common and most effective is sandblasting, where fine silica particles are blown under pressure onto the surface of the metal. Small areas may be sanded by hand. The primer should be rust-inhibitive and specially formulated for that specific metal.

Masonry

Masonry usually has a porous surface and will not give a smooth top coat unless a block filler is used. The product analysis of the block filler shows a much larger percentage of calcium carbonate than titanium dioxide. (Notice in Table 1–6, the small area covered by one gallon of paint due to the heavy calcium carbonate content acting as a filler). One problem encountered with a masonry surface is *efflorescence*, which is a white powdery substance caused by an alkaline chemical reaction with water. An alkaline resistant primer is necessary if this condition is present. However, the efflorescence must be removed before the primer is applied.

WRITING PAINTING SPECIFICATIONS

The specifier should learn how to read the technical part of the product guide, or find the same information on the label of the can. Some manufacturers state in the product description that it is a short-, medium-, or long-oil coating. A long-oil paint has a longer drying period and is usually more expensive. One of the properties of a long-oil product is that it coats the surface better than a short-oil product because of its wetting ability. The volume of solids is expressed as a percentage per gallon of paint. This percentage can vary from the 40s to the high teens. If, for the sake of comparison, a uniform thickness of 1 1/2 **mils** is used, the higher percentage volume paint would cover 453 square feet and the lower percentage only 199 square feet. This, of course, means that more than twice as much paint of the lower volume would have to be purchased when compared to the higher volume. Thus, the paint that seems to be a bargain may turn out to cost more in order to achieve the same result.

Painting specifications are a way of legally covering both parties in the contract between the client and the painting contractor. There will be no misunderstanding of responsibility if the scope of the paint job is clearly spelled out, and most major paint companies include in their catalogues sample painting specifications covering terms of the contract. Some of these are more detailed than others. Table 1–4, Coverage According to Method of Application, and Table 1–5, Average Coat Requirements for Interior Surfaces, will aid the designer in calculating the approximate time required to complete the painting contract.

A time limit and a penalty clause should be written into the contract. This time requirement is most important, as painting is the first finishing step in a project and, if it is delayed, the final completion date is in jeopardy. The penalty clause provides for a deduction of a specific amount or percentage for every day the contract is over the time limit.

Information on surface preparation may be obtained from the individual paint companies. The problems created by incorrect surface treatment, priming, and finishing are never corrected by simply applying another coat of paint.

High-performance paints should be selected if budget restrictions permit, as high-performance paints last several times longer than regular paints. This longer durability means business or commercial operations will not have to be shut down as frequently. So the increase in cost will more than offset the loss of business. The words "high performance" should be included in the product description.

Method of application should be specified: brush, roller, or spray. The specifier must be sure that the method suits the material to be covered and the type of paint to be used. Also, primers or base coats must be compatible both with the surface to be covered and the final or top coat. When writing painting specifications, items to be excluded, are just as important as items to be included. If other contractors are present at the site, their work and materials must be protected from damage. One area should be designated as a storage for all paint and equipment, and this area should have a temperature at or near 70°F, the ideal temperature for application of paints. All combustible material should be removed from the premises by the painting subcontractor.

The specifier should make certain that inspections are made prior to the application of each coat, as these inspections will more properly cover both client and contractor. If some revisions or corrections are to be made, they should also be put in writing and an inspection should be made before proceeding.

Cleanup is the responsibility of the painting contractor. This means that all windows and glass areas will be free of paint streaks or spatters. The area should be left ready for the succeeding contractor to begin work without any further cleaning.

Some states do not permit interior designers to sign the contract on behalf of clients, while other states do allow this. The specifier will have to check state laws to see whether he/she or the client must be the contractual party.

How to Use the Manufacturer's Painting Specification Information. All paint companies have slightly different methods of laying out their descriptive literature, but a designer with the background material of this chapter will soon be able to find the information needed.

First, the material to be covered is listed, then the use of that material, and then the finish desired. Let us use wood as an example: The material is wood, but is it going to be used for exterior or interior work? If interior, is it to be used on walls, ceilings, or floors? Each different use will require a product suitable for that purpose. Floors will obviously need a more durable finish than walls or ceilings.

Another category will be the final finish—flat,

Table 1-4
Coverage according to method of application

Method	Coverage per Hour
Brush	50–200 sq. ft.
Roller	100–300 sq. ft.
Spray	300–500 sq. ft.

Table 1-5
Average coat requirements for interior surfaces

Surface	Vehicle	Number of Coats
Woodwork	Oil gloss paint	2–3 coats
	Semigloss paint	2–3 coats
Plaster	Alkyd flat	2–3 coats
Drywall	Alkyd flat	2–3 coats
	Vinyl latex	3 coats
Masonry	Vinyl latex	3 coats
Wood floor	Enamel	3 coats

semigloss, or gloss? Will you need an alkyd, a latex, or, for floor use, a urethane? This is sometimes classified as the vehicle or generic type. The schedule then tells you which primer or sealer is to be used in order to be compatible with the final coat. After the primer, the first coat is applied. This may also be used for the final coat or another product may be suggested. Drying time for the different methods of application may also be found in these catalogues. Two different times will be mentioned, one "dust-free," or "tack-free," meaning the length of time it takes before dust will not adhere to the freshly painted surface. In some cases, a quick drying paint will have to be specified, due to possible contaminants in the air. "Recoat" time may also be mentioned; this is important so that the application of the following coat can be scheduled.

The calculated spreading rate per gallon will enable a specifier to calculate approximately how many gallons are needed for the job, thus enabling him/her to estimate material costs. Sometimes, in the more technical specifications, an analysis of the contents of the paint is included both by weight and by volume (see page 6). However, the most important percentage is the volume amount because weight of solids can be manipulated while volume cannot. This is the only way to compare one paint with another. It is the type and percentage of these ingredients that makes paints differ in durability, application, and coverage.

If paint is to be sprayed, there will be information on lowering the **viscosity** and, for other methods of application, the maximum reduction permitted without spoiling the paint job. Most catalogues also include a recommended thickness of film when dry which is expressed as so many mils **DFT**. This film may be checked with specially made gauges. The DFT cannot be specified by the number of coats. The film thickness of the total paint system is the important fact and not the film thickness per coat.

Table 1–6 is an example of information that may be found in three major paint catalogues. It is not a comparison chart as printed, but could be utilized as such if similar products were used.

PROBLEMS WITH PAINT AND VARNISH AND HOW TO SOLVE THEM

Temperature should ideally be around 70°F, but it can vary from 50°F up. Cold affects viscosity, causing slower evaporation of the solvents, which results in sags and runs. High temperature lowers viscosity, also causing runs and sags. High humidity may cause less evaporation of the solvent, giving lower gloss and allowing dirt and dust to settle and adhere to the film. Ventilation must be provided when paints are being applied, but strong drafts will affect the uniformity of luster.

Today, most paint starts out with a base and the pigments are added according to charts provided to the store by the manufacturer. Sometimes it may be necessary to change the mixed paint in hue and this can be done by the judicious addition of certain pigments. Therefore, it is vital that the designer be aware of the changes made by these additions.

BIBLIOGRAPHY

Painting and Coating Systems for Specifiers and Applicators. Cleveland, Sherwin Williams, 1989

Banov, Abel. Paintings and Coatings Handbook. Farmington, MI Torstar Corporation, 1973

"50,000 Years of Protection and Decoration," History of Paint and Color. Pittsburg, PA: Pittsburg Plate Glass Company.

Glidden Specification Guide. Section 09900 Painting. Cleveland, OH: Architectural Services Departments, Glidden Coatings & Resins.

Innes, Jacosta. Painting Magic. New York: Pantheon, 1986

Morgans, W.M. Outlines of Paint Tecnology. Vol I- Materials. London & High Wycombe. 2nd ed. Charles Griffin & Co. Ltd. 1982

"Paints and Coatings, A guide for Professional Performance. S.San Francisco, CA: Fuller O'Brien, 1975

Product and Painting Guide. Pittsburg, PA: Pittsburg Paints, 1981.

Rose, A.R. "With Paint . . . It's the Dry film That Counts." Decorative Products World, November 1981, pp. 58–59 New York: Time-Life Books, 1976

GLOSSARY

Binder. That part of a paint which holds the pigment particles together, forms a film, and imparts certain properties to the paint. It is part of solids and is also known as vehicle solids.

Calcium carbonate. An extender pigment.

Table 1-6

Paint specifications

Material	Surface	Vehicle or Type	Luster or Finish	Primer	Final Coat	Type of Application	Dust Free Touch	Recoat	Thinner or Solvent	Coverage Sq. Ft. Per Gal / Dry Mils	Solids by Volume	Company
Concrete Block	Walls	Latex	Flat	1 coat Prohide Plus Block Filler		Airless spray	½ hr.	2 hrs.	Water	50 sq. ft. per gal. 11 mils.	36%	Pratt & Lambert
		Vinyl acrylic latex	Satin		2 coats ProHide Plus Latex Satin Enamel	Airless spray	1 hr.	4 hrs.	Water	500 sq. ft. per gal. 1.5 mils.	39%	Pratt & Lambert
Drywall	Walls or ceilings	Latex	Flat	1 coat Supreme E-Z Kare Latex Primer/Sealer		Airless spray	1 hr	24 hrs.	Water	400 sq. ft. per gal.	38.16%	TruTest paints
		Alkyd	Semi-gloss		1 coat Supreme Low Fog airless spray	Airless spray	10–30 mins.	2–4 hrs.	Mineral spirits	400 sq. ft. per gal.	38.16%	TruTest paints
Wood	Trim	Alkyd		1 coat ProMar 200 alkyd enamel undercoater		Airless spray	1–2 hrs.	16–24 hrs.	Mineral spirits	320 sq. ft. per gal. 2 mils	47.36%	Sherwin Williams
		Alkyd	Semi-gloss		2 coats ProMar 200 alkyd semi-gloss enamel	Airless spray	2–4 hrs.	24 hrs.	Mineral spirits	400 sq. ft. per gal. 1.7 mils	43%	Sherwin Williams

Chalk resistance. A paint with a binder that resists decomposition caused by weathering. The pigment is loose or powdery on the surface.

Coalescence. The merging into a single mass.

DFT. Dry film thickness. The mil thickness when coating has dried.

Faux. French for fake or false. These include marbling or other imitation finishes.

Flagged bristles. Split ends.

Flatting. Lowering of the gloss.

Flexibility. Ability of paint film to withstand dimensional changes.

Gloss. Luster. The ability of a surface to reflect light. Measured by determining the percentage of light reflected from a surface at certain angles (see Table 1–1).

Gum. A solid resinous material that can be dissolved and that will form a film when the solution is spread on a surface and the solvent is allowed to evaporate. Usually a yellow, amber,or clear solid.

Gypsum wallboard. Thin slabs of plaster covered with a heavyweight paper covering.

Hiding power. The ability of paint film to obscure the substrate to which it is applied. Measured by determining the minimum thickness at which film will completely obscure a black and white pattern.

Humidity. The amount of water vapor in the atmosphere.

Kiln dried. Controlled drying in an oven to a specific moisture content.

Luster. Same as gloss.

Mill scale. An almost invisible surface scale of oxide formed when iron is heated.

Mils. Measurement of thickness of film. One one-thousandth of an inch. One mil equals 25.4 microns (micrometers).

Oxidation. Chemical combination of oxygen and the vehicle of a paint that leads to drying.

Reduction. Lowering the viscosity of a paint by the addition of solvent or thinner.

Resins. A solid or semisolid material that deposits a film and is the actual film-forming ingredient in paint. May be natural of synthetic. See Gum.

Solvent. A liquid that will dissolve something, commonly resins or gums or other binder constituents and evaporates in drying. Commonly an organic liquid.

Substrate. The piece or object that is to be painted.

Titanium dioxide. A white pigment providing the greatest hiding power of all white pigments. Nontoxic and nonreactive.

Tooth. The slight texture of a surface that provides good adhesion for subsequent coats of paint.

Vehicle. All of a paint except the pigment; the liquid portion of a paint.

Viscosity. The resistance to flow in a liquid. The fluidity of a liquid, i.e., water has a low viscosity and molasses a very high viscosity.

Wick. To bleed the color.

0–25 flame spread. Lowest acceptable rating for commercial and public buildings.

2

Carpeting

HISTORY OF CARPETING

The origins of carpet weaving have been lost in antiquity. The first wool carpet may have been crudely handwoven in Ninevah or Babylon around 5,000 B.C. An Egyptian fresco, depicting workers at a loom, provides concrete evidence of skillful weaving as far back as 3,000 B.C. The most ancient records, including the Bible, mention the use of carpets. Nomadic tribes of central Asia were known to have woven hand-knotted rugs—not only to cover the cold ground in their tents, but for saddle blankets and tent flaps as well. As treasures were brought back from Eastern conquests by the Greeks and Romans, Persian rugs were among the most sought after and valued possessions. Exactly when hand-knotted Oriental rugs were first woven is uncertain. Marco Polo, however, brought the news of their incredible beauty with him on his return to Italy from the Orient in 1295. The Saracens had been weaving carpets in France as early as the 8th century. No royal support was given until Henry IV set up a workroom for weaving in the Louvre in 1604. Royal support not only meant the development of carpets that reflected courtly taste,

but also ensured the protection and growth of the industry. Often credited with the "invention" of the weaving industry is Englishman Thomas Whitty of Axminster who developed the first machine loom that could weave carpets. The resulting product: Axminster carpets.

In Colonial America, the first floor coverings were herbs, rushes, or sand spread on the floor. Later, rag rugs made from clothing scraps, and hooked or braided mats were used. Affluent settlers, however, introduced America to prized Oriental rugs which they brought with them to the New World. Oriental rugs may have as many as 500–600 knots per square inch. It is interesting to note that while Europeans buy old Oriental rugs, Americans prefer to buy new ones.

The first U.S. carpet mill was started in Philadelphia in 1791. America's most important historic contribution to the industry was the invention of the power loom by Erastus Bigelow in 1839. Years later, the first Brussels-type carpet was made here, utilizing **Jacquard** method of color pattern control, and with further modification the first **Wilton** carpets were also woven in the United States. By the later 19th century, much machinery and skilled labor found its way to our shores, and the roots of many of today's major carpet manufacturing firms were firmly established. For centuries, a hand-made wool rug has been a status symbol. The high price of a wool rug or carpet was probably due to the tremendous labor involved; an ancient weaver needed 900 days to complete an Oriental carpet! [1]

As can be seen from the historical background, carpets were originally for the wealthy. Today, carpeting, due to modern technology, is one product that gives more value for the money than in the past.

This chapter will deal with *carpet,* defined as fabric used as a floor covering, rather than rugs (carpet cut unto room or area dimensions and loose laid). Area rugs include; Oriental rugs, **Rya** rugs, **dhurries**, American Indian rugs, etc. Much of the information on weaves, pile, etc. may also apply to area rugs.

Area rugs are gaining in popularity due to the mobility of our population. Rugs can be used in many ways: as accents over existing carpet, to highlight a wood floor, or to spotlight area groupings.

✱ FUNCTIONS OF CARPETING

- **Quiet.** Carpet absorbs ten times more airborne noise than any other flooring material and as much as most other types of standard acoustical materials.

- **Beauty.** Carpet provides a tremendous choice of colors, textures, and designs to suit every taste. Custom-designed carpet for commercial installation is also available at reasonable prices. Carpet has a way of framing the furnishings in a room or office which makes them look more important and distinctive.

- **Atmosphere.** Carpet dramatically enhances the feeling of quality in interior design—a major consideration in hotels and motels, for example.

- **Warmth.** Physically, the pile construction of carpet is a highly efficient thermal insulator. Mechanical demonstrations have shown that over a cold cement slab, carpet's surface temperature is substantially higher than that of hard surface tile. Thus, carpet relieves coldness at foot and ankle levels and lends a psychological warmth as well.

- **Safety.** The National Safety Council reports that falls cause most indoor accidents. Carpet is a soft surface in case of a fall.

- **Comfort.** Carpet reduces "floor fatigue." This characteristic is important to salespeople, teachers, nurses, waiters—all those who spend many hours on their feet during the course of their work.

The three Cs—Color, Comfort, and Cost—are probably the major factors in residential choice, whereas in commercial and institutional projects, durability, traffic, cost, and ease of maintenance are more important features.

The properties considered in the selection of carpeting include type of fiber, density of pile, depth of pile, the method of construction, and cleanability.

FIBERS

The fiber selected is the major decision. Each fiber has its own characteristic and modern technology has greatly improved the features of synthetic fibers. The cost and characteristics of the fiber need to be considered together so that the final selection will fulfill the client's need.

The main natural fiber used in carpeting is wool, but in some rare instances silk, linen, and cotton may be used. Man-made fibers are always more colorfast than natural fibers as the dye can be introduced while the fiber is in its liquid state in order to produce colored fibers. Wool, in its natural state, is limited to off white and black/grays and various shades in between.

Carpet manufacturers do not produce the actual fibers described but rather buy the fibers from the various chemical companies.

Nylon accounts for nearly 90 percent of all carpeting sold today. Nylon is the generic name of a fiber in which the fiber-forming substance is any long chain synthetic polyamide having recurring amide groups as an integral part of the polymer chain. There are numerous types of nylon. Since 1947, the carpet industry has moved through five generations of nylon carpet fibers; however, all, to some degree, are still found in carpet manufactured today. The generation can best be distinguished by technical advances in the performance of the nylon fiber.

The first generation nylon fibers were round, clear, and readily showed soil. Being round and clear, the fibers actually magnified the soil. Inherent static build-up was and still is a disadvantage of this type of fiber.

The second generation of nylon fibers effectively reduced soil magnification by changing the fiber shape or cross section from round to non-circular configuration. This second generation nylon fibers are sometimes referred to as *soil-hiding* types.

The third generation nylons are characterized by improved soil-hiding properties and built-in static protection. The soil-hiding characteristics were improved, in some cases, by further modifying the cross sections and by adding a delustering agent to the fiber.

The fourth generation nylons go one step further by adding carpet protectors to the fiber to make them *soil-resistant*. Fifth generation nylon is the same as the fourth generation with the addition of the acid dye resistor. Features of the fifth generation are: Non-magnifying shape of the fiber to reduce apparent soiling, resistant to static electricity to the level of human detection, acid dye resistor applied after regular dyeing, and fluorochemical coating (see fluorochemical coatings on page 15).

The anti-static properties can also be brought about by the use of conductive **filaments** (metallic or carbon based) incorporated within the nylon fibers.

Some fiber producers have also included anti-microbial treatment in or on the fiber. The anti-microbial aspect is very important when dealing with hospital and healthcare facilities. This involves obtaining a written document from the manufacturer that the carpet has been treated to meet the low bacteria count required by hospitals.

Being a man-made fiber, nylon absorbs little water and, therefore, stains are on the surface rather than penetrating into the fiber itself. Dirt and soil are trapped between the filaments and are removed by proper cleaning methods. Nylon has excellent abrasion resistance. The reason for worn or thin spots is that the yarn has physically been damaged by grit and soil ground into the carpet. This problem can be taken care of with proper maintenance.

Wool has, for many years, represented the standard of quality against which all other carpet fibers were measured and it still is to some degree. Most important is wools aesthetics and inherent resilience. The best wool for carpeting comes from sheep that are raised in the colder climates. Although wool has a propensity for high static generation, treatments are available to impart static-protection properties. Wool retains color for the life of the carpet despite wear and cleanings. Wool has good soil resistance due to its naturally high moisture content and has excellent pile resilience.

Wool gives good service. When price is no object, the best carpet fiber is wool. Wool blends, usually 80 percent wool and 20 percent nylon have a larger market segment than a decade ago. However, wool will stain or bleach in reaction to some spills and is not as easy to clean as nylon.

Acrylic is the man-made fiber which most feels like wool. Acrylic carpets have a low soiling rate, clean well, are highly static resistant, have very good to excellent abrasion resistance and excellent colorfastness. In properly constructed carpets, pile resilience is good.

In the 1960s and early 70s, acrylic was a very popular fiber for commercial and residential carpeting because of its good performance. However, new dyeing processes introduced in the 1970s favored nylon due to its high dyeing rate and resistance to deformation under hot-wet conditions. Now, producer-dyed acrylic is being offered which should again make acrylic a viable fiber for commercial and residential installations.

Polyester is offered for carpet in **staple** form only. Polyester is an important carpet fiber, but more in residential styles than for commercial carpet applications. Polyester is a soft fiber with good soil and wear resistance, but has a tendency to crush with wear.

Olefin (Polypropylene) is the lightest commercial carpet fiber and has excellent strength and toughness. The fiber is offered as both **continuous filament** and a staple. It is sold as a **solution dyed** fiber or yarn, but because olefin is **hydrophobic**, dyes are difficult to apply and should be solution dyed. Because of its very low moisture absorbency and the fact that the color is sealed into the fiber, olefins have excellent resistance to stains. They have resistance to sunlight fading and generate low levels of static electricity. They do, however, have fair to poor resilience of pile. Polypropylene should not be used for outdoor use unless specifically recommended by the carpet manufacturer. It is also used in carpet backing.

Cotton is an expensive natural fiber most often used for flat woven rugs such as Indian dhurries.

MANUFACTURING PROCESS

In the beginning, looms were only available in 27–inch widths. Although that width is still available, most carpeting is usually available in 12–foot widths. Some come in 15–foot widths and may be custom-sized for large installations.

The main manufacturing processes in order of

quantity of carpeting produced are tufting, weaving, needle-punch, and others.

Tufting

In a tufted piece of goods, the back is woven first and then the face is tufted into it and backed with additional material. It is a much faster process than the traditional weaving method and has greatly reduced the cost of carpeting, thereby making it available to more buyers. The technique is fast, efficient and simple. More than 90 percent of all carpet sold in the United States is tufted.

Weaving

Weaving is a fabric formation process used for manufacturing carpet in which yarns are interlaced to form cloth. The weaving loom interlaces lengthwise (warp) and widthwise (filling) yarns. Carpet weaves are complex, often involving several sets of warps and filling yarns. The back and the face are produced simultaneously and as one unit. When describing an area rug, the term "tapestry weave" is sometimes used.

Velvet carpets are the simplest of all woven. They are made on a velvet loom, which is not unlike the Wilton loom, without the Jacquard unit. The rich appearance of velvets is due to their high-pile density. Velvets can be cut or looped pile.

Knitted

Knitted carpets were not made by machine until 1940. Their quality is generally high, depending on the yarns used and their density. Knitting a carpet involves at least three different facing yarns and perhaps a fourth for backing. Face yarns are knitted in with warp chains and weft forming yarns in a simple knitting process. Variations of colors, yarns and pile treatment (cut or looped, high or low) create design choices for knitted carpets. Knitting today is a speedy process that produces fine quality carpeting.

Needle Punching

Needle-punched carpet is a felt-like product manufactured by entangling a fiber fleece with barbed needles. A latex coating or attached padding is applied to the back.

Tufted

Wilton Weave

Velvet Weave

Axminster Weave

Knitted

Figure 2-1
Construction methods. Drawings courtesy of Monsanto Contract Fibers.

Aubusson

Aubussons are flatly woven tapestries and carpets in silk or wool, named for the French town where they originated (circa.1500). Tapestries bear narratives or portraits while carpets feature architectural designs in rich colors, or flowers in muted pastels.

Axminster and Wilton

While the appearance of the Axminster and Wilton may be similar, the construction is very different. In an Axminster, pile tufts are individually inserted from colored yarns arranged on spools making possible an enormous variety of colors and patterns. The Wilton looms have Jacquard pattern mechanisms which use punched cards to select pile height and yarn color. In a Wilton, unwanted yarn colors are buried under the surface of the carpet, limiting the color selection to five of six colors. The carpets are often patterned or have multilevel surfaces. The traditional fiber in Axminster and Wilton construction is wool, but a blend of 80 percent wool and 20 percent nylon is sometimes used. One way to distinguish between the two is by rolling across the warp and weft. A Wilton will fold in both directions; an Axminster only in one.

DYEING

Color is the most important aesthetic property of carpet. Designers should be familiar with the major methods of color application to carpet. This increases their ability to specify the most appropriate carpet for a given application.

Solution-dyed yarns and fibers are pre-colored by the fiber manufacturer who introduces pigments into the molten polymer before extrusion into fiber. Solution-dyed fibers have outstanding fade resistance and wet fastness. Stabilized with ultraviolet inhibitors, they are excellent for outdoor applications. The most common solution dyed-carpet fiber is polypropylene, but polyester and nylon are also available.

Stock Dyeing

Stock dyeing is the application of color to fibers before conversion into **spun yarn**. This method of dyeing is probably the oldest method of coloring yarns, and is still important today for dyeing wool. Other fibers, such as acrylic, polyester, and some nylon can also be dyed in this manner. In stock dyeing, bulk staple fiber is placed in a large drum-like kettle where a prepared dye liquor is forced through the fiber. By controlling the temperature and, in some cases, the pressure, the dyeing is continued until the dyestuff has been completely exhausted from the bath onto the fiber. The kettle is then drained, and the fiber is rinsed, followed by centrifuging to remove excess water. It is then dried and ready for spinning. Fiber blending during the spinning operation produces uniform color throughout the yarn lot.

Stock dyeing is a valuable styling device for contract carpet designers. Heather blends and **berber** effects are produced by combining stock-dyed fibers of various colors.

Skein Dyeing

Skein dyeing is a technique which applies color to yarn. Almost any yarn and fiber may be dyed this way if the yarn has sufficient strength and scuff resistance to withstand skein winding and back winding onto tufting cones. The method is applicable to spun yarns, bulked, continuous filament yarns, heat-set yarns, and non-heat-set yarns of many fiber types. Although a high labor cost is involved, skein dyeing is especially suited to small volume production of custom colorations.

Piece Dyeing

Piece dyeing is the application of color from an aqueous dyebath onto unfinished carpet consisting only of primary backing and undyed yarns. Piece dyeing is generally for solid colors. However, two or more colors can be produced in tweed, moresque, or stripe patterns in the same carpet from a single dyebath. This is achieved by using fibers of modified and/or altered dye affinity.

Carpeting Printing

Carpet printing is accomplished with machinery that is essentially enlarged, modified textile printing equipment. Printed carpet is available in a wide variety of patterns or textures ranging from low-level loop carpet to saxony, cut-loop, and shag. Printed carpets can simulate woven patterns at much lower cost.

Jet printing uses machinery consisting of rows of color jets arranged across the width of the carpet. The jets are closely spaced, about an eighth to a tenth of an inch apart. Each jet may be opened or closed by computer controlled valves as the carpet moves under the row of jets. Controlled patterns are produced without screens or physical contact of machinery against carpet. Each row of jets applies a different color. Pattern changes are rapid, requiring only computer program modifications. The jets squirt color onto the carpet surface, but unlike screens, do not crush the pile, resulting in superior texture. The machinery is costly, but the obvious advantages suggest that various types of the jet printing technology may gain importance in the carpet industry.

FABRIC PROTECTORS

Fabric protectors can be introduced after the dyeing process.

"There are three basic types of fabric protectors. These are:
- Colloidal silica, which fill pores, thus preventing soil from becoming embedded:
- Silicones, which provide a water repellent coating; and
- Florochemicals, which form an invisible shield on the fibers that helps prevent soil and stains from sticking.

Fluorine is very inert and wants nothing oily, watery, solid, or liquid to adhere to it. Colloidal silicas were first introduced in the early 1950s, and usually show good dry soil performance over short periods of time but have no oil or water repellency at all. In addition, colloidal silica finishes generally detract from the luster of carpet and may give a harsh hand to the fiber.

Products based upon silicones form a water-repellent coating on the fiber. But even though they are good water repellents, silicone finishes have no resistance to oily substances and, consequently, they frequently show poor dry soil performance. In fact, they often attract some types of soil resulting in a carpet that appears dirtier than one without a protective finish. The silicone products are formulated in organic solvents that are usually flammable and sometimes odor causing. The product should be used only in well-ventilated areas and never used around an open flame or while smoking. Silicone products offer a viable alternative to Fluorochemical products when cost is the main concern.

Fluorochemical products form a protective coating on the carpet fibers that helps keep dirt from lodging itself within the fibers. These unique products are characterized by outstanding dry soil resistance and resistance to wet soil. They provide very good resistance to both water- and oil-based liquids. Dirt or soil tends to remain on top of fabrics treated with fluorochemicals and can usually be vacuumed away.

The fluorochemicals will work in basically two ways. When a fluorochemical product is applied, it will disperse and wick to cover all of the fiber surfaces as long as it is applied properly. The coverage is spread throughout the fabric and the dirt and stain repellency will work even at the base of a carpet as long as the product is there. The fluorochemicals also impart a high degree of surface tension. This surface tension is created by an electrical charge that will hold a liquid on the surface of the fiber. The surface tension can be broken easily by physically forcing the liquid into the fabric. If the liquid is dropped onto the surface from a distance, it will usually break the surface tension. When this surface tension is broken, the liquid is being forced into the air spaces rather than being absorbed into the fiber protected with a fluorochemical.

Fluorochemical protectors fall into two categories—water-base and solvent-based. The two main manufacturers of the water-based fluorochemicals are 3M with Scotchgard®, and DuPont with Teflon®.

The 3M Company sells the Scotchgard product while DuPont allows for the private labeling of their products. Therefore, many products containing DuPont Teflon have appeared in the marketplace. Make sure the recommended concentration of Teflon is being used.[2]

Fire-retardant products also may be used especially for commercial installations where firecodes require it. Wool self-extinguishes when the source of ignition is removed, and merely chars, leaving only a cold ash which can be easily brushed away with no permanent scars. Man-made fibers melt.

FLAMMABILITY TESTING

It is extremely important for designers to realize the legal ramifications of flammability specifications because of possible damage and liability law suits. Designers should require carpet suppliers to submit written documentation of firecode compliance.

Monsanto Contract Fibers has a special report on flammability resistance:

With the Federal regulations which govern the manufacturing of all carpet, it is now against the law to make or sell any carpeting which does not pass the Methenamine Tablet Test (DOC FF 1–70).

All fires have three distinct stages: ignition, flashover, and expansion. In the *ignition stage*, the fire has started but is contained in a small area of one room. *Flashover* occurs when the fire spreads beyond its point of origin and everything in the room is burning. In the *expansion stage*, the fire leaves the room and spreads over into other rooms or down a corridor. If the fire can be contained during the ignition stage, minimal damage will occur.

This is the rationale behind the Methenamine Table Test, or pill test, as it is more commonly known. In this test, eight identical carpet specimens are placed in a draft-free environment. A methenamine tablet is positioned in the center of each specimen and ignited. If two or more of the specimens burn for three inches in any direction the carpet fails the test and cannot be sold in the United States.

Another method for testing the flame resistance of carpet is the Steiner Tunnel Test (ASTM E-84). Here, a carpet sample 20-inches wide and 25-feet long is placed on the ceiling of the test tunnel with its pile facing down. The carpet is exposed to a gas jet flame in a temperature range of 1,600°F to 1,800°F for 10 minutes or until the carpet has been completely burned. The flame spread is observed every 15 seconds, and the longest distance of flame spread is measured. This distance is then used to determine a flame spread rating. This test is being replaced by the Radiant Panel Flooring Test in most states because of its greater accuracy.

The Chamber Test (UL-992) is a variation of the Tunnel Test. Here, the carpet sample and any padding or other underlayment are placed on the floor of the test tunnel and exposed to a high heat burner and a draft of air. This test is not widely accepted, because its results are inconclusive.

A more accurate test is the Radiant Panel Flooring Test (ASTM E-648), which simulates conditions that could cause flame-spread in a carpeting system, but applies only to carpeting installed in corridors. In this test, the carpet sample and underlayment are positioned inside a test chamber. A radiating heat panel, not a direct flame, is placed at a 30° angle above one end of the sample. This panel generates heat at the carpet surface ranging from 1.1 watts/cm^2 directly beneath the panel to about 0.1 watts/cm^2 at the far end of the sample. The total distance the sample burns is measured and then converted to watts/cm^2. This number is called the *critical radiant flux* (CRF). Each sample is tested three times and an average CRF is derived. The higher the CRF, the more resistant a carpet system is to flame spread. For example, oak flooring has a CRF of about 0.35 to 0.40 in comparison to carpet which may have a CRF above 1.1

As relates to smoke generation by solid materials, the latest edition of the *Life Safety Code* states that it is neither necessary nor practical to regulate interior floor finishes on the basis of smoke development. However, if a smoke requirement is deemed necessary, it is recommended that floor covering of all occupancies have a maximum specific optical density of 450 (flaming) when tested in accordance with the NFPA Standard no.258 (ASTM E-662–79).[3]

TYPES OF PILE

Loop pile has a surface consisting of uncut loops (see Figure 2–2). Variations include high and low loops, colors, and highly twisted yarns.

Cut pile (plush) may be made from **unset yarns** (frizzy ends) for an even velvety texture, or from **set yarns** (firm-ended) to give a velour texture with tuft definition. These carpets look more luxurious than loop, but they also tend to show footsteps or flaws more readily. Patterned wovens or printed tufteds will offset such characteristics. Area rugs, particularly those with borders, or a colored pattern, quite often use a sculptured cut pile. Where two colors meet, the pile is cut at in a V-shape to delineate the pattern and produce a three-dimensional effect. Plain carpet may also be carved in any design.

Frieze (hard twist) is cut pile from a highly twisted yarn set in a snarled configuration. It will hide footsteps, shedding, and the **shading** that occurs when pile lays in opposite directions.

Semi-shag (splush) is soft, cut pile with shorter piles than shags. Ends of yarn stand up so that the carpet has a pebbled look.

Shag is soft carpets with long pile, such as the Scandivnavian Rya rug where different yarns may be used, but always with the side of the yarn exposed so as to give a shaggy look.

Tip-sheared is a loop pile carpet with some loops sheared on the surface to create areas of cut pile and a luxurious, sculpted look.

Berber was named after the original hand-woven wool squares made by the North African tribes. Now made by machine in country style with natural colors and homespun effect. Usually coarse loop pile, but also made in cut pile, shags, and a variety of designs. Berber is very often used in contemporary rooms. This system is the oldest in the history of rug making. It may be as old as the second millennium B.C. Hand-loomed woven rugs are still being produced by the American Indians, as well as in India, China, Iran, and elsewhere.

Along with the quality of the fiber, the amount of it is crucial to a carpet's durability. The depth of pile is not as important as its **face weight**, that is, the density of fiber in the pile. If asked, sales staff will disclose (if sometimes reluctantly) the face weight of

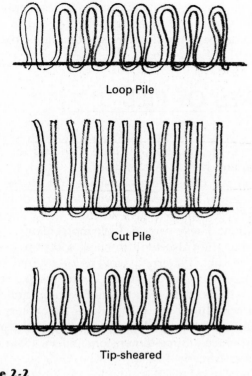

Figure 2-2
Piles.

a carpet. In terms of durability carpets are often divided into four grades:

1. Grade One is intended for residential or domestic use;
2. Grade Two is for normal contract (commercial) use;
3. Grade Three is for such public areas as lobbies, where face weight is especially important; and
4. Grade Four is for stairs, offices containing chairs with casters, and institutions. Many Grade Four Carpets have uncut loop pile for greater resilience.[4]

CARPET CUSHIONING

The padding or cushioning is the "unseen" but indispensable element of a carpet installation. There are four types of carpet cushion. Fiber, sponge rubber, prime urethane foam, and bonded urethane foam (see Table 2–1).

There are two basic types of fiber carpet cushion: natural fiber (such as felt, animal hair, and jute) and synthetic fiber (like nylon, polypropylene, and poly-

ester). The grade of fiber cushion is determined by its weight in ounces per square yard. Fiber cushions tend to have a firm "walk" or "feel" and can be used in light, moderate, and heavy traffic areas. Available in weights from 18 ounces to 86 ounces per square yard.

There are two specific types of sponge rubber carpet cushion: flat sponge (smooth or flat surface) and waffled sponge (waffle or rippled surface). Flat sponge offers a firm feel; waffled sponge is softer. Sponge rubber cushion is available to meet light, moderate or heavy traffic conditions. Again, grades are measured by weight in ounces per square yard. Available in weights from 36 oz. to 120 oz. per square yard.

There are also two types of prime urethane foam carpet cushion: prime and densified prime cushion. Prime urethane is manufactured by a chemical mixing reaction process. In densified prime, the chemical structure is modified during the manufacturing process to produce a product with specific performance characteristics. Grades of prime urethane are determined by foam density or weight of a cubic foot of material. For light, moderate, and heavy traffic areas, they are available in densities from approximately 1 to 5 pounds per cubic foot for softer more resilient cushions, and up to 20 pounds per cubic foot for firmer feels.

Bonded foam cushions are made by combining shredded pieces of urethane (and sometimes other plastic foams) through an adhesive and heat fusion process into a single sheet of material. Bonded foam grades are also measured by density and are available for light, moderate and heavy traffic applications. Densities range from approximately 4 to 5 pounds per cubic foot for softer cushions, and up to 14 pounds per cubic foot for firmer products.[5]

WRITING CARPET SPECIFICATIONS

Construction

A carpet construction specification prescribes how a carpet is to be manufactured without reference to its end-use or performance. There are many factors in construction which help define the finished quality of carpet. Those most frequently written into construction specifications are listed below:

1. Construction type—tufted, woven, knitted, etc.
2. **Gauge** (pitch).

Table 2-1
Contract cushion selection

Labeling for traffic makes contract cushion selection easier.

To help you compare "apples to apples" in various types of cushion, the Carpet Cushion Council has established recommended minimum contract cushion criteria for three levels of traffic. Any cushion which carries a CCC Traffic label can be expected to perform satisfactorily at that traffic level under normal conditions, when used with a carpet made for the same specified traffic.

[Red Label] [Green Label] [Blue Label]

carpet cushion council

THIS PRODUCT MEETS OR EXCEEDS THE RECOMMENDED MINIMUM CRITERIA FOR

USE IN: COMMERCIAL
TYPE OF INSTALLATION

MODERATE
TRAFFIC LEVEL

ACCORDING TO THE CARPET CUSHION COUNCIL TRAFFIC CLASSIFICATION PROGRAM.

carpet cushion council

THIS PRODUCT MEETS OR EXCEEDS THE RECOMMENDED MINIMUM CRITERIA FOR

USE IN: COMMERCIAL
TYPE OF INSTALLATION

HEAVY
TRAFFIC LEVEL

ACCORDING TO THE CARPET CUSHION COUNCIL TRAFFIC CLASSIFICATION PROGRAM.

carpet cushion council

THIS PRODUCT MEETS OR EXCEEDS THE RECOMMENDED MINIMUM CRITERIA FOR

USE IN: COMMERCIAL
TYPE OF INSTALLATION

EXTRA HEAVY
TRAFFIC LEVEL

ACCORDING TO THE CARPET CUSHION COUNCIL TRAFFIC CLASSIFICATION PROGRAM.

Look for these labels. They assure you that the manufacturer certifies the cushion to meet or exceed Carpet Cushion Council traffic recommendations.

Minimum recommended criteria for satisfactory carpet cushion performance in contract installation.

TYPES OF CUSHION	CLASS I MODERATE TRAFFIC	CLASS II HEAVY TRAFFIC	CLASS III EXTRA HEAVY TRAFFIC
Commercial Application	**Office Buildings:** Executive or private offices, conference rooms **Health Care:** Executive, administration **Schools:** Administration **Airports:** Administration **Retail:** Windows and display areas **Banks:** Executive areas **Hotels/Motels:** Sleeping rooms **Libraries/Museums:** Administration	**Office Buildings:** Clerical areas, corridors (moderate traffic) **Health Care:** Patients' rooms, lounges **Schools:** Dormitories and classrooms **Retail:** Minor aisles, boutiques, specialty **Banks:** Lobbies, corridors (moderate traffic) **Hotels/Motels:** Corridors **Libraries/Museums:** Public areas (moderate traffic) **Convention Centers:** Auditoriums	**Office Buildings:** Corridors (heavy traffic), cafeterias **Health Care:** Lobbies, corridors, nurses' stations **Schools:** Corridors, cafeterias **Airports:** Corridors, public areas, ticketing areas **Retail:** Major aisles, check outs, supermarkets **Banks:** Corridors (heavy traffic), teller windows **Hotels/Motels:** Lobbies and public areas **Library/Museum:** Public areas **Country Clubs:** Locker rooms, pro shops, dining areas **Convention Centers:** Corridors and lobbies **Restaurants:** Dining areas and lobbies
FIBER, oz/sq. yd.			
Natural (Hair, jute, etc.)	Wt: 32 oz. Th: ¼"+ 5% max.	Wt: 40 oz. Th: ⁵/₁₆"+ 5% max.	Wt: 50 oz. Th: ³/₈"+ 5% max.
Synthetic, Needled	Wt: 22 oz. Th: ⁵/₁₆"+ 5% max.	Wt: 28 oz. Th: ³/₈"+ 5% max.	Wt: 36 oz. Th: ³/₈"+ 5% max.
SPONGE RUBBER, oz./sq. yd.			
Flat Sponge	Wt: 56 oz. Th: .225"+ 5% CLD @ 25%: .75 psi	Wt: 64 oz. Th: .250"+ 5% CLD @ 25%: 1.0 psi	Wt: 80 oz. Th: .250"+ 5% CLD @ 25%: 1.5 psi
Ripple Sponge	Wt: 64 oz. Th: .350"+ 5% CLD @ 25%: .75 psi	Wt: 80 oz. Th: .400"+ 5% CLD @ 25%: 1.0 psi	Wt: 80 oz. Th: .250"+ 5% CLD @ 25%: 1.5 psi
Reinforced Foam Rubber	Wt: 56 oz. Th: .225"+ 5% CLD @ 25%: .75 psi	Wt: 64 oz. Th: .235"+ 5% CLD @ 25%: 1.0 psi	
POLYURETHANE FOAM, lbs/cu.ft. (pcf)			
Bonded Urethane	Polyester foam content not to exceed 50% Particle size not to exceed ½" D: 5.0 pcf ± 5% Th: ³/₈" ± ¹/₃₂" CLD @ 65%: 4.0 psi	Polyester foam content not to exceed 50% Particle size not to exceed ½" D: 6.5 pcf ± 5% Th: ⁹/₁₆" ± ¹/₃₂" CLD @ 65% (⁷/₁₆"): 5.0 psi	Polyester foam content not to exceed 50% Particle size not to exceed ½" D: 8.0 pcf ± 5% Th: ¼" ± ¹/₃₂" CLD @ 65% (1"): 7.0 psi
Modified Prime Urethane	D: *2.5 pcf ± 5% Th: ¼" + ¹/₃₂" ILD @ 25%: 100 lb. ± 10%	D: *2.7 pcf ± 5% Th: ¼" + ¹/₃₂" ILD @ 25%: 100 lb ± 10%	D: *3.2 pcf ± 5% Th: ³/₁₆" + ¹/₃₂" ILD @ 25%: 120 lb. ± 10%
Densified Prime Urethane	D: *2.1 pcf Th: .350" ± ¹/₃₂" CLD @ 65%: .85 psi	D: *3.5 pcf ± 5% Th: .265"-.015" + .031" CLD @ 65%: 1.8 psi	D: *4.5 pcf Th: .265"-.015" + .031" CLD @ 65%: 2.3 psi

*Weights are /cu.ft. polymer density only

Used with permission of Carpet Cushion Council.

3. Stitches per inch (wires per inch).
4. Pile height (wire height).
5. Pile fiber (generic type-nylon, polypropylene, polyester, wool).
6. Yarn ply, count, and heat set.
7. Face weight per square yard.
8. Backing material:
    a. In woven carpet—type and weight per square yard.
    b. In tufted carpet—types and weights per square yard for both primary and secondary backs.
9. Back coating type and weight per square yard.
10. Finished weight per square yard.

NOTE: Parentheses refer to woven carpet specifications in items 2, 3, 4.

Construction specifications can be proprietary, identifying a specific carpet by grade, name, and manufacturer. An "or equal" specification could also identify a specific grade, listing its construction factors so that other manufacturers can bid for the order competitively. In this case, the usual procedure is to approve "or equals" in advance of the actual bidding. Full attention can then be given to price and delivery information when bid documents are analyzed.

Performance

To clarify the difference between performance and construction specifications, performance specifications define what characteristics the carpet must deliver in use.

Put another way, a performance specification tells the manufacturer what the carpet must do without telling him how it must be made. By contrast, a construction specification tells the manufacturer, in very precise terms, how the carpet is to be manufactured without stipulating performance needs.

Specifying performance rather than construction can also take other important pressures off the specifier. If the specifier does not deal with carpet regularly, he/she may not be totally familiar with all of the latest technology and materials available to the carpet industry. Therefore, he/she might not choose the best, most economical construction to ensure the performance he/she desires. Whether written for construction or performance, most carpet specifications also incorporate requirements governing the following items:

1. Type of installation (tackless or glue-down).
2. Cushion type and grade, if required.
3. Installation procedures and accessories.
4. Certification that materials meet federal, state, and local government ordinances* including fire codes and others.
5. Delivery and installation schedules.
6. Carpet maintenance (usually a request for maintenance instructions from the manufacturer).

Special requirements for different types of installation sites can be very complex and technical. For example, in window-wall architecture, fade resistance could be a matter of primary concern. In a hospital medical dispensary, stain resistance and anti-microbial properties might be placed high on the list of performance priorities. Special static protection properties may be necessary for computer and date-processing areas.

The following questions should be answered.

1. Budget.
2. Surface texture, pattern or design.
3. Color—solid, tweed, figured.
4. Traffic load—light, medium, heavy.
5. Maintenance levels that will be sustained—good, better, best.
6. Minimum life expectancy.
7. Installation requirements.

Performance factors to consider:

1. Ease of maintenance.
2. Stain resistance—anti-microbial properties.
3. Resistance to cigarette burns.
4. Resistance to excessive wear.
5. Very firm—for ease of rolling objects.
6. Superior sound absorption.
7. Superior impact insulation.
8. Superior static control.
9. Low moisture absorbency.
10. Luxurious appearance.
11. Superior dimensional stability.
12. Superior resistance to sunlight.

*Particularly for flammability

Figure 2-3
A winner in the 1990 Antron carpet competition in the health care division shows how the designers, Jain Malkin Inc., used contrasting borders in "Texturescape," "Stati-tuft," "Providence," and "Newport II" from Karastan-Bigelow to delineate the waiting area in the Kaiser Permanente Vendever Medical Office building in San Diego, CA.
Photograph: Jonathan Hillyer Photography. Photograph courtesy of Du Pont.

13. Flammability requirements. All carpet over 4 feet by 6 feet must meet the requirements of CPSC: FF1–70.

MEASURING

Before estimating the amount of carpet needed for a particular job, there are several points that the designer needs to remember. First of all, if carpet is available in other widths besides the usual 12 foot, then all the carpet must be of that width. DO NOT COMBINE DIFFERENT WIDTHS because of differences in dye lots. Second, the nap or pile of the carpet needs to be considered and all pieces must

have the nap running in the same direction, toward the entrance, unless otherwise specified, or the seams will be obvious.

Third, seaming and nap direction must be shown on all carpet seaming plans. Placement of furniture will often decide where seams should be placed. Seams should never be in the middle of high traffic areas such as at right angles to a doorway, across a hallway, in front of often used office machines such as copiers and drinking fountains. In residential seaming layouts, do not have seams which will fall directly in front of seating areas.

Carpets which have to be seamed at right angles will also have an obvious seam, however, seams placed under a door are quite often necessary. The nap on stairs should run downwards. The warp (nap) should always run the longer direction.

The precise measuring of the carpet should be done by the installer on site, with a carpet seaming diagram submitted to the designer for approval. However, the designer should have an understanding of what and how it is done.

Carpeting usually comes in 12-foot widths, but 6-foot, 9-foot, and 15-foot widths are sometimes available. Whatever width is selected, it will be necessary to piece or seam the carpet. The fewer the seams the better the appearance which may mean purchasing slightly more yardage.

Although carpet comes in widths measured in feet, the amount ordered is always square yards, so be sure to divide a square foot answer by 9 to arrive at the square yardage needed. (From experience, the author finds this is the most common error made by design students.)

Each measurer seems to have their own method of calculation. Some suggest using templates, others have complicated formulas and some answers are very close with little waste and others have few seams and much waste. The amount of seams does depend on each job. A master bedroom may have a seam one foot in from a wall where a dresser and other pieces of furniture are to be placed because it will not be visible, but in an art gallery a one foot piece would be unacceptable. Whichever method is used, the installer is responsible for the accuracy of the measurements.

In todays computerized design offices, programs are available to assist the designer in producing an economical and yet viable plan. Some programs actually produce a floor plan with measurements, nap directions, and seam placements. The program can provide an estimate needed with the 12 foot width going across the room or at right angles. A pattern repeat can be programmed so that the repeat is taken into consideration. Some programs do the calculation but do not provide a line drawing of the seams and cuts, just a summary of how many pieces are needed.

PROBLEMS

Sprouting. Occasionally, a tuft will rise above the pile surface of a carpet. Just snip off these tufts level with other tufts. DO NOT PULL THEM OUT!

Ripples. Ripples in carpet usually are the result of improper stretching during installation, stretching of the back yarns after the carpet was installed, or elongation of the backing fibers from moisture. With a jute-backed carpet, it is not uncommon to have ripples during periods of high humidity which disappear during periods of low humidity. A de-humidifier may help to eliminate this problem. Using waffled sponge cushioning under a woven carpet will also cause this problem.

Mildew. Mildew can be a problem on carpet and rugs, but it does not have to be. If a carpet is going to be used where mildew or other bacteria growing conditions are present some or all of the time, then a carpet with all man-made fibers (both front and back) should be used.

Indentations. When a heavy object such as a piano, piece of furniture, etc. is allowed to remain for an extended period of time in one spot on a carpet, indentation or crush marks will develop. In most cases, the crushed areas can be either restored or greatly improved. The crushed pile can be lifted by working gently with a coin. The yarn should be lifted to its original appearance without fuzzing or distorting the yarn. After the yarn has been raised, moisten the area with a steam iron, held at least four inches above the pile. The procedure can be repeated if the original appearance was not obtained the first time. Moving furniture a few inches, will help to prevent permanent indentations. Moving the furniture will also help prevent damage to the back of the carpet from small furniture legs and rollers.

To help prevent matting, Monsanto Company has created Wear-dated® carpet. Their new Traffic Control™ fiber system employs a unique dual fiber design. By taking tough nylon fibers and interweaving them with acrylic fibers, they have built in a new type of resilience.

Corn rowing. Corn rowing is a characteristic which should be expected in carpet with higher tufts and lower density pile. Corn rowing develops in the traffic areas or those areas subjected to mechanical action such as in front of chairs, television sets, etc. Vacuuming alone will not raise the fallen yarns. Specially designed carpet rakes will lift the yarns but will not keep them erect as the yarns will be crushed again when subjected to foot traffic.

Shedding or fluffing. When a newly installed carpet is vacuumed, a large amount of fiber may be found in the vacuum. This is a normal process. A carpet made with staple fibers will not have all the the fibers anchored into the back or tightly held in the yarns. Mechanical action will work some of the fibers loose. As the carpet is vacuumed, some of the loose fibers will be removed. Many styles of carpet are sheared as one of the final steps in manufacturing. Most fibers are removed at the factory, but some of these sheared fibers will fall into the carpet pile. The shorter the fiber and the longer the tuft, the greater the number of loose fibers in the yarns. The yarns with less twist will not hold the loose fibers as tightly. Therefore, they are easier to remove. A deep brushing action produces the maximum removal.

Static Electricity. Static is caused by the rubbing together of two different types of materials which result in a transfer and a build-up of electrical charges. Most carpets have some type of treatments built into them which will eliminate the static electricity problem. Moisture in the air will help the problem but may produce a condensation problem on window glass in the colder climates.

Shading. Shading is a natural characteristic of plush carpet and should be expected to develop. It is not something which is due to neglect during manufacturing, nor is it something which the manufacturer can eliminate in a plush or velvet type of construction. Shading helps to break up the plainness or sameness in solid color, dense, cut pile carpet. It is a characteristic which occurs in good quality carpet, and it should be enjoyed, but the client should be made aware of this characteristic. When the carpet is manufactured and rolled, the ends of the face yarns will all lean toward the end of the roll. After the carpet is installed and vacuumed, the pile will have a uniform appearance. This uniformity is due to the light being reflected from a uniform surface.

Some changes can be expected after the carpet is used. The traffic areas will appear a little different from the adjacent, unwalked on areas. This difference is because the carpet pile has been compressed by the pressure from footsteps. Vacuuming and brushing will help to raise the crushed pile. However, an occasional vacuuming cannot equalize the continual compressing of the carpet. The consumer will have to work to keep the pile erect. Sometimes these shaded spots will occur even in areas with little or no traffic and may be called shading, watermarking, pooling, highlighting and pile reversal. Vacuuming and brushing the pile all in one direction, or professional cleaning, may temporarily improve the condition, however, this changes only the top portion of the pile, and shading will soon redevelop. With some plush carpet, vacuum cleaner marks and footsteps may show after the carpet has been freshly cleaned.

INSTALLATION

There are three principal methods of contract carpet installation. They are stretch-in, tackless strip installation; direct glue-down (including attached cushion); and double glue-down. *Tackless installations are stretched in over a separate cushion.* They are best suited to areas which must have maximum underfoot comfort and luxury.

Glue-down installations can be made with two types of carpet—carpet with attached cushion or carpet without attached cushion. These installations are well suited to heavy traffic and to rolling traffic. The Carpet and Rug Institute (CRI) recommends adhesive installations for carpet in areas that will be exposed to rolling traffic.

Double glue-down installations combine cushion and carpet in a floorcovering system by first gluing the cushion to the floor and then, the carpet to the cushion. This method, often referred to as *double-stick*, has grown in popularity due to combining the stability of direct glue-down of carpet with the cushioning benefits of separate cushion. The cushion materials must be designed specifically for this method of installation in order to achieve a successful installation. A 14-pound density with a maximum thickness of 1/4 inches should be used for glue-down installations. Depending on the type of adhesive used, the cushion can be easily removed if necessary.

This type of installation eliminates restretching problems, with no movement of pattern-type carpeting or bordering. Direct glue-down and double glue-down installations can be made on any subfloors including wood, concrete, metal, terrazzo, ceramic tile, and other suitable surfaces, Generally, most are on concrete, therefore, proper preparation of subfloor is needed for adequate adhesion. Testing concrete for moisture and alkalinity is necessary for best results.

The glue-down method may also be used for **carpet modules** which come in 12-inch by 12-inch and 18-inch by 18-inch size, though 24-inch by 24-inch are occasionally used, with 36-inch by 36-inch tiles rarely being used. Due to the heavy backing, however, carpet tiles may be loose laid. Carpet modules can be freely rotated and/or replaced without detracting from overall like-new appearance of the installation, particularly in the health care, institutional, retail stores, and hospitality areas with their heavy use and traffic.

They are also useful in furnishing the upper floors of tall buildings, where delivering heavy, cumbersome rolls of broadloom may present a problem. This is particularly true in the case of refurbishing when construction cranes and elevators used to lift the original carpets are no longer available.

Direct glue-down of carpet must utilize the correct trowel size, usually $1/8 \times 1/8$ inch, and the recommended adhesive specially formulated for use with hot-melt bonded carpet.

The tackless strips are narrow pieces of wood with two to four rows of pins, long enough to penetrate the backing, set at a 60 degree angle. The strips are nailed or glued down around the perimeter of the room a slight distance from the wall. When installing carpet over a cement floor, two rows are used. For stairs, the strips are placed at the base of the riser and the back of the tread. After the tackless strip is nailed down, the padding is cut to fit inside the strips. The principle of the tackless installation is that the carpet is stretched by means of a knee kicker or power stretcher so that it hooks over the pins in the wooden strip. The excess carpet is cut off and the small amount remaining is tucked into the slight gap between the strip and the wall. The base is then installed to cover this area.

The most important aspects of stretched-in tackless strip installation are:

1. Sufficient stretching of carpet.
2. Proper selection of cushion.
3. Correct environmental conditions, prior, during, and after the installation is completed.

The Carpet and Rug Institute finds that most complaints about wrinkling or buckling in tackless installations result from inadequate stretch during initial installation or from a cushion that does not provide adequate support for the carpet.

Guidelines for proper stretch for various carpets are in "How to Specify Commercial Carpet Installation," published by The Carpet & Rug Institute. Additional information concerning the amount of stretch for each carpet can be obtained from either its manufacturer or the secondary backing manufacturer. Always use the best carpet installer available.

Construction and density of the cushion are equal in importance to adequate stretch. Firm, low profile cushion should be used in commercial traffic areas. Cushions that are too thick and soft will permit carpet backings to stretch and eventually wrinkle. Recommendations from both cushion and carpet manufacturers should be considered prior to tackless stretch-in installations.

Seaming is another important consideration. Most modern installations employ hot-melt tape which is generally adequate. Follow the carpet manufacturer's recommendations for seaming. Woven carpet constructions may require hand sewing or other specialized seaming techniques. In all cases, cut edges must be buttered with appropriate seam sealer prior to sealing.

The Carpet and Rug Institute finds that the major cause of separation from the floor in a glue-down installation is an insufficient amount of carpet floor adhesive. Adequate open time for adhesives to develop tack (to partially set) prior to laying carpets into adhesives is also very important for many of today's carpet backing systems. Additionally, the specified amounts of adhesives must be applied to floors to obtain the required 100 percent adhesive transfer into the carpet back. The quantity applied is controlled by the size of notches in the installers' floor adhesive trowels. If too little is used, carpet will not adequately adhere to the floor.

Carpet with an attached cushion, secondary, unitary or woven backings may be adhered to floors, whereas, separate cushion stretch-in installations are usually limited to woven construction or tufted carpet with secondary backings. For heavy and rolling traffic, and other severe conditions, direct glue-down of carpet with either secondary, unitary, woven or attached cushion backing is preferred.

In tackless installations in commercial areas, firm cushions with minimum deflections are recommended. Adequate stretch conforming to manufacturer's recommendations should be applied. Power stretchers are mandatory to ensure adequate stretch. Knee kickers are permissible only in areas so small that power stretchers do not fit, such as closets.

The following should be included in installation contracts.

1. Scope including description of area involved as well as details on measurements, seam locations, diagrams, etc.

2. Qualifications required of contractor and installation specialists and references for similar jobs.

3. Storage and delivery responsibilities.

4. Preparatory work responsibilities (installer, general contractor, or owner) including:
   a. inspection and cleaning of subfloors;
   b. vertical transportation;
   c. removal and replacement of furniture;
   d. removal and disposition of existing floorcovering.

5. Submittal and approval of installation materials, edge mouldings, etc.

6. Method of installation:
   a. Stretch-in with separate cushion;
   b. Direct glue-down—
      I. without cushion,
      II. with attached cushion,
   c. Double glue-down.

7. Specify that installation should be in accordance with CRI 104, Standard for Installation of Commercial Textile Floorcovering Materials for all aspects not specifically covered.

8. Responsibility for cleanup.

9. Disposition of excess carpet.

10. Details of guarantee.

11. Time of installation, completion date, final acceptance inspection by specifier and installer prior to acceptance.

MAINTENANCE

Carpet is the only textile product on which people walk. This is why construction and installation specifications are so critical. The third critical specification element is maintenance. Specification of any one of these three elements without knowledge or consideration of the other two increases the risk that the carpet will not perform up to potential or expectation.

Even properly specified carpet can wear out or appear to be worn out if it is not maintained adequately. Dirt is unsightly but it can also be abrasive. As foot traffic deposits soil and causes the pile yarns to flex, embedded grit cuts the face fibers. The carpet begins to lose density and resilience. Threadbare spots appear and the carpet wears out. Moreover, allowing soil to build up and to spread may give the carpet a worn out appearance even if the face fibers are essentially intact.

If carpet is not vacuum cleaned regularly, the dirt builds up and begins to spread. To guard against build-up, a well-planned program is essential in commercial installations with their high traffic loads. Planned maintenance is the key to extending the life expectancy of carpet. The maintenance plan is no less important than the initial carpet specification and installation.

The maintenance plan should be developed as the carpet specifications are being considered. (In fact, a plan should be prepared in case the carpet is installed prior to completion of construction.)

When preparing the maintenance plan, keep in mind that one of the advantages of carpet compared to hard floors is that carpet localizes soil. Carpet tends to catch and hold soil and spills where they occur instead of allowing them to spread quickly. This feature of carpet suggests, then, that the best maintenance plan will identify in advance the most likely areas for soiling and spilling. The plan will specify maintenance schedules and procedures for these areas as well as the remainder of the carpet.

Specifically, heavy traffic areas, like entrances and lobbies, will not only require the most substantial carpet, they will probably have to be vacuumed once a day. In other instances, much of the traffic will come directly from a parking lot. Greasy staining from tracked-in motor oil should be anticipated.

Kitchen smoke in restaurants and cafeterias will contribute heavily to overall soiling. Stains and spills in restaurants and hospitals will be very common. Routine procedures for attending to these as quickly as possible are necessary.

Whatever the nature of the installation, it is wise to anticipate dealing with soilage from the very first day the carpet is installed. Otherwise, abrasive dirt may build up faster than it can be handled.

Two elements essential to an efficient maintenance program include daily procedures encompassing both regular vacuuming and spot cleaning, and scheduled overall cleanings to remove discoloring grime and to refresh the pile.

Overall grime not only causes discoloration, it presents another undesirable quality. Carpet that is not cleaned and reconditioned regularly, no matter how faithfully it is vacuumed, will tend to permanently crush and mat down. As greases present in smoke or pollutants in the air settle on the carpet, pile yarns may become gummy enough to stick to

each other and flatten in use. Matted carpet appears to be worn out, even if there is no real pile loss. Obviously, carpet which must be replaced because it looks worn out is no less costly than carpet which must be replaced because it is worn out!

The color of the carpet can contribute significantly to minimizing the appearance of dirt, particularly for entrances and lobbies, which get the bulk of tracked-in soil. If possible, colors should be chosen which blend with the color of the dirt brought in from outside.

Since the most common dirt colors are grays, beiges, browns, and reds, carpet colors for entrances should be chosen from these tones. The best choice would be a tweed coloration combining two or more of the colors.

Another choice might be a multicolored, patterned carpet which would add visual interest while helping camouflage dirt and spills until they can be removed. Such highly patterned carpet is a popular choice for hotel lobbies and restaurants.

Lighter, more delicate colors are best reserved for inside spaces—offices, guest rooms, lounges—where soiling rates are obviously lower and danger of accidental spills are more remote.

Elevators should also be carpeted, even if the entrance lobby is not. It is certainly wise to have soil wiped off in the elevator carpets rather than having it tracked over the carpet elsewhere.

As a matter of preventative maintenance, **walk-off** mats should be installed in all entrances to collect dirt before it reaches the carpet inside. Walk-off mats can be constructed of stiff bristles, they can be made from pieces of the inside carpet itself, or they can be one of a variety of types specially made for commercial use. Some have aluminum strips between the carpet. It is common to have two sets of walk-off mats and removable carpets available. Because they take such heavy abuse, one set is kept in place while the other is being cleaned. Another method of dirt control is to use a recessed mat or grating inside exterior doors. These gratings feature a system of self-cleaning recessed treads that are closely spaced to prevent the smallest heel from catching, yet allow dirt and sand to collect below the surface. The grate removes easily for cleaning.

Vacuuming Schedules

Of all the carpet maintenance procedures, vacuuming takes the most time and attention . . . yet is the most cost effective. The carpet should be inspected for stains during vacuuming. Stains should be removed as soon as possible. The longer they are allowed to set, the more permanent they may become.

The following is a normal vacuuming schedule:

High Traffic —Vacuum daily
Medium Traffic —Vacuum twice weekly
Light Traffic —Vacuum weekly

This broad guide recommends minimum schedules only. In order to reduce this general rule to specifics, some definitions will be useful. *Track-off areas* are where carpet collects foot soil tracked in from the outdoors or from hard-surfaced floors indoors.

Funnel areas where foot traffic is squeezed into or through a concentrated area, such as a doorway, stairwell, in front of drinking fountain, vending machine, etc. These areas readily can be identified in advance of soiling. Planned vacuuming in these areas, **even when soil is not visible,** will help prevent soil build-up. Also it will help focus maintenance attention on the places where it is known that soil will be tracked.

In the final analysis, an adequate schedule must key on the individual installation and its own traffic load and soiling rate. For example, soil may accumulate so rapidly at entrances (track-off areas) that carpet at those location will have to be vacuumed several times a day. In another instance, rooms may be entered directly from an uncarpeted corridor. Under the circumstances, even light traffic may cause heavy soiling, and the carpet may have to be vacuumed several times a week. Only experience will tell whether more frequent vacuuming is indicated.

Vacuum Cleaning Equipment

Vacuum cleaning equipment are of two types. The first of these, a heavy-duty wide track machine is recommended for large open areas. Because of its size, maintenance time can be measurable reduced with commensurate savings in labor costs. Such large industrial vacuums should be equipped with a stiff cylindrical brush, a beater-bar, to whip embedded dirt to the surface, and a powerful suction. A second machine, an industrialized version of the domestic upright vacuum cleaner belongs in every maintenance program. It too should have a good brushing action, a beater- bar and powerful suction. If possible, it should also have a hose and wand attachment for cleaning under heavy furniture not normally moved.

Otherwise, a canister vacuum, preferably with a power head, may also be needed for hard-to-reach places.

Stain Removal

Identification and immediate action are the keys to effective stain removal procedures. To minimize time and effort, it is helpful to know what causes a stain so that treatment can begin without guesswork. In most installations, stain identification may not be difficult because the possibilities are limited. In others, it could be a real problem.

A drug dispensing area in hospitals, for example, is susceptible to hundreds of staining agents. Employees must be instructed to report spills as they occur and to identify the spilled material.

It is also important to clean up stains as quickly as possible. The longer a stain sets, the more difficult it may be to remove. If it sets too long, it might react with the carpet dyes and cause permanent discoloration. Hence, an alert staff and well-stocked stain removal kit are important to good carpet maintenance. Always test a re-agent to determine its effect upon the carpet dye, fibers, and stain before applying larger amounts to the stain.

Detergent solutions to be used on wool should have a neutral pH. Natural fibers absorb moisture and are apt to be somewhat more vulnerable to chemical damage from acids or alkalis.

Man-made fibers on the other hand, are less moisture absorbent. Detergents which are alkaline in nature, between 7.0 and 10.0 pH, cut grease and suspend soil better and can be used satisfactorily on man-made fibers but should be tested on each color. Some detergents may leave a sticky residue that will cause rapid resoiling on the face of the carpet. The better detergents will dry to a crisp flake some of which can be vacuumed away.

There are many factors which will influence the frequency of cleaning, but a maintenance plan should be in effect BEFORE the traffic or high use areas start to show discoloration. If the traffic areas are allowed to become excessively soiled, on location cleaning may not remove sufficient soil to restore them to an acceptable level. It may be possible to clean only the high use areas occasionally in order to maintain an over-all high level of the carpet. This should all be part of the maintenance plan.

There are many methods of cleaning carpet, however, it is not possible to become an instant expert by reading descriptions, advantages, and disadvantages of each method. Successful carpet firms will use different methods and debate that their system is superior. The important factors are to have trained operators running the equipment, the equipment kept in proper working condition, using the correct chemicals at the right concentrations. A reputable carpet cleaner will be able to assist in deciding which method is best for that particular installation. These methods may be wet or dry or even a combination of these and the extraction methods may also vary.

Beware of the bargain carpet cleaning companies who will clean a whole house for a ridiculously low price. They often hire untrained people and, in the case of water extraction, they may soak the carpet so that it takes a long time to completely dry especially in high humidity areas. The time invested in developing a plan for carpet maintenance will pay off in longer use from the carpet. CLEANING SHOULD BE DONE BEFORE THE CARPET SHOWS SIGNS OF SOIL.

BIBLIOGRAPHY

Bridgepoint Corp. "Protector Course," Salt Lake City, UT: Bridgepoint Corporation, 1990.

Burlington Industries, Inc. *Carpet Maintenance Guide for Hospitals and Health Care Facilities.* King of Prussia, PA: Burlington Industries Inc., Carpet Division, 1987.

The Carpet and Rug Institute. *Carpet Specifier's Handbook.* Dalton, GA: The Carpet and Rug Institute, 1987.

Monsanto Contract Fibers—Concepts Ideas for Specifiers. Atlanta, GA: Monsanto Fiber and Intermediates Co.

Revere, Glen. *All About Carpets.* TAB Books Inc., Blue Ridge Summit, PA, 1988.

Reznikoff, C.S. *Specifications for Commercial Interiors.* Whitney Library of Design, an imprint of Watson-Guptil Publications, a division of Billboard Publications, NY, 1989.

The Wool Bureau, New York, NY.

ENDNOTES

[1] *Wool Bureau Library*, Volume 6, Rugs and Carpets.

[2] *Concepts, Ideas for Specifiers*, Monsanto Fiber and Intermediates Co., page 11.

[3] *Material Wealth—Living with Luxurious Fabrics* by Jack Lenor Larsen, published by Abbeville Press, New York, 1989, pages 195 and 197. Permission to reprint granted by John Calman & King Ltd., London, England.

[4] Carpet Cushion Counil. *The Supporting Facts About Carpet Cushion*, Riverside, CT.

[5] *Material Wealth—Living with Luxurious Fabrics* by Jack Lenor Larsen, published by Abbeville Press, New York, 1989, pages 192 through 193. Permission to reprint granted by John Calman & King Ltd., London, England.

GLOSSARY

BCF-*Bulked continuous filament.* The name given to continuous strands of synthetic fiber which are first spun into yarn and then texturized to increase bulk and cover.

Berber. A looped pile rug from North Africa. May be patterned or natural colored. Today Berbers are mostly textured natural earth tones.

Carpet modules. These are cut into 18 inch by 18 inch squares or other suitable dimensions.

Continuous filaments. Continuous strand of synthetic fiber extruded in yarn form without the need for spinning which all natural fibers require. (*See* **Spinneret**.)

Corn rowing. A characteristic which should be expected in carpet with higher tufts and lower density pile, resulting in the pile laying flat.

Dhurrie. A tapestry woven, flat rug with no pile that may be turned over. Originally from India, today comes mostly in pastel colors.

Filaments. A single continuous strand of natural or synthetic fiber.

Gauge. This is the distance between needles in tufted carpets as measured in fractions of an inch. Gauge is also the number of yarn ends across the width of the carpet.

Hydrophobic. Will not absorb liquids.

Indentations. Marks left in the carpet from heavy pieces of furniture remaining in one place.

Jacquard. An apparatus on a carpet weaving loom that produces patterns from colored yarns. The pattern information is contained on perforated cards. The holes in the cards activate the mechanism that selects the color to be raised to the pile surface.

Mildew. Discoloration caused by fungi.

Nap. Carpet or rug pile surface.

Ripples. Waves caused either by improper stretching or humidity.

Rya. A Scandinavian handwoven rug with a deep resilient comparatively flat pile. Usually of abstract design.

Sculpturing. A patterned carpet made by using high and low area.

Set yarns. Straight yarns.

Shading. Apparent color difference between areas of the same carpet. The physical cause is the difference between cut end luster, and side luster of fibers.

Shedding. Normal process of excess yarns coming to the surface in a freshly installed carpet.

Solution dyes. In man-made fibers, the dye is part of the liquid chemical which forms the filament resulting in a colorfast fiber.

Spinneret. A metal plate with fine holes, through which the chemical solution is forced in man-made filaments.

Sprouting. Protrusion of individual tuft or yarn ends above pile surface. May be clipped with scissors.

Spun. Drawing out and twisting of numerous staple fibers into yarn.

Staple fiber. Short lengths of fiber which may be converted into spun yarns by textile yarn spinning processes.

Static electricity. Shoe friction against carpet fiber causes production of electrostatic change which is discharged from carpet to person to conductive ground (e.g., a doorknob).

Unset. Frizzy yarns.

Walk-off mats. Mats on which most of the exterior soil is deposited.

Yarns. A continuous strand composed of fibers or filaments and used in the production of carpet and other fabrics.

Floors

WOOD

Wood was used in ancient times for flooring. According to the Bible, Solomon's Temple had a floor of fir, whereas the Romans only used wood on the upper floors of their buildings, using stone on the main floor. These stone floors persisted throughout the Dark Ages. In peasant homes, of course, a dirt floor was spread with straw; however, heavy, wide oak planks predominated in larger domestic structures.

The first wood floors were called *puncheon floors*, which were split logs, flat side up, fitted edge to edge, and smoothed with an ax or an adz. When saws became available to cut the wood into planks, white pine plank flooring of great widths was used in the Colonial period in the United States and was pegged in place.

In 18th and early 19th century America, sand was frequently spread over the wood floor to absorb dirt and moisture. Later, these floors were stained and then covered by Oriental rugs in wealthy homes; in more modest homes, they were either left bare or covered by homemade rugs. When renovating an old pine plank floor, the knots, which are much harder than the surrounding wood, have a tendency to protrude above the level of the worn floor and must be sanded to give a smoother surface. In some early floors that have not been renovated, it is actually possible to trip over these knots because they extend so far above the level of the floors.

In the early 19th century, **stenciling** was done directly on the floor in imitation of rugs, parquet floors, and marble and tile patterns. Painted floors and **floorcloths** came to be highly regarded until the carpet industry spelled the decline of floorcloths in the 1830s and 1840s. Incidently, these floorcloths are now making a comeback with textile designers such as Mayer Romanoff.

From the early 1700s in France, **parquetry and marquetry** were used. One of the most famous examples of this period is the beautiful parquet floor at the Palace of Versailles.

In 1885, the invention of a machine capable of making a **tongue and groove** in the edge of the wood, plus the use of **kilns**, combined to produce a draft-proof hardwood floor.

In the Victorian era, inlaid border patterns using contrasting light and dark wood were put together in a very intricate manner.

End-grain wood was even used to pave streets at the beginning of the 20th century.

In the early 1920s, unit block flooring was introduced, making parquet floors more reasonably priced because each piece did not have to be laid down individually but rather in a block.

Wood as a material for floors has definitely made

a comeback in recent years, particularly in contemporary homes. This is due in part to the use of polyurethane and urethane varnishes, which give an almost maintenance-free finish. Previously, a wood floor had to be stripped of wax build-up and frequently resanded and refinished. Also contributing to the popularity of wood floors are the warranties. Bruce Hardwood Floors for example has a 5-year residential and a one-year non-residential warranty on the surface wear layer. Hartco has a 25-year warranty for their acrylic impregnated flooring either in Pattern Plus™ or their parquet.

Wood is divided into two broad categories: the hard woods from the deciduous trees, which lose their leaves in the winter, and the soft woods, which come from the conifers or evergreens. Actually, there is an overlapping of hardness because some woods from the evergreens are harder than those from the broad-leafed trees.

The harder woods will, of course, be more durable and this durability, together with color and texture, must be considered in both flooring and furniture construction. Ease of finish should also be considered when the wood is to have an applied finish.

Weight is usually a good indicator of the relative strength of wood. Because wood is a natural material, it absorbs or eliminates moisture depending upon the humidity to which it is exposed. Most shrinkage or swelling occurs in the width of the wood; the amount depends on the manner of the cut. **Quarter sawn** woods are the least troublesome.

Warping is the tendency of wood to twist or bend when drying. This may be in the form of a bow, crook, twist, or cup and, as these are terms frequently referred to in construction, they are illustrated in Figure 3–1. The moisture problem can be reduced to a minimum by using kiln-dried lumber, where wood is stacked in an oven in such a manner that heated air can circulate around the whole plank in order to obtain a uniform moisture content. Seven to 8 percent is acceptable in flooring and furniture making, and 12 to 19 percent is acceptable for construction grades.

Wood is composed of many cells that run vertically, thus giving wood its straight **grain**. At frequent intervals, **medullary rays** thread their way between and at right angles to the vertical cells. They are most noticeable in plain oak and beech.

We have all seen pictures or drawings of the circular rings of trees. Some of the giant sequoias of California and the ancient oaks of Great Britain have been dated by rings showing hundreds of years of growth. These rings show the seasonal growth and are comprised of spring-wood—formed early in the growing season—and the summer wood or late wood. In some trees, the different time of growth is very obvious, such as in ash or oak, while in others, such as birch and maple, the seasonal growth is more blended. When there is an obvious difference in growth time, there is also a difference in weight and hardness. The faster-growing trees, usually those in more moderate climates, are softer than the same trees grown in northern areas where the growing season is shorter. Next to the bark is the sapwood that contains the food cells and is usually lighter in color. Heartwood contains the now-inactive cells and

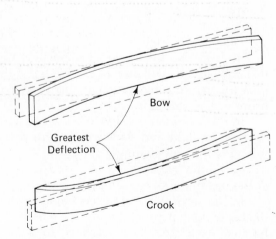

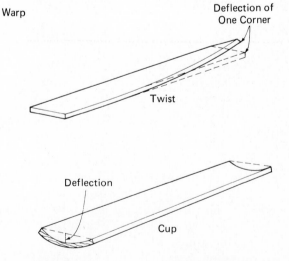

Figure 3-1
Warp.

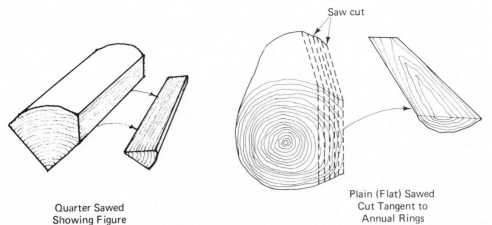

Quarter Sawed
Showing Figure

Plain (Flat) Sawed
Cut Tangent to
Annual Rings

Figure 3-2
Quarter sawed and plain sawed.

is slightly darker due to chemical substances that are part of the cell walls.

Figure is the pattern of the wood fibers, and the wood grain is determined by the arrangement of the cells and fibers. Some are straight and others are very patterned; this is enhanced by the method of cutting the boards.

There are two principal methods of cutting lumber. One is plain sawed for hardwoods, and flat grained for softwoods. The second is quarter sawed for hardwoods, or edge grained for softwoods. When referring to maple as used as a flooring material, the words "edge grained" are used, even though maple is a hardwood. Oak is quarter sawn, but fir cut in the same manner is called "vertical grain." As interior designers will probably be dealing mainly with hardwoods, the terms "plain sawed" and "quarter sawed" will be used from now on, with the exceptions mentioned above. Each method has its own advantages: plain sawed is the cheapest, easiest, and most economical use of wood, while quarter sawing gives less distortion of wood from shrinkage or warping.

Each method of cutting gives a different appearance to the wood. Plain sawing gives a cathedral effect, while quarter sawing gives more of a straight-line appearance. Saw mills cut logs into boards producing 80 percent plain to 20 percent quartered lumber. Quartered oak flooring, therefore, is extremely hard to find and is expensive. Most of all production is mixed cuts (see Figure 3–2).

Veneer is a very thin sheet of wood varying in thickness from 1/8 to 1/100 of an inch. Wood over 1/4 inch thick is no longer considered veneer. The manner in which the veneer is cut also gives different patterns. The three methods are rotary sliced, flat sliced, and quarter sliced. (These will be discussed

in more detail in the wall paneling chapter). **Laminated** wood is used for some floors and is a sandwich with an eneven number of sheets of veneer, layered at right angles to prevent warping, with the face having the better veneers. Water-resistant glue should be used for bonding the layers together, and the sandwich is placed in a hot press where pressure of 150 to 300 pounds per square inch (**psi**) is applied. Heat around 250° permanently sets the adhesive and bonds the layers together into a single strong panel.

The more expensive and rarer cuts of wood are used as the face veneer, thus holding down the cost and preserving the supply of these rarer woods. Mannington Wood Floors uses the same wood for all five plies of their laminated wood floors.

Grades of oak are determined by appearance alone. Flooring that is generally free of defects is known as *clear*, though it still may contain burls, streaks, and pinworm holes. *Select* is almost clear, but this grade contains more of the natural characteristics including knots and other marks. The *common* grades have more marking than either of the other two grades and are often specified because of these natural features and the character they bring to the flooring.

The three different types of wood flooring are strip, random plank, and parquet.

TYPES OF WOOD FLOORING *Two Types*

• Strip

Strip flooring comes in narrow widths, 2–1/4 inches or narrower, and is tongue and grooved on both

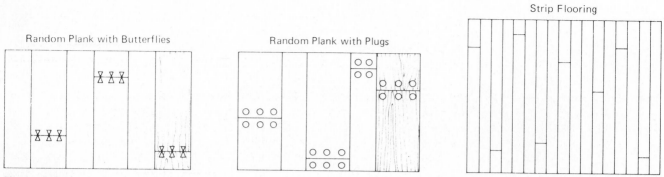

Figure 3-3
Types of flooring.

sides and ends. This type of flooring is most commonly made of oak, although some other woods may be used, such as teak and maple. The strip flooring may be laid parallel to the wall or diagonally. Gymnasium floors are always constructed of maple, but require a special type of installation that provides a slight give to the floor.

Harris-Tarkett manufactures a prefinished laminated plank product, Longstrip Plank™. The company's exclusive lamination features a top layer of fine hardwood, which is pressure glued to a hardwood core. This product is installed with a "floating" installation system. The precisely milled tongue-and-groove planks are tapped together over a 1/8-inch foam underlayment. No attachment to a subfloor is necessary, a good method when humidity may vary considerably.

For residential installations, Mannington Wood Floors has a Lifetime Structural Guarantee, as long as you own your house, on the following. Separation of bonded parts, unsightly cupping of planks, buckling due to expansion and warping or twisting. In addition, if you do not like the appearance of any plank before installation, the company will replace it free of charge. There is a full five-year warranty against subfloor moisture problems.

Perma-Grain® has an acrylic-impregnated plank flooring for high traffic areas, available in warm oak or the unique tupelo. Because it is offered as a five-ply laminate Timeless™ is the most stable plank flooring available, and is backed by a 20–year full replacement wear warranty. This type of flooring has been treated with a liquid acrylic that has been forced under pressure into the porous structure of the wood. The wood is then subjected to irradiation, which causes the liquid acrylic to harden and thus to impart to the wood/plastic an extremely abrasion-resistant finish, which exists throughout its thickness. Also available in a parquet.

Dyes and fire retardants may be added to the acrylic, if required. The stain penetrates throughout the wood so that worn areas need only be retouched with a topcoat. The floor never needs sanding, staining, or refinishing. With all these impregnated woods, it must be remembered that the color cannot be changed as it has penetrated the whole depth of the wood. This can be an asset or a liability, depending upon your requirements.

Regular strip flooring is sold by the board foot and 5 percent waste allowance is added to the total ordered.

Random Plank

Random width plank is available in widths from 3 to 8 inches; most installations are comprised of three different sizes. The widths selected should correspond to the dimensions of the room in order to keep the flooring in proper scale: the narrower ones for small rooms and wider ones for the larger rooms. Random plank comes with a **square** or **beveled edge** and may be **prefinished** at the factory or finished after installation.

Plank floors also have a tongue and groove side. The prefinished tongue and groove installation does disguise any shrinkage, as the V-joint becomes a fraction wider, whereas with a square edge, the crack caused by shrinkage is more obvious. This is why it is important that all wood be stored in the climatic conditions that will prevail at the installation site. This will allow the wood to absorb or dissipate moisture and reach a stable moisture content. A white finish will also emphasize any shrinkage.

In the past, some plank floors were installed using wooden pegs or plugs. A hole (or several holes in the case of a wide plank), was drilled about 1–1/2 to 2 inches from the end of the plank and a dowel was pounded into the floor joist and glued into place.

Any excess dowel was cut and sanded flush with the floor. Many times, these plugs were constructed of a contrasting wood and became a decorative feature of plank flooring. In later years, screws were countersunk and short dowels of walnut, other contrasting woods, or even brass were glued in to cover the screws for decorative purposes only. Today, unfortunately, some prefinished floors may even have plugs made of plastic, which seems incongruous in a wood floor. Another decorative joining procedure was the butterfly or key, where a dovetail-shaped piece of wood was used at the end joint of two boards.

Plank flooring is sold by the square foot and a 5 percent waste allowance is generally added to the total square footage.

Parquet

Parquet is individual pieces of wood (generally oak) 3/8, 5/16, 1/2, or 3/4 of an inch thick, joined together to form a variety of patterns. These small pieces are held together by various methods: using a **metal spline**, gluing to a mesh of paper, or gluing to a form of cheesecloth. This holds the small pieces of wood in the pattern.

There are many patterns, as can be seen from Figure 3–4, and most manufacturers make a similar variety of patterns, but the names may vary. One company will name a pattern Jeffersonian, another Monticello or even Mt. Vernon, but they are basically variations of the same pattern. This particular design is made with a central block surrounded by **pickets** on all four sides. The center may be made of solid wood, a laminated block, or contain five or six strips going in the same direction. Or there may be a standard unit of four **sets** in the center.

A word of warning about using some of the parquet patterns. Some parquets have direction, an example would be the herringbone pattern. Depending on whether the pieces are laid parallel to the

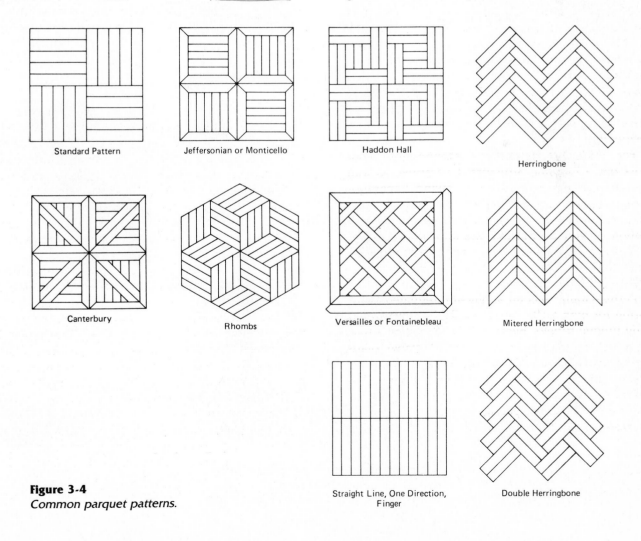

Standard Pattern

Jeffersonian or Monticello

Haddon Hall

Herringbone

Canterbury

Rhombs

Versailles or Fontainebleau

Mitered Herringbone

Straight Line, One Direction, Finger

Double Herringbone

Figure 3-4
Common parquet patterns.

wall, or at an angle, your client may see "Ls," "zig-zags," or arrows. The important thing is the clients expectations.

To minimize the expansion problems caused by moisture, the oak flooring industry has developed several types of parquets. These include the acrylic-impregnated and the laminated floor, some of which are warranteed for 25 years provided that correct installation methods are used.

The laminated block is a product that displays far less expansion and contraction with moisture changes and, therefore, can be successfully installed below grade (see Figure 3–7) in basements, in humid climates, and even fit tight to vertical obstructions. The blocks can be glued directly to the concrete with several types of adhesive. One of the concerns in the past has been the ability of a laminated block to be sanded and refinished. Because the face layer is oak, with proper maintenance, the initial service life can be expected to be 20 to 30 years. Any of the laminated products on the market today can be sanded and refinished, using proper techniques and equipment, at least twice, so the expected life of a laminated block floor is 60 to 90 years.

Parquet floor comes packed in cartons with a specific number of square feet. When ordering parquet flooring, only whole cartons are shipped, so the allowance for cutting may be taken care of with the balance of the carton.

Most woods for flooring are quarter sawed or plain sawed, but some species are cut across the growth rings (end-grained).

Another end-grain pattern is formed by small cross-cut pieces that are attached together into blocks or strips with the end grain exposed. The thickness may vary from 1 to 4 inches, depending upon the manufacturer. Some use tentachlorophenol to penetrate the blocks, while others use a penetrating oil finish. One and a half inches of end-grain block has insulating qualities equal to 23 inches of concrete. Some end-grain block floors are still in use after more than 40 years of heavy industrial use. These blocks absorb noise and vibration and have been installed in museums and libraries.

Special custom designed borders are available for use in a Victorian setting or for a contemporary custom look. These borders are made of contrasting woods and vary in width from 4 inches up to 20

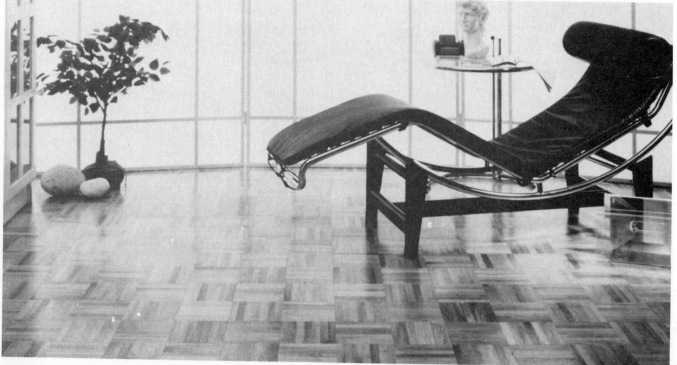

Figure 3-5
Prefinished parquet from The Oakweld™ Collection from Tarkett features the traditional mosaic pattern, a contrasting background for the chaise designed in 1928 by Le Corbusier. The parquet is available in two species Parawood and Malaysian Merbau. Photograph courtesy of Tarkett, Hardwood Division—North America.

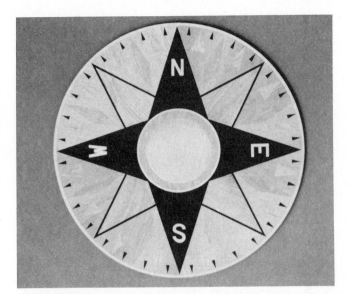

Figure 3-6
A custom inlay floor treatment for a residential or commercial entry area. This specific inset combines oak, ash, cherry, wenge, and brass for a truly unique approach. Inlays such as this are available in a wide range of designs, species, and scales for that special custom hardwood flooring accent area. Photograph courtesy of Kentucky Wood Floors.

inches. Thin strips of semiprecious stones or metals such as brass or aluminum may also be incorporated into the design.

Custom Borders from Kentucky Wood Floors are preassembled modules which can be glued down flush with 5/16-inch thick flooring or on top of underlayment with 3/4-inch thick flooring. Corner blocks are also available. Kentucky Wood Floors also handcrafts Custom Classics using a variety of species manufactured to the designers specifications (see Figure 3–6). Optional surface and finish treatments include beveled edges, a wire-brushed texture, a hand-distressed texture, or pre-finishing the floor. Matching architctural millwork is available, such as quarter-round, baseboard, nosing and **reducer strip**.

Grade Levels

Figure 3–7 illustrates the difference between on, above, and below grade. *Above grade* is not a problem for installation of wood floors because no moisture is present. As mentioned earlier, moisture is the major cause of problems with wood. *On grade* means that the floor is in contact with the ground. The floor usually has a drainage gravel as a base, covered by a polyethelene film to prevent moisture from migrat-

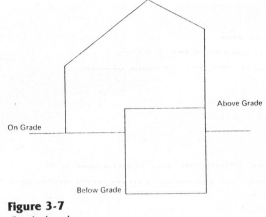

Figure 3-7
Grade levels.

ing to the surface. The concrete is then poured on top of this polyethelene sheet.

Below grade means a basement floor and the presence of moisture is an even greater problem. The polyethelene film should be lapped at the joints. Reinforcing rods are placed on top of the film and then the concrete is poured. All freshly poured concrete should be allowed to **cure** for 30 to 60 days. The rubber mat test will show if moisture is present. A rubber mat is placed on the cement surface and left for 24 hours. When removed, if the concrete surface is dry, there is no moisture present. This test should be done even if the slab has been in place over two years. The polyethelene film is of the utmost importance in insuring a subsurface that is properly moisture-free for installation of any floor.

Only laminated wood floors may be installed below grade, but the manufacturer's installation procedures must be followed exactly. Laminated products expand very little so may fit to a vertical surface.

Installation Procedures. Substrates must be clean (free of dust, grease, or oil stains), dry, and level. As we stressed in the paint chapter and will repeat throughout this book, SURFACE PREPARATION IS EXTREMELY IMPORTANT. The completed floor is only as good as the subfloor. Any high spots should be ground down and low spots filled in using the correct leveling compound. One floor installer related a story about a client who complained of a loose wood floor installed over a slab. When the loose wood was removed, not only did the wood come up, but attached to it was the material used as a filler for the low spots. The person who leveled the floor had used the wrong leveling compound.

Solid strip products are nailed down and parquet products are glued down. Laminated plank is the only product that can be either nailed or glued.

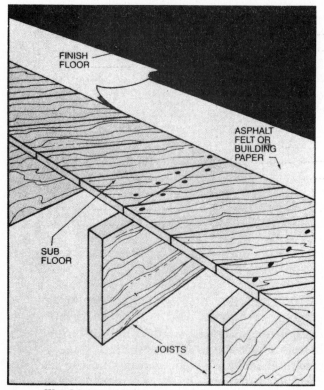

Wood joist construction using square-edge board subfloor.

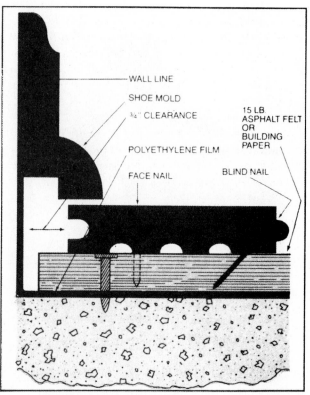

Plywood-on-slab method of installing strip oak flooring.

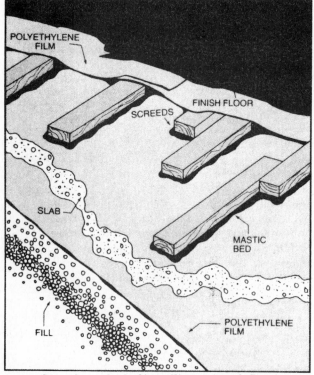

Screeds method of installing strip oak flooring on slab.

Use of the power nailer for installing strip flooring.

Figure 3-8
Installation methods for wood floors.

The National Oak Flooring Manufacturers Association (NOFMA) suggests that several factors may contribute to an unsatisfactory installation. First, the wood floor installation should be scheduled at the very end of construction. Since most other work is completed, the floors will not be abused. The building should now be dry, with any moisture introduced during construction gone. Second, a subfloor of minimum specifications will usually result in a minimum installation. The thicker, well fastened subfloor gives the better installation. Third, the wood flooring should be well nailed; there should be no skimping on the number of nails per strip, plank, etc. The photographs in Figure 3–8 are taken from NOFMA's Hardwood Flooring Installation Manual and show correct installation procedures.

Walls are never used as a starting point because they are never truly square. Wood parquet must always be installed in a pyramid or stair step sequence, rather than in rows, to avoid a misaligned pattern. The 3/4-inch parquet may be laid either parallel to or at a 45° angle to the wall.

Reducer strips may be used at the doorway if there is a difference in level between two areas, and are available to match the wood floor. Most wood floor **mastics** take about 24 hours to dry, so do not walk or place furniture in the room during that period. Laminated planks must be rolled with a 150-pound roller before the adhesive sets. An unfinished wood floor is sanded with the grain using progressively finer grits until the floor is smooth and has an almost shiny appearance. After vacuuming to eliminate any dust particles, finishing materials specifically manufactured for use on wood floors are applied. For open-grained wood such as oak, a filler with or without stain may be used after sanding to provide a more highly reflective surface.

There are two main types of finish applied to wood floors: polyurethane and Swedish finish. A polyurethane finish will yellow with time, while the Swedish finish will not. Glitsa, a brand name Swedish finish is now VOC compliant. When a very light finish is desired, the wood may be bleached or pickled.

Maintenance. It is the general housekeeping type of cleaning that prolongs the life of a wood floor. The main problem with maintenance of any floor is grit. This can be removed by dust mop, broom, or vacuum. Another problem is the indentations caused by heels, especially ladies high heels. A 125-pound woman with high heels exerts 2,000 psi pressure and, therefore, indentations should be expected. If the floor is the type that may be waxed, a thin coat of wax should be allowed to dry and harden. Then an electric bristle brush buffer is used. Because old wax holds dirt and grease and a buildup of "scuffs," it should be removed periodically by means of a solvent type of wax remover specifically designed for wood floors. Food spills may be wiped up with a damp cloth.

Most factory-finished or prefinished wood floors have a wax finish that may be renewed with a paste wax. However, custom finishes such as polyurethane and Swedish should not be waxed. Manufacturers of acrylic wood provide special cleaning materials for their products.

MARBLE

Marble is a **metamorphic** rock derived from limestone. Pressure and/or heat created the metamorphic change that turned limestone debris into marble. Today all rocks that are capable of taking a polish come under the heading of marble. Dolomitic limestone ("hard" limestone) although technically limestone, is known commercially as marble. Travertine and onyx are related stones; travertine being the more important for flooring purposes because it is easier to work. Onyx is brittle and is mostly relegated to decorations. Serpentine is of a different chemical

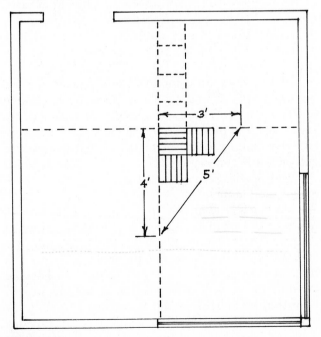

Figure 3-9
Method of laying out a tile or parquet floor.

makeup but because it can be polished it is classified as marble.

The colors of marble are as varied and numerous as the areas from which it is quarried. One of the famous Carrara marbles is pure white. Michaelangelo used this marble for many of his sculptures. Other Carrara marble may have black, gray, or brownish veinings. The name verd antiques is applied to marbles of prevailing green color, consisting chiefly of serpentine, a hydrous magnesium silicate. Verd antiques are highly decorative stones, the green being interspersed at times with streaks or veins of red and white. The pinks, reds, yellows, and browns are caused by the presence of iron oxides, whereas the blacks, greys and blue-greys result from bituminous deposits. Silicate, chlorite, and mica provide the green colors.

Marble is the most ancient of all finished materials currently in use today. Some authorities believe that the onyx marble of Algeria was employed by the Egyptians as early as 475 B.C. Biblical references indicate that marble was used in King Solomon's Temple at Jerusalem and in the palace of Sushun more than one thousand years before Christ. Parian marble from the Aegean Sea was found in the ruins of Ancient Troy.

Pentelic marble was used in the Parthenon in Athens, and is still available today. Phidias used this same marble for the frieze of the Parthenon and portions of this frieze knows as the **Elgin Marbles** are intact today and greatly treasured by the British Museum. Makrana marble, a white marble, was used in the Taj Mahal in India. Inside, the sunlight filters through marble screens as delicate as lace and the white marble walls are richly decorated with floral designs picked out in onyx, jasper, carnelian, and other semiprecious stones.

Knoxville, Tennessee was known at the turn of this century as the "marble capital." Marble is found in many states from Vermont to Georgia and in some of the western states. *True* marble is quarried in Georgia and Vermont. *Dolomitic* marble is quarried in Tennessee and Missouri. The famous Yule Quarry in Marble, Colorado (from which came the columns of the Lincoln Memorial and the massive block forming the Tomb of the Unknown soldier) has just been repoened. The white from this quarry may be the "purest" marble in the world.

Marble floors were used in the Baroque and Rococco periods in Europe. During the French empire, black and white marble squares were used, and they remain a popular pattern for marble floors today. In the formal halls of Georgian homes, the marble floors

Figure 3-10
Cast Marble Tile, Armstone™ from Armstar in the Atrium lobby of Bellevue Place, Wintergarden, Bellevue, Washington. 24-inch by 24-inch by ⅜-inch polished in three colors with accents of 8-inch by 8-inch black granite. Architect Kober/Sclater Associates. Photograph courtesy of Armstar.

were appropriate for the mahogany tables and chairs. In his Barcelona Pavillion, Mies Van der Rohe used great slabs of marble as free-standing partitions. Today, marble is used for furniture, floors, and both interior and exterior walls (see marble floors in Figures 3–10 and 4–3).

Marble does not come in sheets of equal size and must be mined with care. Blocks of marble are mined by drilling holes outlining the block and then wedges are driven into the holes and the blocks are split from the surrounding rock. Diamond blades are used to cut the blocks into the sizes required. Marble chips are used in the production of **terrazzo** and agglomerated marble tiles.

Marble is a relatively heavy and expensive material for use on floors due to the necessity of using the conventional, thick-bed installation method. One method of cutting down weight and cost is to use a layer of fiberglass and/or epoxy resins as a backing for thin layers of marble. Another method uses a 1/4-inch thick layer of marble backed by a 1-inch thick piece of Styrofoam. This latter method also provides a marble floor that is warmer to the touch than than one made of thicker marble. A third method is from

Stone Panels, Inc. and uses a thin veneer of natural stone, then an impervious fiber-reinforced epoxy skin, above an aluminum honeycomb which is backed by a high-strength fiber-reinforced epoxy skin, a 15/16-inch sandwich.

The agglomerated marble tiles consist of 90 to 95 percent marble chips combined with 5 to 10 percent resins and formed into blocks in a vacuum chamber, and are available as floor tile or marble wall veneers. Agglomerated marble may be classified as cast marble but the term "cast" is also used to describe a polyester product containing ground marble.

The following properties need to be considered for marble floors:

- **Density.** Averages 0.1 pound per cubic inch. This figure may be used to calculate the weight of the marble.
- **Water absorption**. Measured by total immersion of a 2-inch cube for 48 hours and varies from 0.1 to 0.2 percent, which is less than other natural stones. The maximum absorption as established by ASTM C503 is 0.20 percent.
- **Abrasion resistance.** Measured by a scuffing method that removes surface particles in a manner somewhat similar to the action of foot traffic. Abrasion resistance for commercial flooring should be at least a hardness value of 10 as measured by ASTM C241. The Marble Institute of America (MIA) recommends a hardness value of 12. This value is not necessary for one family homes.

Marble is also classified A through C, according to what methods of fabrication are considered necessary and acceptable in each instance, as based on standard trade practice.

A polished or glossy finish may be used in a residential installation but is not for commercial installations. Smooth satin or honed (a velvety, smooth surface with little or no gloss) or sand-rubbed (a flat nonreflective surface with little or no gloss) should be specified for commercial floors (see Figure 4–3).

When using marble or any other of the natural stones, it is necessary to calculate the weight of these materials and be sure the subfloor is strong enough to support the extra weight. This, of course, is where the 3/8 inch materials come into use, especially for remodeling, where the floor was probably not constructed to bear these heavy stones. Any deflection in the floor will result in cracks in the marble.

One of the newer materials used to provide rigidity to the sub-floor is HARDIBACKER® board, a lightweight, dimensionally stable cement-based board that is water resistant for residential or commercial construction. Because this board is only 1/4 of an inch thick, it reduces the height variations where different types of flooring materials meet, such as ceramic tile and carpeting. Other backerboards vary in composition, thickness, weight and compressive strength. The subfloor suggested is a 1/2-inch minimum thickness plywood firmly fastened to 16-inch **o.c.**, floor joists, with nails and construction adhesive. The backer board is nailed in place every 6 inches, using suggested mechanical fasteners, which penetrate through to the floor joists. The subfloor is now ready for the installation of materials requiring the thin-set method.

- **Installation Methods.** Several associations are responsible for codes and standards based on the consensus of their membership. The natural stones such as marble, travertine, and slate use the specifications and test methods contained in the American Society for Testing and Materials (ASTM), Section 4 Construction; volume 04.08 Soil and Rock; Building Stones. The ceramic tile industry uses the American National Standards Institute (ANSI) A108.5 for installation specifications. A copy of these specifications and test methods may be obtained from the respective organizations (see Appendix B).

As this is the first hard surface material covered in this book, installation methods will be detailed. Basically the same methods are used for all natural stones, ceramic tile, quarry tile, and other types of flooring.

Setting materials only account for 10 percent of the installation cost but account for 90 percent of the problems, so proper specification and a workmanlike installation will eliminate most problems.

The Tile Council of America states:

There are two equivalent methods recognized for installing ceramic tile with a portland cement mortar bed on walls, ceilings and floors. They are (1) the method covered by ANSI A108.1, which requires that the tile be set on a mortar bed while it is still plastic, and (2) the method covered by ANSI A108.5, which requires the tile to be set on a cured mortar bed with Dry-Set or latex-portland cement mortar. When absorptive ceramic tile are installed on a plastic mortar bed using a neat cement bond coat they must be soaked before setting.[1]

Thick-set or thick bed MUST be used for setting materials of uneven thickness such as flagstone and slate. It may also be used for hard-surfaced materials of uniform thickness. The thick bed, 1–1/4 inches, facilitates accurate slopes or planes in the finished tile work. Tiles are placed on the mortar and tapped into place until the surface is level. The mortar used on floors is a mixture of portland cement and sand, roughly in proportions of 1:6.

Portland cement mortars can be reinforced with metal lath or mesh, can be backed with membranes and can be applied on rough floors. They are structurally strong, are not affected by prolonged contact with water, and can be used to plumb and square surfaces installed by others. Installation and material specifications are contained in ANSI A108.1.

Dry-set or thin-set mortar is only for materials of even thickness such as pavers or tiles. Dry-set mortar is suitable for use over a variety of surfaces. It is used in one layer, as thin as 3/32 of an inch, after tiles are beat in, has excellent water and impact resistance, is water-cleanable, nonflammable, good for exterior work, and does not require soaking of tile. Another thin-set method is to use an adhesive which is spread with a trowel, first using the flat edge for continuous coverage and then the notched edge for uniform thickness. Oil-based adhesives should be avoided when installing marble as they stain the marble. Again it must be repeated thin bed should only be used where the substrate is solid and level.

There are differences between a marble setter and a tile setter. One is that the former **butts** tiles together, resulting in 1/16 of an inch width space which may be filled in with portland cement if desired or left unfilled. A tile setter, however, is accustomed to working with **cushion-edged** tile and so will leave a wider space between the tiles. It is necessary to state the spacing of the marble tile and whether or not **grout** is to be used. Another difference is that marble setters prefer a stiffer 1:3 mortar mix.

Normal Maintenance. The following information is taken from the booklet "How to Keep Your Marble Lovely," which is available from the Marble Institute of America, Inc. (See Appendix B.) Marble floors should be washed with clean luke warm water, and if badly soiled, a mild detergent can be used. The floor is rinsed thoroughly with clean water. Any residue left could made the floor slippery. All stones and many man-made, hard-surfaced materials are to some degree porous and should, therefore, be protected from oil and water-borne stains.

Most old stains require the use of a poultice which consists of molding plaster, untreated white flour, white chalk, or white tissue paper soaked to form a paste. The poultice should be soaked in the proper solution depending on the type of stain and covered with a sheet of plastic which has been taped down around the edges to keep the moisture from evaporating while the stain is drawn out of the marble-from up to 48 hours, depending upon the type of stain.

To remove organic stains such as tea or coffee, and leached colors from paper or textiles, the surface is washed with clean water and a poultice is applied soaked in either hydrogen peroxide (20 percent volume) or household ammonia (full commercial strength). Oil stains and mustard are soaked in Amyl Acetate or Acetone. (Caution: Amyl Acetate and Acetone are highly flammable and should only be used in a well-ventilated area and kept away from flame or sparks). For rust stains, a poultice is soaked in commercial rust remover.

• TRAVERTINE

Travertine is a porous limestone formed from the precipitation of mineral springs and has holes in it as a result of escaping gas. When it is to be used on the floor, travertine should be filled with an epoxy resin. As travertine is creamy colored, this resin may be opaque, of a creamy color, or transparent. The opaque filler does not reflect the light as well as the surrounding polished travertine, whereas the clear epoxy gives a three-dimensional appearance to the holes and takes on the shine of the travertine.

Maintenance. The maintenance of travertine is the same as for marble.

• GRANITE

Granite is technically an igneous rock having crystals or grains of visible size. These grains are classified as fine, medium, or coarse.

Colors are white, gray, buff, beige, pink, red, blue, green, and black, but within these colors, the variegations run from light to dark. The color gray, for example, may be light, medium, or dark or vary between dark and purplish gray, or dark and greenish gray. It is important to see an actual sample of the type of granite to be used. The National Building Granite Quarries Association recommends submitting duplicate 12-by-12 inch samples to show the full range of color, texture and finish, with the designer retaining one set and the other being returned to the granite supplier for his guidance.

In addition to color, finish is important. The following definitions were set up by the NBGQA.

- **Polished.** Mirror gloss, with sharp reflections.
  Honed. Dull sheen, without reflections.
  Fine rubbed. Smooth and free from scratches; no sheen.
  Rubbed Plane. Surface with occasional slight "trails" or scratches.
  Thermal. Plane surface with flame finish applied by mechanically controlled means to insure uniformity. Surface coarseness varies, depending upon grain structure of the granite.

As with other stones, polished granite should not be used for floors because the mirror gloss and color will eventually be dulled by the abrasion of feet. Flamed or thermal texture are used to create a nonslip surface where water may be present.

The same method of veneered construction used to make thinner and lighter weight marble squares is also used with granite, and for the same reasons. Permetage® is an American made, 96 percent natural marble or granite **agglomerate**, reinforced by high-technology resin, which is inherently stain resistant and is much stronger than natural stone materials in similar size. Tiles are a nominal 3/8-inch thick and are available in the standard 12-by-12 inch tile up to a 24-by-24 inch unit. This product is available in 19 different colors including four travertine patterns where random veining is produced in the manufacturing process. The other colors are granite, from reds, greys, to white and black.

Armstar® has three finishes—polished, honed with a softer more elegant look, and textured with a more natural context (see Figure 3–10).

When a feeling of permanence and stability is needed, granite is a good choice.

Installation. Granite is installed using the same methods as for marble, especially for the honed-face stones. When some of the more textured finishes are specified, and when the granite has not been cut to a definite size, a mortar joint is used.

Maintenance. Granite floors, particularly those with rougher surfaces, require ordinary maintenance by means of a brush or vacuum cleaner. The more highly finished granite surfaces should be maintained in a manner similar to marble.

GROUT

Grout is the material used to fill the joints between tiles. The type of grout employed, if any, depends on which variety of tile is being used. Therefore, not only is the type of grout important, but also the spacing of the tile. Proper joint placement is very important so that both sides of the room have equal size pieces. The use of crack isolation membranes in thin-bed installations is necessary to prevent cracks in the substrate from cracking marble and ceramic tile installed over them.

The Tile Council of America states that portland cement is the base of most grouts and is modified to provide specific qualities such as whiteness, mildew resistance, uniformity, hardness, flexibility, and water retentivity. Noncement-based grouts such as epoxies, furans, and silicone rubber offer properties not possible with cement grouts. However, special skills on the part of the tile setter are required. These materials can be appreciably greater in cost than cement-based grouts. The commercial portland cement grout for floors is usually gray (colors are available), and is designed for use with ceramic **mosaics**, quarry and paver tile. Damp curing is required which is the process of keeping the grout moist and covered for several days, resulting in a much stronger grout.

Grouts with sand are not used with highly reflective tiles, as the roughness of the grout is not compatible with the high gloss. For glazed tiles, use unsanded grout or mastic grout. There are special grouts available that are chemical resistant, while some are fungus and mildew resistant, and others of a latex composition are used when any movement is anticipated.

Latapoxy® SP-100 is a 100 percent solid epoxy grout. Stainless, sanitary and colorfast with uniform color and highly chemical resistant and may be used for both walls and floors. Consult the manufacturers of grout and mortar for recommendations of products for specific applications as new products are constantly being developed.

FLAGSTONE

Flagstone was used on the floors in Tudor England (1485–1603). *Flagstone* is defined as thin slabs of stone used for paving walks, driveways, patios, etc. It is generally fine-grained **sandstone**, **bluestone**, **quartzite**, or slate, but thin slabs of other stones may be used. One-inch-thick bluestone flagging in random

Table 3-1
Grout guide

GROUT GUIDE

Printed through the courtesy of the Materials & Methods Standards Association	**GROUT TYPE** See pages 6 & 7 for complete description								
A rubber faced trowel should be used when grouting glazed tile with sanded grout.	Commercial Portland Cement		Sand-Portland Cement	Dry-Set	Latex Port-land Cement (3)	Epoxy (1) (6)	Furan (1) (6)	Silicone or Urethane (2)	Modified Epoxy Emulsion (3) (6)
	Wall Use	Floor Use	Wall-Floor Use	Wall-Floor Use					
TILE TYPE — GLAZED WALL TILE (More than 7% absorption)	•			•	•			•	
TILE TYPE — CERAMIC MOSAICS	•	•	•	•	•	•		•	•
TILE TYPE — QUARRY, PAVER & PACKING HOUSE TILE	•	•	•		•	•	•		•
AREAS OF USE — Dry or limited water exposure	•	•	•	•	•	•	•	•	•
AREAS OF USE — Wet areas	•	•	•	•	•	•	•	•	•
AREAS OF USE — Exteriors	•	•	•	•	•(4)	•(4)	•(4)		•(4)
PERFORMANCE — Stain Resistance (5)	D	C	E	D	B	A	A	A	B
PERFORMANCE — Crack Resistance (5)	D	D	E	D	C	B	C	A Flexible	C
PERFORMANCE — Colorability (5)	B	B	C	B	B	B	Black Only	Restricted	B

(1) Mainly used for chemical resistant properties.
(2) Special tools needed for proper application. Silicone, urethane and modified polyvinylchloride used in pregrouted ceramic tile sheets. Silicone grout should not be used on kitchen countertops or other food preparation surfaces unless it meets the requirements of FDA Regulation No. 21, CFE 177.2600.
(3) Special cleaning procedures and materials recommended.
(4) Follow manufacturer's directions.
(5) Five performance ratings—Best to Minimal (A B C D E).
(6) Epoxies are recommended for prolonged temperatures up to 140F, high temperature resistant epoxies and furans up to 350F.

Source: 1991 Handbook for Ceramic Tile Installation. Copyright © Tile Council of America, Inc. Reprinted with permission of Tile Council of America and the Materials and Methods Standards Association.

multiple pattern compares very favorably in price to premium vinyl tiles.

The stone may be irregularly shaped as it was quarried, varying in size from 1 to 4 square feet, or the edges may be sawed to give a more formal appearance. Thickness may vary from 1/2 to 4 inches; therefore, the flagstone must be set in a thick mortar base in order to produce a level surface.

The extra thickness of the flagstone must be taken into consideration when positioning the floor joists. One client had flagstone drawn and specified on her blueprints, but the carpenter misread the plans and assumed that it was to be a flagstone patterned floor and not the real thing. The client arrived at the house one day to discover that the entry way did not have the lowered floor necessary to accommodate the extra thickness of the stone. The contractor had to cut all the floor joists for the hall area, lower them 4 inches, and then put in additional bracing and supports in the basement—a very costly error.

Another point to remember with flagstone is that the surface is usually slightly uneven because it comes from naturally cleaved rock; therefore, flagstone is not suitable for use under tables and chairs as the legs will rock. An entrance hall of flagstone is very durable but needs to be protected from grease.

The grout used is a sand-portland cement type and fills all areas where flagstones adjoin.

Maintenance. There are sealing compounds on the market that make flagstone **impervious** to any staining and wear. These compounds are available in gloss and matte finishes and protect the treated surface against the deteriorating effects of weathering, salts, acids, alkalies, oil, and grease. The gloss finish does seem to give a rather unnatural shiny appearance to the stone but where the impervious quality rather than the aesthetic quality is of prime importance, these sealers may be used. Vacuuming will remove dust and siliceous material from the surface and a damp mop will remove any other soil from the sealed surface.

SLATE

Slate was also used as a flooring material in Tudor England (1585–1603) and in 17th century France, slate was combined with bands of wood. Slate is a very fine-grained metamorphic rock cleaved from sedimentary rock shale. One of the characteristics of slate is that this cleavage allows the rock to be split easily into relatively thin slabs. The most common colors for slate range from gray to black, but green, brown, and red are also available. In areas of heavy traffic, the honed black slate does have a tendency to show the natural scuffing of shoes, and the scratches give the black slate a slightly grayish appearance. All stones will eventually show this scuffing and, therefore, highly polished stones should be avoided as a flooring material.

Different finishes are available in slate, as in other stones. The Structural Slate Company describes the following finishes:

Natural cleft. The natural split or cleaved face. It is moderately rough with some textural variations. Thickness will have a plus or minus tolerance of 1/8 of an inch
Sand-rubbed. This has a slight grain or stipple in an even plane. No natural cleft texture remains. Finish is equivalent to **60–grit** and is obtained by wet sand on a rubbing bed
Honed. This finish is equivalent to approximately **120–grit** in smoothness. It is semipolished, without excessive sheen

The standard thickness of sawed flooring slate is 1/2 inch. Also available are 3/4– and 1-inch thicknesses, and these are suitable for both interior and exterior use.

One half inch slate weighs 7 1/2 pounds per square foot, 3/4 inch weighs 11 1/4 pounds, and 1 inch weighs 15 pounds. The absorption rate of slate is 0.23 percent. One-quarter-inch slate is used for interior foyers in homes and commercial buildings using the thin-set method. This thickness is an excellent remodel item over wood or slab, and gives a rug level effect when it adjoins carpet. One-quarter-inch slate only weighs 3 3/4 pounds per square foot.

The thicker slate is available in rectangles and squares in sizes from 6-by-6 inches to 24-by-24 inches in multiples of 3 inches, whereas the sizes for 1/4-inch slate are 6-by-6 inches to 12-by-12 inches, also in multiples of 3 inches.

As can be seen from the above types, slate is available for both thin-set and thick-set applications. When thin-set mastic or adhesive is used, a 1/4-by-1/4 inch notched trowel held at a 45° angle is suggested.

There are, however, several points to remember with both types of installations. If grout is used with slate (the spacing varies from 1/4 to 1/2 of an inch), it is important that any excess be cleaned off, because grout that has dried on the slate surface will probably never come off. If grout is not used, the slate tiles are butted against each other. Joint lines are staggered so no lines are more than 2 to 3 feet in a straight line.

Thick-bed installation is similar to flagstone. All joints should be 1/2-inch wide flush joints and should be **pointed** with 1:2 cement mix the same day the floor is laid to make joints and setting bed **monolithic**.

Maintenance. A slate floor is easily maintained with mild soap and water. While waxing is not harmful, it detracts from the natural beauty of the stone, turns the floor a darker shade, and may yellow the grout.

CERAMIC TILE

Due to the fact that ceramic tile was one of the most durable materials used by ancient civilizations, archaeologists have been able to ascertain that thin slabs of fired clay, decorated and glazed, originated in Egypt about 4700 B.C. Tile was, and frequently is, used in Spanish architecture to such a degree that a Spanish expression for poverty is "to have a house without tiles." The Spanish also use ceramic tile on the **risers** of stairs.

In England, many abbeys had tile mosaic floors and the European cathedrals of the 12th century also had tile floors. The ancient tiles were used to make pictures on the walls, with the pattern covering many tiles. A good example is the bulls and dragons in the Ishtar Gate from Babylon now in the Pergamon Museum in Berlin. Later, each tile was decorated with very intricate patterns or four tiles were used to form a complete pattern. Eighteenth and 19th century tiles used a combination of these two types.

Tiles were named after the city where they originated.—Faience from Faenza in Italy, Majolica from Majorca, and Delft tiles from the town of Delft in Holland. Delft tiles, with their blue and white designs, are known worldwide.

Most glazed ceramic tiles for interior use are produced by the dust-press process. A mixture of damp, white-burning clays and other ceramic materials are forced into steel dies under heavy pressure. After pressing, the tile is inspected for smoothness, size, and imperfections. It may then be fired at a high temperature to form a **bisque**, a tile ready to be glazed. A glaze of ceramic materials and mineral pigments is sprayed on the bisque and a second firing at a lower temperature fuses the glaze to the bisque. Some glazed tiles are produced with a single firing. In this process, the tile is pressed, allowed to cure, given a coat of glaze, and then fired in the kiln.

Tiles are also made by extrusion, a slush-mold process, or a ram-press process. In the extrusion process, the clay is mixed the consistency of thick mud and forced through a die. The machine cuts the clay to proper lengths as it comes from the die. In the slush-mold process, a wet mixture of clay is poured into molds and allowed to set. The tiles are then removed from the molds, glazed, and fired in a kiln. In the ram-press process, tiles are formed between two steel dies. This method produces larger tiles of any shape or surface texture. The tiles are glazed and fired in the same manner as dust-pressed tiles.[2]

It is the temperature and the proportions of the ingredients that dictate the use; walls, floors, interior or exterior, and residential or commercial.

Porcelain tiles are inherently impervious and are used frequently in heavy-use commercial and retail areas. These are used in light colors which give an airy and spacious feeling to the installation. One problem may be that light-colored tile often means light-colored grout and, therefore, stain-resistant grout should be specified. Due to the low absorption rate of porcelain tiles, bond-promoting additives are added to the mortars and grouts.

There are many types of finishes and patterns

Table 3-2
Porosity variances

Type	Water Absorption Rate
Impervious	0.5% or less
Vitreous	More than 0.5% but less than 3%
Semivitreous	More than 3% but less than 7%
Nonvitreous	More than 7%

available in ceramic tile, ranging from a very shiny, highly reflective glaze to a dull matte finish and even an unglazed impervious tile. Tile may be solid color or hand painted with designs (see Figure 3–11).

The surface texture of the tile has a great deal to do with the reflectance qualities. For example, a perfectly smooth tile will have a much higher reflectance rate than a rough surface tile, even though they may have identical glazes. Ceramic tiles are available in many different shapes and sizes. Instead of the

Figure 3-11
American Olean introduces new Triad™, combining decorated tile in a variety of geometric designs with field tile in either a granite glazed or marbleized surface. Photograph courtesy of American Olean Tile Company.

FLOOR TILING INSTALLATION GUIDE
Performance-Level Requirement Guide and Selection Table
Based on results from ASTM Test Method C-627 "Standard Method for Evaluating Ceramic Floor Tile Installation Systems."

SERVICE REQUIREMENTS	FLOOR TYPE — Numbers refer to Handbook Method numbers			
Find required performance level and choose installation method that meets or exceeds it.	Concrete	Page	Wood	Page
EXTRA HEAVY: Extra heavy and high impact use in food plants, dairies, breweries and kitchens. Requires quarry tile or packing house tile. (Passes ASTM C627 cycles 1 thru 14.)	F101, F102 F111, F112, F113 F114, F115 F121[b] F131, F132, F133 F134	12 13 14 15 16 17	F143[a]	18
HEAVY: Shopping malls, stores, commercial kitchens, work areas, laboratories, auto showrooms and service areas, shipping/receiving and exterior decks. Heavy tile except where noted. (Passes ASTM C627 cycles 1 thru 12.)	F103[b] F111 (ceramic mosaic) F112 (ceramic mosaic) F113 (ceramic mosaic) F121[b] (ceramic mosaic) F125 RF918[c]	12 13 13 13 15 15 34	RF913, RF915[c]	34
MODERATE: Normal commercial and light institutional use in public space of restaurants and hospitals. Ceramic mosaic or heavier tile. (Passes ASTM C627 cycles 1 thru 10.)	F112 (cured bed) F115 F122[d] (quarry tile) RF914, RF916[c]	13 14 15 34		
LIGHT: Light commercial use in office space, reception areas, kitchens, bathrooms. Ceramic mosaic or heavier tile. (Passes ASTM C627 cycles 1 thru 6.)	F122[d] RF911, RF912, RF917[c]	15 34	F121[b] F141 F143[a], F144	15 17 18
RESIDENTIAL: Kitchens, bathrooms, foyers. Ceramic mosaic or heavier tile. (Passes ASTM C627 cycles 1 thru 3.)	F116 (ceramic mosaic or glazed floor tile) TR711[e]	14 30	F142	17

Notes:

Consideration must also be given to (1) wear properties of surface of tile selected, (2) fire resistance properties of installation and backing, (3) slip-resistance.

Tile used in installation tests listed in Selection Table were unglazed ceramic mosaic and ½" thick quarry tile unless otherwise noted. Unglazed Standard Grade tile will give satisfactory wear, or abrasion resistance in installations listed. Glazed tile or soft body decorative unglazed tile should have the manufacturer's approval for intended use. Color, pattern, surface texture and glaze hardness must be considered in determining tile acceptability on a particular floor.

Selection Table Notes:

Tests to determine Performance Levels utilized representative products meeting recognized industry standards:

a. ANSI A118.3 epoxy mortar and grout.

b. Rating extrapolated from other test data.

c. Data in Selection Table based on tests conducted by Tile Council of America, except data for F144 and RF900 Methods, which are based on test results from an independent laboratory through Ceramic Tile Institute.

d. ANSI A118.1 latex portland cement mortar and grout.

e. Tile bonded to existing resilient flooring with epoxy adhesive.

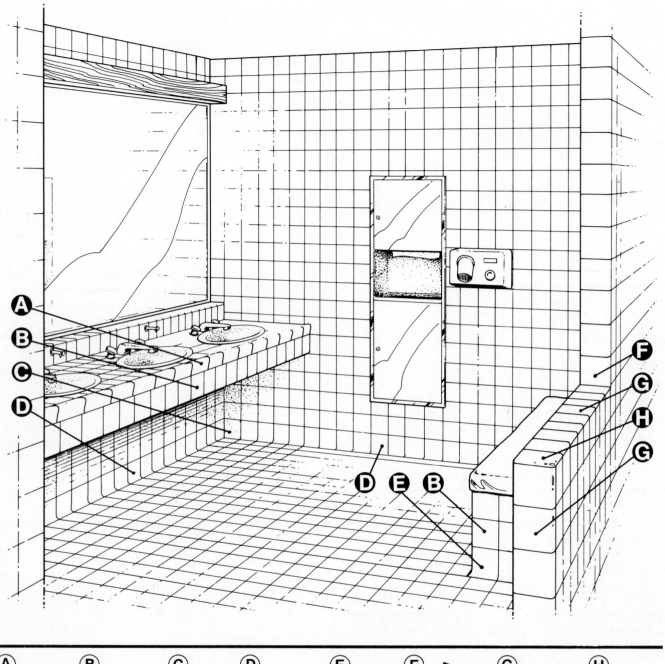

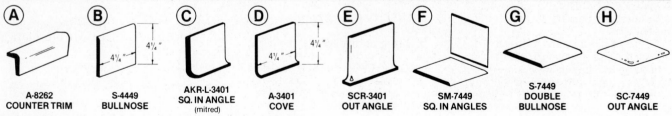

A	B	C	D	E	F	G	H
A-8262 COUNTER TRIM	S-4449 BULLNOSE	AKR-L-3401 SQ. IN ANGLE (mitred)	A-3401 COVE	SCR-3401 OUT ANGLE	SM-7449 SQ. IN ANGLES	S-7449 DOUBLE BULLNOSE	SC-7449 OUT ANGLE

Figure 3-12

Tile Trim reprinted with permission of American Olean.

4 1/4-by-4 1/4 inch tile, the 8-by-8 inch tile is being more widely used (see Figure 8–5). A 60-by-60 cm tile is shown in Figure 4–1.

When ceramic or quarry tile is used on the floor, it is usually finished with a **base** or combination trim tile having a **bullnose** at the top and a **cove** at the bottom in the same material as the floor tile (see Figure 3–12). If ceramic tile is to be continued onto the wall surface, a cove base is used.

CERAMIC MOSAIC TILE

Ceramic mosaic tile is usually formed by the dust pressed method, 1/4 to 3/8 of an inch thick, with a facial area of less than 6 square inches. Pigments and, if required, abrasives are added to the porcelain or clay mixture and, therefore, the color is dispersed throughout the tile. Ceramic mosaic tile is fired in kilns with temperatures reaching 2,150°F. It is im-

Figure 3-13
A restaurant in Greektown, Michigan has 1 inch by 1 inch and 2 inch by 2 inch mosaic tile laid to imitate the keys of a piano. The contrast of color and size provide an interesting combination on both walls and floor. Architects: Beatty & Beatty. Tile Contractor: Virginia Tile Co. Photograph courtesy of American Olean.

pervious, stainproof, dentproof, and frostproof. Because of a mosaic tile's small size, the individual tiles are mounted on a sheet to facilitate setting. Backmounted material may be perforated paper or a fibermesh. Face-mounted tiles have paper with a water-soluble adhesive applied to the face of the tile, which is removed prior to grouting (see Figure 3–13).

A paver tile has the same composition and physical properties as a mosaic tile, but is thicker and has a facial area of more than 6 square inches.

Hastings Tile has a new collection of modular marble mosaic designs, in 12-inch long sections, mesh-mounted for one-piece installation on walls or floors, for borders or trim in combination with marble or ceramic tiles or used in allover mosaic designs. (See Figure 3–14.)

Highly glazed tile is not recommended for floor use for two reasons. First, the surface can become extremely slippery when wet; second some wearing and scratching can occur over a period of time, depending on type of use. Of course, if moisture and wear are not a problem, then glazed tile may be used.

Ceramic Tile. *The Installation Handbook* is published by the Tile Council of America, Inc. each year and contains Table 3–3, which will help the designer to choose the correct tile for every type of use, and from that table be able to specify a Handbook Method Number, grout, and setting method. This handbook is also a guide in developing job specifications.

As can be seen from Table 3–3, ceramic tile for floor use may be installed by both thick and thin-set methods.

Specialty Tiles

Conductive tile is made from a special body composition by adding carbon black or by methods resulting in specific properties of electrical conductivity while retaining other normal physical properties of tile. These tiles are used in hospital operating rooms, certain laboratories, or wherever sparks from static electricity could cause an explosion, due to the presence of oxygen. Conductive tile should be installed using a conductive dry-set mortar with an epoxy grout.

Pregrouted tiles usually come in sheets of up to 2.14 square feet that have already been grouted with silicone rubber. Pregrouted tiles save on labor costs because the only grouting necessary is between the sheets, rather than between individual tiles.

Slip-resistant tiles contain abrasive particles that

Figure 3-14

Italian classics updated . . . Hastings displays a variety of ¾ inch modular marble mosaic designs for borders or trim. (Photograph courtesy of Hastings Tile & Il Bagno Collection.)

are part of the tile. Other methods of slip-resistance may be achieved by grooves or patterns on the face of the tile.

Some tiles are self-spacing because they are molded with **lugs**. Other means of spacing are achieved by using plastic spacers to insure alignment of tiles and an even grout area.

When ordering any tile, add 2 percent extra of each color and size for the owner's use. This will make replacements due to damage immediate and the color will match exactly.

QUARRY TILE

Quarry tile is strong, hard-body tile made from carefully graded shale and fine clays, with the color throughout the body (see Figure 3–15). Depending upon the geographic area where the clays are mined,

the colors will vary from the warm brown-reds to warm beiges. The face of quarry tile may be solid colored, variegated with lights and darks within the same tile, or *flashed* where the edges of the tile are a darker color than the center. Quarry tile is extruded in a 1/2-inch thick ribbon and then cut to size. The quality of the clays and temperatures at which they are fired (up to 2,000°F) provide a wide variety of finished products. Quarry tile is generally considered stain resistant but not stain proof.

The rugged, unglazed surface of quarry tile develops an attractive **patina** with wear. An abrasive grit surface is available where slip resistance is important. Almost all quarry tile is manufactured unglazed in order to retain the natural quality of the tile, but some quarry tile is available glazed.

Quarry tile may be installed by either thick or thin-set methods. The grout is either a sanded portland cement mix, or an epoxy grout with a silica filler.

Figure 3-15
The atrium of Harborside, a financial office complex in Jersey City, NJ used three colors of Summitville's Old Towne Quarry in the 6-inch x 6-inch x ½-inch size. Photograph courtesy of Summitville Tile Co.

Maintenance. Ceramic or quarry tile may be cleaned with a damp mop if the soil is light, or with water and a detergent if the soil is heavier. It must be remembered that tile and grout are two different materials, with grout being the more porous. Any soil that is likely to stain the grout should be removed as soon as possible.

It is the reponsibility of the tile installer to remove all excess grout as part of the installation contract.

MEXICAN TILE

Clay, taken directly from the ground, is shaped by hand into forms. Mexican tile differs from ceramic and quarry tile in that the proportion of ingredients in the clay are not measured. It is allowed to dry in

Figure 3-16
Mexican tile laid in a Jefferson pattern, together with a terracotta pot and terracotta base give a country feeling to a room. Photograph courtesy of Solarq, Mexico.

the sun until it is firm enough to be transported to the kiln. As Mexican tile is a product of families working together, it is not uncommon to find a child's handprint or a dog or cat paw imprinted in the surface of the tile. Leaf prints may also be noticed where they drifted down when the tile was drying. These slight imperfections are part of the charm of using Mexican tile.

Due to the relatively uneven thickness of Mexican tile, it should be installed using the thick-set method (see Figure 3–16). If being used in a greenhouse or similar area where drainage is possible, Mexican tile may be laid in a bed of sand, which will accommodate any uneveness of the tile. All cracks or joints are then filled in with sand.

Mexican tile is extremely porous—the most porous of all tile—due to its natural qualities. This does present a problem during installation and grouting, as grout stains will show if not removed promptly. A sealer may be used and then four coats of polyurethane varnish, however, this does impart to the tile a very shiny finish. For a more natural appearance the following can be used.

The most durable and least porous finish is obtained by using a generous amount of boiled linseed oil. A second coat of linseed oil is used to even up the absorption of the tile. The porous parts are recoated until an even layer is obtained. Any excess oil is mopped up (*Caution:* Oil rags are combustible).

A clear paste Tre-wax is applied by scrubbing the tile with a fiber scrub brush, using approximately one pound per 125 square feet. Just before the wax dries it should be buffed. If an antique look is desired, brown paste Tre-wax is used, but it should be applied to only one tile at a time so the color is evenly spread. It should dry for 20 to 30 minutes. The brown wax does not dry cloudy as does the clear, so it should be buffed just before it is dry. A sealing coat may then be applied.

Maintenance. Keep the floor free of dust and dirt by sweeping or vacuuming and, when the wax shows signs of wear, apply another coat of wax and buff.

GLASS BLOCK

The glass block used for floors is an 8-inch square of solid glass that is 3 inches thick. VISTABRIK® provides excellent light transmission and good visibility, with high-impact strength. These blocks may be used as pavers and as covers for light fixtures recessed in floors. This material is also used where special light effects are required.

Figure 3-17
The glass block walkway utilizes a Circle Redmont grid system. Glass block, from Pittsburgh Corning, was also used for the two-story curved wall. The walls are polished granite. Capital Bank, Miami. Architects: Gensler and Associates, Photography: Nick Merrick. © Copyright Hedrich-Blessing.

Maintenance. Simple cleaning with clean water and a sponge or mop should suffice. Any oily deposits should be removed by using soap and water and then rinsing with clean water.

CONCRETE

Concrete is a mixture of water, portland cement, and an **aggregate** that may be sand, gravel, rocks (1 1/2 inches in diameter or larger), or it may be a combination of sand and rocks. The final product will vary considerably, depending on the type and size of the aggregate used and the chemical and physical properties of the cement binder.

A concrete floor is low-cost as compared to other materials and is very durable. However, it is difficult to maintain unless the surface has been treated with a floor sealer specially manufactured to produce a dust-free floor. Color may be added when the concrete is mixed. A concrete floor looks less like an

unfinished floor or subfloor if it is grooved into squares. Also, any cracking is more likely to occur in these grooves and be less visible. Concrete floors are being used in passive solar homes because the large mass absorbs the rays of the sun during the day and radiates the heat back at night.

Concrete floors may be painted with an epoxy, oil-base, or latex paint. Generally, epoxy paints are the best for adhesion although, when the concrete is often wet, latex paints provide a less slippery surface. Custom colored cast concrete squares may be seen in Figure 8–3.

Maintenance

Dry concrete will absorb alkaline salts, such as carbonates and trisodium phosphate. These absorbed salts will crystalize in the pores of the cement and increase in size as they pick up moisture. Subsequent harsh washings cause additional damage and complicate the problem of maintenance. Prewetting, there-

Figure 3-18
Wausau Tile Precast Terrazzo in black, grey and white provides an interesting foil for the exposed architectural members. Photograph courtesy of Wausau Tile, Inc.

fore, should be standard procedure before using any cleaning solution on a concrete floor. . . Wetted concrete should be washed with a hot synthetic detergent, as soap will react with the lime and cause a scum . . . Well-sealed, dense concrete is easy to maintain and is less subject to injury from routine washing and scrubbing.[3]

• TERRAZZO

Terrazzo was used as a flooring material during the Italian Renaissance. However, terrazzo, as we know it today was not produced until after the development of portland cement in the 18th century. Terrazzo is a composite material, poured in place or precast, consisting of marble chips, **seeded** or unseeded with a binder that is cementitious, noncementitious (epoxy, polyester, or resin) or a combination of both. See Figure 3–18 for terrazzo tile.

The National Terrazzo and Mosaic Association explains that the chips are mixed with the **matrix** in a ratio of two parts aggregate to one part matrix before pouring. After the terrazzo topping is poured in place (in a monolithic installation), additional chips are sprinkled or seeded and troweled into the terrazzo topping to achieve the proper consistency.

Terrazzo that is poured into forms should be cured at least three days and then ground on a water-coated surface, first with a coarse grit and then with successively finer grits.

The NTMA gives the following sizes for aggregates:

Standard—1/16- to 3/8-inch chips
Venetian—1/4- to 1 1/16-inch chips
Palladian—3/8-inch thick **spalls** up to 5 inches in breadth.

The binder may be gray or white portland cement, or it may be colored to blend or contrast with the marble chips. Divider strips of brass, zinc, or plastic are attached to the subfloor and are used for several purposes—as expansion joints to take care of any minor movement, as dividers when different colors are poured in adjacent areas, and as a means of enhancing a design motif, logo, or trademark. Precast tiles of terrazzo inlaid in a resilient thermoset resin mortar come in approximately 12-by-12 inches with a 3/16-inch thickness (see Figure 3–18).

Maintenance. The National Terrazzo and Mosaic Association specifically warns that soaps and scrub-

bing powders containing water-soluble inorganic salts or crystallizing salts should never be used in the maintenance of terrazzo. Alkaline solutions will sink into the pores and, as they dry, will expand and break the cells of the marble chips and matrix, causing **spalling**. (This is similar to the problem with cement floors.)

After the initial cleaning, the floor should be allowed to dry and then sealed as soon as possible. This sealing is for the cement portion of the floor. The cleaning program for terrazzo is as follows:

1. daily sweeping,
2. regular damp-mopping to prevent dirt accumulation,
3. machine buffing to remove traffic marks and restore luster,
4. sealing as needed in high traffic areas, and
5. periodic machine scrubbing to remove heavy accumulation of dirt.

Stain removal for terrazzo is the same as for marble.

EXPOSED AGGREGATE

When an exposed aggregate floor is specified, the type of aggregate to be used is extremely important, as this is the material visible on the finished floor. River stone gives a smooth rounded texture. Today, the river stone effect may be achieved by tumbling the stones in a drum to remove the sharp edges.

While the concrete is still **plastic**, the selected aggregate is pressed or rolled into the surface. Removal of the cement paste, by means of water from a hose when the concrete is partially hardened, will expose the aggregate and display the decorative surface. For interior use, most of the aggregate should be approximately the same size and color, but other values within that hue may also be used, with a scattering of white and black stones.

One drawback to the use of exposed aggregate is that, like any other hard-surfaced material, exposed aggregate is not sound absorbent and is hard on the feet for prolonged standing.

A clear polyurethane finish specially formulated for masonry surfaces can be applied. This gives a finish that brings out the natural color of the stone, similar to the way a wet stone has more depth than a dry one. The coated exposed aggregate seldom seems to become soiled. A vacuum brush used for wood floors will pick up any loose dirt from between the stones.

BRICK

Brickmaking is an ancient art, appearing before recorded history. These early bricks consisted of clay and possibly straw mixed with water to form a plastic mass that was put into molds and baked in the sun. The earliest recorded use of brick is in the Bible when the Egyptians made the Israelites work "in mortar and in brick" (Ex. 1:14). Burnt brick was used in the Tower of Babel and also in the wall surrounding the city of Babylon.

The Chinese used brick in the 3rd century B.C. for building part of the Great Wall. The Romans used sun-dried bricks until about 14 A.D. when they started using bricks burnt in kilns. The Romans took this knowledge of brickmaking to Europe and Britain but after they left in 410 A.D., the art died out and was not restored until the 11th and 13th centuries.

The first brick buildings in the United States were built in Virginia around Jamestown by British settlers and on Manhattan Island by the Dutch. The bricks used in Virginia were probably made locally as there are records of brick being exported in 1621. Of course, the Aztecs of Mexico and Central America also used **adobe** bricks for building purposes.

Until about the mid-1850s, brick was molded by hand; from then on it was made using mechanical means. Bricks are made by mixing clays and shales with water and are formed, while plastic, into rectangular shapes with either solid or hollow cores.

During the process of heating the bricks, the clay loses its moisture content and becomes rigid but it is not chemically changed. It is during the higher temperatures used in burning the brick that it undergoes a molecular change. When the temperature is raised further the grains fuse together, closing all pores, and the brick becomes vitrified or impervious.

The color of the brick depends on three factors: chemical composition of the clay, method of firing control and the temperature of the kiln. The red color comes from the oxidizing of iron to form iron oxide. The lighter colors (the salmon colors) are the result of underburning. If a higher, longer heat is applied, the brick will be harder. The harder bricks have lower absorptions and higher compressive strengths than the softer ones. Generally, the denser the brick and the lower the absorption, the easier it is to clean and maintain.

Installation. For areas where spilled liquids are likely, such as in a kitchen or bathroom, a mortared installation may be appropriate. When installing over a wood frame floor, a relatively thin brick paver may be selected to minimize the additional dead weight of the floor assembly. Brick pavers weigh approximately 10 psf (pounds per square foot) per inch of thickness.

Installation methods are shown in Figure 3–19. Pavers are laid in a conventional manner in a 1/2-inch wet mortar bed with mortar joints. When the joints are thumbprint hard, they are **tooled**, compacting the mortar into a tight water-resistant joint.

Where moisture is not a problem, a mortarless method may be used.

Maintenance. Brick may be vacuumed, swept, damp mopped, or spray buffed.

LINOLEUM

Linoleum was first invented more than a hundred years ago and was the only resilient flooring material available for many years. Modern technology has now produced vinyl sheet flooring and linoleum has not been manufactured in this country since 1974. However, many people still persist in calling sheet vinyls "linoleum" out of habit. And although the components of the two products are very different, the end results do appear similar.

ASPHALT TILE

Like linoleum, asphalt tile is another flooring material that is gradually been phased out due to advanced technology. Actually, at the moment there is very little asphalt in this tile. Asphalt tile is very inexpensive but does not have resistance to stains and can be softened by mineral oils or animal fats. The individual tiles are brittle and have poor recovery from indentation. Any of the solvents will permanently damage the surface. Nine-inch-by-9-inch squares are available in the darker shades in a marbleized pattern.

Installation of Resilient Tile. Asphalt, vinyl-composition, vinyl, cork, and other resilient tiles are all installed using the thin-set method. The most important step in this installation procedure is to be

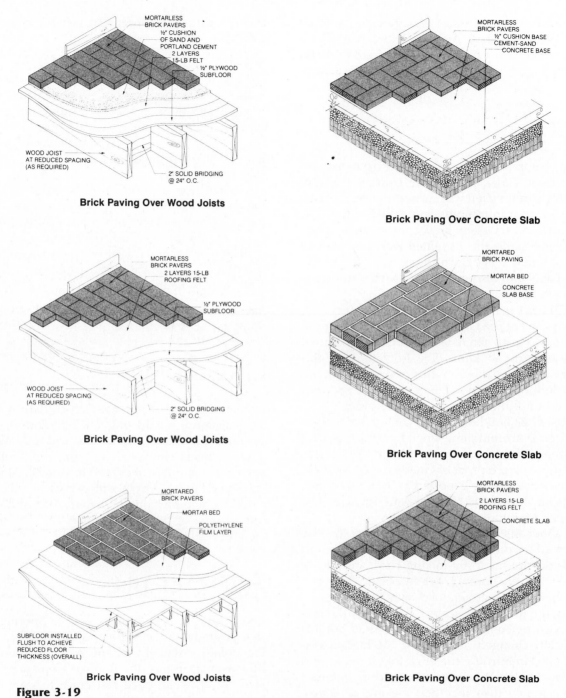

Figure 3-19
Methods of Installing Brick Floors. (Photograph courtesy of The Brick Institute of America.)

sure the subfloor is smooth and level. Due to the thin nature of these tiles, any discrepancies in the subfloor will be visible on the surface of the tile. One friend was extremely disturbed to find that her newly installed floor had developed a wavy and bumpy appearance after only several weeks because the wood subfloor had not been sanded.

The subfloor is troweled with the suggested adhesive and, as with the installation of parquet floors, the walls should not be used as a starting point (see Figure 3–9).

Maintenance. All resilient tile floors should be washed using only a damp mop, as an excess of water is likely to cause raised or uneven tiles due to moisture penetrating through the joints to the subfloor. Asphalt tile may have a factory coating for protection during shipping and installation. If this is present, it should be removed before further treatment. There are many liquid waxes on the market that may be used for residential use, but the solvent types of paste waxes should never be used on asphalt tile. For commercial installations, Hillyard Chemical Company makes cleaners and waxes that may or may not require buffing. This company specializes in floor treatments and supplies finishing and maintenance information for every type of flooring discussed in this book. Many janatorial supply companies also produce suitable maintenance cleaners and waxes for commercial installations.

Vinyl composition and vinyl tile floors are all maintained in the same manner as asphalt tile.

Vinyl composition

Vinyl composition, or reinforced vinyl, is the most commonly used floor tile for less expensive installa-

Figure 3-20
The 12-inch square vinyl tile is shown with 9-inch-by-9-inch corner tiles, one 9-inch border with diamonds and another with stripes, plus a feature strip providing a custom design. Photograph courtesy of Azrock Industries, Inc.

tions. Vinyl composition consists of blended compositions of vinyls, resins, plasticizers, coloring pigments, and fillers formed into thin sheets under heat and pressure. The thin sheets, without backing, are then cut into tiles.

In recent years, asbestos has proven to have adverse health effects. As vinyl composition tiles are no longer made with asbestos fibers, there are no health hazards now. *Note:* If you are removing an old vinyl asbestos floor, OSHA has extremely rigid rules as to the manner in which they may be removed and the safety precautions that must be taken.

The thickness, or **gauge**, as it is sometimes called, is 1/16, 3/32, and 1/8 of an inch. For commercial and better residential installations, the 1/8-inch gauge is the best choice. The advantages of vinyl composition tile are that it (1) is inexpensive, (2) is easy to install and maintain, (3) may be installed on any grade, (4) resists acids and alkalies, and (5) withstands strong cleaning compounds. The disadvantages are that it (1) has low impact resistance, (2) has poor noise absorption, (3) is semiporous as compared to solid vinyls and solid rubber.

Maintenance. See Asphalt Tile.

Vinyl tile

Vinyl tiles are homogeneous or, in other words, solid vinyl with the color throughout the tile. They are available in the traditional marble and travertine designs and also in brick, slate, and stone patterns. Solid color vinyl tiles are used as feature strips or for borders (see Figure 3–20). Borders should be of approximately the same width at all walls. Vinyl tiles are constructed of polyvinyl chloride with mineral fillers, pigments, plasticizers, and stabilizers.

Several companies manufacture a vinyl floor with real wood veneer literally sealed between solid vinyl. The top layer is made of a transparent 0.20 of an inch thick, pure vinyl, which permits the natural color and texture of the wood grain to be visible, yet protected.

Vinyl wall base effectively trims off a resilient floor installation and also helps hide minor wall and floor irregularities. Its distinctive profile consists of a reclining curvature at the top and a descending thin-toe line which conforms snugly with wall and floor. Some vinyl coves can be hand-formed to make the corners, while others come with both inside and outside corners preformed. The cove wall base comes either in 20-foot rolls or 48-inch strips in a 2 1/4-inch or 4-inch heights (see Figure 3–21).

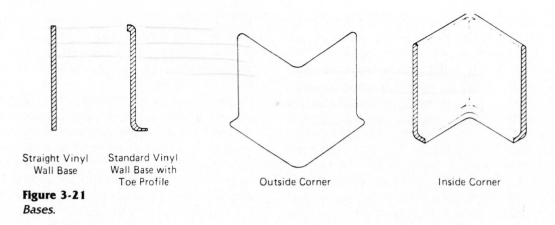

Straight Vinyl
Wall Base

Standard Vinyl
Wall Base with
Toe Profile

Outside Corner

Inside Corner

Figure 3-21
Bases.

Installation. Tiles are installed with a specified adhesive in a pyramid fashion (see Figure 3–9).

Maintenance. The new tile floor should not be washed, just damp mopped for a week to allow the adhesive to set. Spots of adhesive can be removed with a clean white cloth dampened with paste wax or lighter fluid. Periodic sweeping with a soft broom or vacuum will prevent buildup of dust and dirt. Spills should be cleaned immediately. Damp mopping with a mild detergent is sufficient for slightly soiled floors, or scrubbing with a brush or machine for heavy soil. Soap-based cleaners should not be used because they can leave a dulling film. The floor should then be rinsed with clean water. The floor should never be flooded, and excess dirty water should be removed with a mop or vacuum. No-wax floors can be damaged by intense heat, lighted cigarettes, and rubber or foam-backed mats or rugs. If stubborn stains persist, try rubbing the spot with alcohol or lighter fluid.

RUBBER

Rubber flooring is now made of 100 percent synthetic rubber. The multilevel rubber flooring (raised discs or pastilles, solid or duo-colored squares, or even rhythmic curves) has become increasingly popular where excessive dirt or excessive moisture are likely to be tracked inside. The raised portions have beveled edges, causing the dirt to drop down below the wear surface, which lowers the abrasion on the wear surface. The same thing happens with water; most of it flows below the wear surface. While the original purpose of this tile was as stated above, many installations today are done purely for aesthetic rather than utilitarian reasons (see Figure 3–22).

Rubber tiles are available in 9-, 12-, 20- and 39-inch squares, with a thickness of 3/32, 1/8, or 3/16 inch. The tiles are usually marble or travertine patterned, laid at right angles to each other. They may be laid below grade and are extremely sound absorbent.

Maintenance. The RCA Rubber Company, an Ohio Corporation of Akron, Ohio, suggests the following maintenance for its floors. New rubber flooring should be thoroughly machine stripped and scrubbed with black stripping pad and stripper. The floor should be thoroughly cleaned with a good grade of mild detergent cleaner. The stripper or detergent solution should be vacuumed, mopped, or squeezed from floors; The floor should be rinsed with a solution of 10 percent Clorox® in warm water. When the floor is dry, an ultra-high-speed buffer can be used. New floors will require more frequent buffing until a high sheen is acquired. For further maintenance, dry dust or mop floors (but do not use mops treated with mineral oil or other petroleum products). Periodically, repeat the cleaning procedure and rebuff as needed.

SHEET VINYL

The sheet vinyl manufacturers have greatly improved not only the quality but also the designs of their products. Precise information as to construction are trade secrets but the following information is generic to the industry.

Sheet vinyl comes in 6-, 9- or 12-foot widths and is manufactured by two methods—inlaid or rotogravure. Most inlaid sheet vinyls are made of thousands of tiny vinyl granules built up layer by layer, then fused together with heat and pressure. The result is

Figure 3-22
*A bar features the raised disk surface of Crosswalk from Armstrong Industries.
Photograph courtesy of Armstrong Industries.*

a soft, hefty flooring with a noticeable depth of color and a crafted look. Some have extra layers of foam cushioning to provide comfort underfoot and muffle footsteps and other noises. Color and pattern go all the way through the vinyl layer. A fiberglass backing will produce a light flexible flooring that virtually eliminates tearing and creasing as well as the telegraphing of irregularities from the old flooring to the new.

Rotovinyls, also called *rotogravure vinyls,* are made by a rotogravure process which combines photography and printing. Almost any image that can be photographed can be reproduced on a rotovinyl floor. The printed layer is protected by a topping (called the *wear layer)* of vinyl resin (**PVC**) either alone or in combination with urethane. The vinyl resin composition produces a gloss surface, whereas urethane

creates a high-sheen results. A mechanical buffer with a lamb's wool pad will bring back the satin-gloss of the vinyl resin composition wear layers. All rotovinyls are made with an inner core of foamed or expanded vinyl, that means they are cushioned to some extent. But at the lower end of the price scale, cushioning may be quite thin. Most sheet vinyls are flexible enough to be coved up the **toe space** to form their own base (check manufacturers specifications).

The trend in the 90s is a high-gloss finish with manufacturers providing five and, in the case of Mannington Gold Floors, a 10–year warranty that the floor will not wear out.

Installation. Seaming methods vary from manufacturer to manufacturer, but all result in an almost

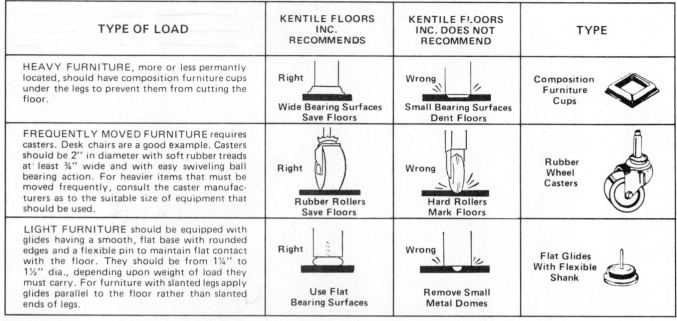

TYPE OF LOAD	KENTILE FLOORS INC. RECOMMENDS	KENTILE FLOORS INC. DOES NOT RECOMMEND	TYPE
HEAVY FURNITURE, more or less permanently located, should have composition furniture cups under the legs to prevent them from cutting the floor.	Right Wide Bearing Surfaces Save Floors	Wrong Small Bearing Surfaces Dent Floors	Composition Furniture Cups
FREQUENTLY MOVED FURNITURE requires casters. Desk chairs are a good example. Casters should be 2" in diameter with soft rubber treads at least ¾" wide and with easy swiveling ball bearing action. For heavier items that must be moved frequently, consult the caster manufacturers as to the suitable size of equipment that should be used.	Right Rubber Rollers Save Floors	Wrong Hard Rollers Mark Floors	Rubber Wheel Casters
LIGHT FURNITURE should be equipped with glides having a smooth, flat base with rounded edges and a flexible pin to maintain flat contact with the floor. They should be from 1¼" to 1½" dia., depending upon weight of load they must carry. For furniture with slanted legs apply glides parallel to the floor rather than slanted ends of legs.	Right Use Flat Bearing Surfaces	Wrong Remove Small Metal Domes	Flat Glides With Flexible Shank

Figure 3-23
Static load for furniture. Courtesy Kentile Floors, Inc.

invisible seam. Sheet vinyls should also be rolled with a 100-pound roller to eliminate air pockets and form a good bond between the backing and the adhesive.

Furniture should be equipped with the proper loadbearing devices; otherwise, indentations will mar the vinyl surface. Most manufacturers recommend limiting the static load to 75 psi (see Figure 3–23).

Heavy refrigerators and kitchen or office equipment must not be dragged across the floor, as this will damage and tear the surface. These items should be "walked" across the floor on a piece of wood or Masonite® runways. Runways must be used even if using an appliance dolly or if the heavy objects are equipped with wheels or rollers.

Maintenance is the same as for vinyl tiles, bearing in mind that no-wax does not mean no maintenance.

CORK

Due to its extremely porous and fragile qualities, cork is not used alone as a flooring material but is combined with resins to provide greater durability and easier maintenance. Plain cork, with no additives, is extremely resilient and has good sound absorbency. When cork is combined with vinyl some of the resiliency and noise reduction is lost, but the added durability and ease of maintenance more than compensate for these losses.

Installation. Cork flooring can be installed on dry, new or existing concrete or plywood subfloors. Use only those subfloor materials and adhesives that are specified by the manufacturer of the cork flooring. Expansion and contraction, due to climatic conditions, will occur, so allow for an approximate 1/8- to 1/4-inch space around the perimeter of the room for this condition. Cover the opening with suitable cove base. Do not install over radiant-heat systems. Depending on the manufacturer and the product, cork flooring may come unfinished, or finished with a polyurethane or wax finish. Because cork is a wood product, the floor tiles should be acclimatized to the installation site for 72 hours before installation.

Maintenance. Sweep or vacuum before washing. Warm water and mild phosphate-free detergent works best. Damp mop, not wet mop, thoroughly and sponge daily. For large areas, a commercial buffing machine is acceptable. Avoid abrasive cleaning pads. Rinse with clear water on a damp mop and allow to dry. The floor should be protected from indentations, as seen in Figure 3–23.

FORMED-IN-PLACE OR POURED FLOORS

Formed-in-place floors come in cans and are applied at the site in a seamless installation. The basis of the "canned floors" may be urethane, epoxy, polyester, or vinyl, but they are all applied in a similar manner. First, as with all other floor installations, the surface must be clean, dry, and level. Second, a base coat of one of the above materials is applied to the substrate according to directions. Third, colored plastic chips are sprinkled or sprayed on the base and several coats of the base material are applied for the wear-layer.

This flooring seems to be popular in veterinary offices, where a nonskid and easily cleaned surfae is desirable. It can also be coved up a base like sheet vinyl, eliminating cracks between floor and base. Of course, this type of flooring may be used in any area where cleanliness is paramount.

Maintenance. Same as sheet vinyl.

DECORATIVE LAMINATE

Where **access flooring** is essential, WILSONART® Perma-Kleen® may be specified. This access floor tile is used in data-processing centers and electronic clean rooms because of its excellent static dissipation and electrical resistance. Perma-Kleen is bonded to oil-free steel, aluminum, wood, or **particle board** access floor components, using moisture-resistant adhesive and following the manufacturer's instructions.

Maintenance. Same as for vinyl tiles.

Figure 3-24
Warm and welcoming Ipocork flooring was used in this contemporary dining room, with a dark tile creating a focal point for the table. Photograph courtesy of Ipocork, Inc.

BIBLIOGRAPHY

American Institute of Maintenance, Floor Care Guide. New York, NY: The Institute, 1982.

Berendsen, Anne. Tiles: A General History. New York: Viking Press, 1967

Dezettel, Louis M. Masons & Builders Library (Vols. I & II). Indianapolis, IN: Theodore Audel, division of Howard W. Sams & Co. Inc., 1984.

Ellis, Robert Y. The Complete Book of Floor Coverings. New York: Charles Scribner & Sons, 1980

The Everything Book of Floors, Walls and Ceilings, New York, NY: Reston 1980

Feirer, John L. Woodworking for Industry, Peoria, IL: Charles A. Bennett, 1979.

Oak Flooring Institute, Hardwood Flooring Finishing/Refinishing Manual. Memphis, TN: 1986

Oak Flooring Institute. Wood Floor Care Guide. Memphis, TN: 1986.

Watson, Don A. Construction Materials & Processes. New York: 2nd Ed. McGraw-Hill, Gregg Division 1978

ENDNOTES

[1] *Ceramic Tile: The Installation Handbook*, Tile Council of America, 1991, p.5.

[2] Watson, Don A. *Construction Materials and Processes.* (New York: McGraw Hill, 1971), p. 271. Reprinted, with minor changes, by permission of the publisher.

[3] Adapted by permission of the American Library association from Bernard Berkeley, Floors: Selection and Maintenance (LTP Publications no. 13), pp. 241–42. Copyright © 1968 by the American Library Association.

GLOSSARY

Access flooring. Raised flooring providing access to the area beneath.

Adobe. Unburnt, sun-dried brick.

Agglomerate. Marble chips and spalls of various size, bonded together with a resin.

Aggregate. The solid material in concrete, mortar or grout.

Base. A board or moulding at the base of a wall that comes in contact with the floor; protects the wall from damage (see Figure 3–21 & 6–1).

Beveled. In wood flooring, the top edge is cut at a 45° angle.

Bisque. Once-fired clay.

Bluestone. A hard sandstone of characteristic blue, gray, and buff colors, quarried in New York and Pennsylvania.

Bow. Longitudinal curvature of lumber (see Figure 3–1).

Bullnose. A convex, rounded edge on tile (see Figure 3–12).

Butts. Close together, leaving no space.

Cove. A concave, rounded edge on tile (see Figure 3–12).

Crook. The warp of a board edge from the straight line drawn between the two ends (see Figure 3–1).

Cup. Deviation of the face of a board from a plane (see Figure 3–1).

Cure. Maintaining the humidity and temperature of freshly poured concrete for a period of time to keep water present so it hydrates or hardens properly.

Cushion-edged. Tiles with a slightly rounded edge.

Elgin Marbles. (Pronounced with a hard "g"). Lord Elgin, the British Ambassador to Turkey from 1799–1802, persuaded the Turkish Government in Athens to allow him to remove the frieze of the Parthenon to the British Museum in London to prevent further damage.

Floorcloths. Printed canvas used in early 1800s.

Gauge. Thickness of tile.

Grain. Arrangement of the fibers of the wood.

Grout. Material used to fill in the spaces between the tiles.

Impervious. Less than 0.5 percent absorption rate.

Kiln. An oven for controlled drying of lumber or firing of tile.

Laminated. Bonding of two or more layers of material.

Lauan plywood. The wood of a Philippine tree which, while not a true mahogany resembles mahogany in grain.

Lugs. A projection attached to the edges of a ceramic tile to provide equal spacing of the tiles.

Marquetry. Veneered inlaid material in wood flooring that has been fitted in various patterns and glued to a common background.

Mastic. An adhesive compound.

Matrix. The mortar part of the mix.

Medullary rays. Ribbons of tissue extending from the pitch to the bark of a tree, particularly noticeable in oak.

Metal spline. Thin metal wire holding the strips of parquet together.

Metamorphic. Changes occurring in appearance and structure of rock caused by heat and/or pressure.

Monolithic. Grout and mortar base become one mass.

Mosaic. A small-size tile, ceramic or marble, usually 1 inch or 2 inch square used to form patterns (see Figure 3–13).

o.c. Abbreviation for *on center*; example: measurement from the center of one joist center of an adjacent joist.

120 grit. A medium-fine grade of sandpaper.

Parquetry. Inlaid solid wood flooring, usually set in simple geometric patterns.

Particle board. Boards or sheets made from a combination of wood particles and a binder.

Patina. Soft sheen achieved by continuous use.

Pickets. Wood strips pointed at both ends, used in parquet floors in patterns such as Monticello.

Pointed. Act of filling the joints with mortar.

Plane. Flat and level surface.

Plastic. Still pliable and soft, not hardened.

PVC. Polyvinyl chloride. A water insoluble thermoplastic resin. Used as a coating on sheet vinyl floors.

psi. Pounds per square inch.

Prefinished. Factory finished when referring to wood floors.

Quarter sawn. Wood sliced in quarters lengthwise which shows the grain of the wood to best advantage (see Figure 3–2).

Quartzite. A compact granular rock, composed of quartzite crystals usually so firmly cemented as to make the mass homogeneous. Color range is wide.

Reducer strip. A tapered piece of wood used at the joining of two dissimilar materials to compensate for difference of thickness.

Riser. The vertical part of a stair.

Sandstone. Sedimentary rock composed of sand-sized grains naturally cemented from mineral materials.

Screeds. 2 by 4s between 18 and 48 inches in length, laid flat side down and randomly placed to support subfloor (see Figure 3–8).

Seeded. Sprinkling of marble chips on top of a base.

Semivitreous. 3–percent, but not more than 7–percent, moisture absorption.

Sets. Groups of parquet set at right angles to each other, usually four in a set.

60 grit. A medium sandpaper.

Spall. A fragment or chip, in this case, of marble.

Spalling. Flaking of floor due to expansion of components.

Square. Edges cut at right angles to each other.

Stenciling. Method of decorating or printing a design by painting through a cut-out pattern.

Terrazzo. Marble chips, of similar size, combined with a binder that holds the marble chips together. This binder may be cementitious or noncementitious (epoxy resin).

Toe space. Area at base of furniture or cabinets that is inset to accommodate the toes.

Tongue-and-groove. A wood joint providing a positive alignment (see Figure 7–2).

Tooled. A mortar joint that has been finished by a shaped tool while the mortar is plastic.

Twist. A spiral distortion of lumber (see Figure 3–1).

Veneer. A very thin sheet of wood varying in thickness from 1/8 to 1/100 of an inch.

Vitreous. 0.5 percent, but less than 3 percent, moisture absorption.

Walls

In floors, the weight of the flooring material was spread over a large area; however, when these same materials are used on walls, they create a heavy dead load. Thus walls, whether constructed or veneered with granite, stone, brick, or concrete, must have a foundation prepared to withstand this additional weight. **Compressive strength** is also important for wall installation materials.

There are two types of walls: loadbearing and nonbearing. The interior designer needs to know the difference. *Loadbearing* walls are those that support an imposed load in addition to their own weight; a *nonbearing* wall is just for utilitarian or aesthetic purposes. The architect deals with both, but the interior designer probably deals more with nonbearing walls. A loadbearing wall should never be removed or altered without consulting an architect or engineer.

STONE

This type of wall is usually a veneer and may be constructed of any type of stone. **Rubble** is uncut stone or stone that has not been cut into a rectangular shape. **Ashlar** is stone that is precut to provide enough uniformity to allow some regularity in assembly. The rubble masonry is less formal and also not as strong as the other types of bonds due to the irregularly shaped bonds. Rubble also requires the use of more mortar. Uniform mortar joints are a mark of good craftsmanship. **Fieldstone** or **cobble** has a more rounded feeling than does ashlar or rubble (see Figure 4–2).

Maintenance. Stonework should be cleaned with a stiff brush and clean water. If stains are difficult to remove, soapy water may be used, followed by a clean-water rinse. Stonework should be cleaned by sponging during construction, which facilitates final cleaning. The acids used to clean brick should never be used on stone walls.

Regular maintenance consists of brushing or vacuuming to remove dust. It is important to remember that, generally, igneous types are impervious, but sedimentary and metamorphic stones are more susceptible to stains. Stone walls should not be installed where grease or any substance that may stain the stone is present.

GRANITE

Granite is used wherever a feeling of stability and permanence is desired. This is probably why one sees so much granite in banks and similar institutions. The properties of granite were mentioned in the previous chapter. The only difference is that granite for walls may be polished or honed as abrasion is not a problem with walls. However, Figure

Figure 4-1
In this 15,000 sq. ft. residence, Nova Studio Ltd. used stone walls of Westchester granite on the exterior and interior to complement the rounded walls in the interior. The tile floor is 60-by-60 cm Buchtal Tile, Keraion series and the ceiling is stained and sealed cedar. Architects: *Peter Keller and John Sandgren.* Interior Design: *Dott. Arch. Dario Caimi and Franco Asnaghi. Photograph by Jon Ortner.*

4–1 shows a rubble granite wall where the stone has been left in its original rough-hewn state.

Installation. Anchors, **cramps**, dowels, and other anchoring devices should be type 304 stainless steel or suitable **nonferrous** metal. A portland cement sand mortar is used and, where applicable, a sealant is used for pointing the joints.

Maintenance. If required, the granite wall may be washed with a weak detergent solution and rinsed with clear water. To restore the shine, buff it with a lamb's wool pad.

MARBLE

Marble has the same elegant and formal properties whether used for walls or for floors (see Figure 4–3). According to the Marble Institute of America, interior marble wall facing may be installed by either mechanical fastening devices utilizing nonstaining an-

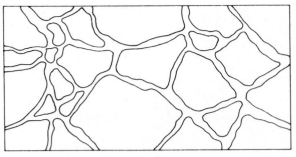

Rubble

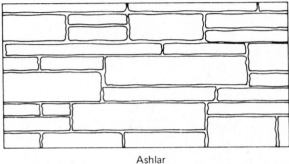

Ashlar

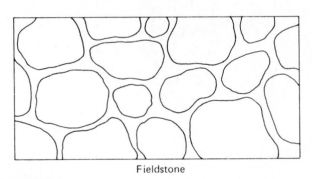

Fieldstone

Figure 4-2
Types of stonework.

Figure 4-3
Architect GMK, Columbia, SC used The Georgia Marble Tile in Pearl Grey® for the floors and walls of the lobby of the AT&T Capitol Center in Columbia, SC. Photograph courtesy of The Georgia Marble Company.

Maintenance. The same as for marble floors, see page 40.

TRAVERTINE

When travertine is used in wall applications, it is not necessary to fill the voids. Unfilled travertine gives an interesting texture to the wall surface but, for a perfectly smooth installation, filling is required. Like flooring, wall applications of travertine may be filled with a clear, translucent epoxy or an opaque epoxy matching the color of the travertine. Filled travertine does tend to have less sheen on the filled area than on the solid area. The surface of the travertine may be left in its rough state, providing texture, or it may be cut and sanded or ground smooth.

Installation. Installation methods of travertine are the same as for marble.

BRICK

The surface of the brick may be smooth, rough, or grooved. Bricks with these surface textures create

chors, angles, dowels, pins, cramps, and plaster spots or in a mortar setting bed to secure smaller units to interior vertical surfaces. The overall dimensions of the marble determine the setting method. Resilient cushions are used to maintain joint widths, which are then pointed with white cement or other approved material.

In addition to the traditional sizes, new thin marble veneers that are backed with lighter weight materials have less weight per square foot and, depending on job conditions, may be set in either a conventional full mortar bed or by any of the several newer thin-bed systems.

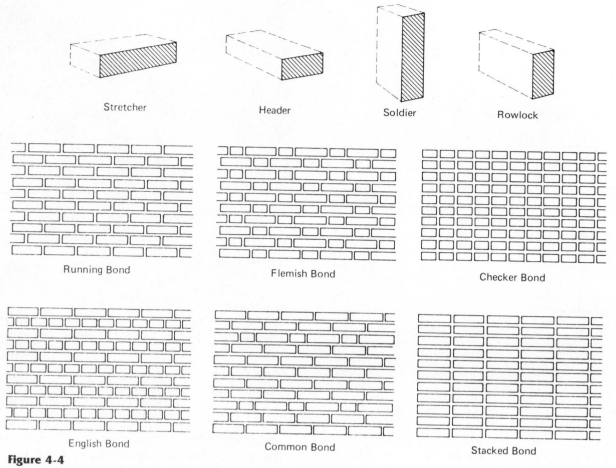

Figure 4-4
Stretchers, headers, and brick bonds.

interesting wall designs with interesting shadows. Bricks are obtainable in whites, yellows, grays, reds, and browns and may be ordered in special sizes or shapes.

The standard brick size is 3 5/8 inches wide by 8 inches long and 2 1/4 inches high. Those laid so as to expose the long side in a horizontal position are called **stretchers**, while vertically they are called *soldiers*. When the end of the bricks show horizontally, they are called **headers**, but vertically they are called *rowlocks* (see Figure 4–4). The bond is the arrangement of brick in rows or courses. A *common bond* is defined as bricks placed end to end in a stretcher course with vertical joints of one course centered on the bricks in the next course. Every sixth or seventh course is made up of headers. These headers provide structural bonding as well as pattern. A bond without headers is called a *running bond*. See Figure 4–4 for types of brick bonds.

Masonry walls may be hollow masonry, where

both sides of the wall are visible, or they may be veneered. When both sides are visible, the **header course** ties the two sides together. A veneered wall is attached to the backing by means of metal ties (see Figure 4–5).

The joints in a wall installation are extremely important as they create shadows and special design effects. The joints of a brick wall are normally 3/8 inch thick. The mortar for these joints consists of a mixture of portland cement, hydrated lime, and sand. The mortar serves four functions:

1. It bonds the units together and seals the spaces between.

2. It compensates for dimensional variations in the units.

3. It bonds to and, therefore, causes reinforcing steel to act as an integral part of the wall.

4. It provides a decorative effect on the wall surface by creating shadow or color lines.

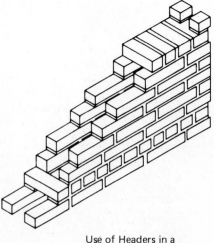
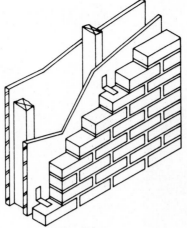

Use of Metal Ties in
Hollow Brick Walls

Use of Metal Ties in a
Brick Veneer Wall

Use of Headers in a
Hollow Brick Wall
Visible from Both Sides

Figure 4-5
Metal tiles.

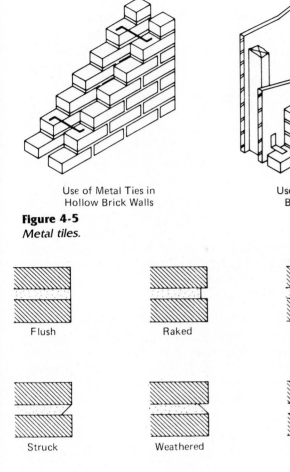
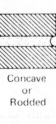
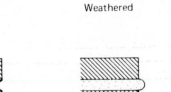

Flush Raked Stripped

Struck Weathered Concave
or
Rodded

V Joint Beaded Flush
may also be
Inset Shoved

Figure 4-6
Mortar joints for brick walls.

Mortar joint finishes fall into two clases: troweled and tooled joints. In the *troweled joint,* the excess mortar is simply cut off (struck) with a trowel and finished with the trowel. For the *tooled joint,* a special tool, other than the trowel is used to compress and shape the mortar in the joint.

Installation. Brick and concrete block are both installed by masons. Bricks are placed in a bed of mortar and mortar is laid on the top surface of the previous course, or row, so as to cover all edges. The mortar joint may be any of the types shown in Figure 4–6.

Maintenance. The major problem with finishing brick walls is the **mortar stain,** which occurs even if the mason is skilled and careful. To remove mortar stain, the walls are cleaned of surplus mortar and dirt then scrubbed with a solution of trisodium phosphate, household detergent, and water, then rinsed with water under pressure. If stains are not removed with this treatment, a solution of muriatic acid and water is used. The acid should be poured into the water to avoid a dangerous reaction. Just the bricks themselves should be scrubbed. The solution should not be allowed to dry but should be rinsed immediately with clean water. For cleaning light colored bricks, a more diluted solution of muriatic acid and water should be used to prevent burning.

Regular maintenance for bricks includes brushing and vacuuming to remove dust that may have adhered to the rough surface. Masonry walls that may come in contact with grease, such as in kitchens, should either be impervious or sealed to prevent penetration of the grease.

CONCRETE

Currently, many architects of contemporary buildings, particularly in the commercial, industrial, and educational fields, are leaving poured concrete walls exposed on the interior. The forms used for these walls may be patterned or smooth, and this texture

Figure 4-7
A contrast of textures is shown by the use of a brick wall surrounded by a circular piece of etched and plain glass. The floor is black and white marble tile. Photograph courtesy of Clark Leaming Co., Salt Lake City, UT.

is reflected on the interior surface. The ties that hold the forms together do leave holes which, if properly placed, may provide a grid design.

From the interior designer's point of view, a poured concrete wall is a *fait accompli*. The surface may be left with the outline of the forms showing, or it may be treated by the following methods to give a different surface appearance: bush hammering, acid etching, and sandblasting. Bush hammering is done with a power tool that provides an exposed aggregate face by removing the sand-cement matrix and exposing the aggregate. Sandblasting provides a textured surface. Bush hammering produces the heaviest texture, while the texture from sandblasting depends on the amount and coarseness of sand used. Acid etching just removes the surface.

The main problem facing the designer is using materials and accessories that will be compatible with cast concrete. Obviously, they need to imply weight and a substantial feeling, rather than any delicacy or formality.

CONCRETE BLOCK

Concrete block is a hollow concrete masonry unit composed of portland cement and suitable aggregates. Walls of this type are found in homes, but are more frequently used in commercial and educational interiors. There are several problems with concrete block. First, it has extremely poor insulating qualities if used on an exterior wall. Second, if used on an outside wall and moisture is present, efflorescence will form. Third, it has a fairly rough surface which is difficult to paint, although this may be accomplished by using a specially formulated paint and a long-nap roller.

Installation. The mason erects a concrete block wall in a similar manner to a brick one except that, while a brick wall is viewed only from one side, a concrete block is often visible from both sides; therefore, the joints need to be finished on both sides of the block. A concrete block wall may be erected in either a running bond pattern or stacked.

Maintenance. Concrete block is not cleaned with acid to remove mortar smears or droppings, as with brick. Excess mortar should be allowed to dry and then chipped off. Rubbing the wall with a small piece of concrete block will remove practically all the mortar. For painting instructions, see Chapter 1.

GLASS BLOCK

In the 1920s and 1930s, the use of glass block seemed to be limited to the side of the front door and bathrooms, but it is now one of the revived materials for use in the 1990s. This is due to modern technology and the innovativeness of today's architects and designers. The use of glass block is only for nonload-bearing installations. This, however, should not be a limiting factor in the utilization of glass block.

Glass block, by definition, is composed of two halves of pressed glass fused together. The hollow in the center is partially **evacuated**, which provides a partial vacuum with good insulating qualities. The construction of the block is such that designs may be imprinted on both the inside and the outside of the glass surfaces. In all of their applications, glass block permit the control of light—natural or artificial, day or night—for function and drama. Thermal transmission, noise, dust and drafts may also be controlled (see Figure 4–8).

Figure 4-8
The Glass Block Wall provides light as well as a visually interesting curve in contrast to the black marble walls. ARGUS® from PC GlassBlock® Products, Pittsburgh Corning Corporation. Crocker National Bank, Houston, TX. Architect: Gensler & Associates Architects. Photograph courtesy Pittsburgh Corning Corporation.

Standard glass block is 3 7/8 inches thick, with the Thinline Series PC GlassBlock® being 3 1/8 inches thick. Glass block is obtainable in the 6-, 8-, and 12-inch squares, and some styles come in a 4-by-8-inch rectangular block. The Thinline block has the additional advantage of 20 percent less weight.

Pittsburgh Corning Corporation, the only domestic manufacturer, produces a variety of glass block that may be used for both exterior and interior purposes. These include the Vue® which is clear for greatest combination of light transmission and visibility and is excellent for passive solar collection, to the Essex® with its fine grid design of closely spaced ridges at right angles to each other on each face with moderate light transmission while providing greatest privacy of all PC GlassBlock patterns.

Specialty blocks such as VISTABRIK® are solid glass and provide maximum protection from vandalism and forcible entry. "LX" inserts, of fibrous glass sheet, are sealed into the PC GlassBlock unit to provide significant light and thermal control by tempering glare, brightness, light transmission and solar heat gain. For a one-of-a-kind design, PC® Signature block can be custom-manufactured with a coporate logo or design.

Glass block may also be of curved panel construction. It is suggested that the curved areas be separated from the flat areas by intermediate expansion joints and supports. (See Table 4-1.)

Also available is HEDRON®, a corner or hexagonal block which can be used not only for corners but also to form very interesting zigzag partitions. EndBlock finishing units feature a rounded, finished surface on one of its edges.

Installation. The mortar-bearing surfaces of glass block have a coating that acts as a bond between the block and the mortar. Additionally, the coating acts as an expansion-contraction mechanism for each block. An optimum mortar mix is 1 part portland cement, 1/2 part lime, and 4 parts sand. Panel reinforcing strips are used in horizontal joints every 16 to 24 inches of height, depending on which thickness of block is used. Expansion strips are used adjacent to **jambs** and **heads**. Joints are **struck** while plastic and excess mortar is removed immediately. Mortar should be

Table 4-1
Radius minimums for curved panel construction

Block Size	Outside Radius in Inches	Number of Blocks in 90° Arc	Joint Thickness in Inches	
			Inside	Outside
6 × 6	52½	13	⅛	⅝
4 × 8	36	13	⅛	⅝
8 × 8	69	13	⅛	⅝
12 × 12	102½	13	⅛	⅝

Courtesy of Pittsburgh Corning Corporation.

removed from the face of the block with a damp cloth before final set occurs.

Maintenance. Ease of maintenance is one of the attractive features of glass block. Mortar or dirt on the face of glass block may be removed by the use of water, but not with abrasives (steel wool, wire brush, or acid).

PLASTER

The Egyptians and ancient Greeks used plaster walls which were then painted with murals. The frescoes of early times were painted on wet plaster, which absorbed the pigment and dried as an integral part of the plaster. The frescoes of Michelangelo's Sistine Chapel still retain their original brilliant color even after 400 years. Plaster was also used for very intricate mouldings and decorations. Today, plaster covered walls are only used in commercial installations and the more expensive custom-built homes.

Lath is the foundation of a plaster wall. In the Pyramids in Egypt, the lath was made of intertwined reeds. The construction of the half-timbered homes of the English Tudor period is often referred to as *daub and wattle* (the daub being the plaster and the wattle the lath,) this time a woven framework of saplings and reeds. When any restoration work is done on houses built prior to the 1930s, the lath will probably be found to be thin wood strips nailed to the studs about 3/8 of an inch apart.

Modern lath is either gypsum board, metal, or masonry block. The gypsum lath consists of a core of gypsum plaster between two layers of specially formulated, absorbent paper. The gypsum lath is 3/8 or 1/2 an inch thick, 16 inches wide by 48 inches long, and is applied horizontally with the joints staggered between courses. Other sizes are also available. Special types of gypsum lath may have holes drilled

in them for extra adhesion or have a sheet of aluminum foil on one side for insulating purposes.

Metal lath is used not only for flat areas but also for curved surfaces and forms. Metal lath is a mesh that is nailed to the studs. The **scratch coat** is troweled on and some plaster is squeezed through the mesh to form the mechanical bond, whereas the bond with gypsum board is formed by means of **suction**. **Beads** or formed pieces of metal are placed at exterior corners and around **casings** to provide a hard edge that will not be damaged by traffic.

Plaster used to be troweled on the lath in three different coats. The first coat bonded to the lath; the second was the brown coat; and the third, the finish coat, was very smooth. The first two coats were left with a texture to provide tooth. A three-coat plaster job is still done sometimes, but two coats or even one may be used to complete the finished surface.

As mentioned in the chapter on paint, due to its extreme porosity, plaster must be sealed before proceeding with other finishes.

GYPSUM WALLBOARD

Gypsum wallboard has the same construction as the gypsum board lath. Sheets are normally 4-feet wide and 8-feet long, but may be obtained in lengths of up to 16 feet. The edges along the length are always tapered, but some types are tapered on all four edges. This allows for a filled or taped joint. This wallboard is also obtainable with a foil back which serves as a vapor barrier on exterior walls. Another method of vapor barrier preparation is the use of a polyethylene sheet stapled to the studs before erecting the gypsum wallboard.

In new construction, 1/2-inch thickness is recommended for single-layer application, or for laminated two-ply applications, two 3/8-inch thick sheets are used.

The horizontal method of application is best adapted to rooms in which full-length sheets can be used, as it minimizes the number of vertical joints. Today, screws are usually used rather than nails, as they can be installed by mechanical means and will not pull loose. They are placed 6 to 8 inches o.c. with the heads slightly below the surface. The ceilings are done first and then the walls. A very good **dry wall** installation may also have an adhesive applied to the studs before installing the panels, in which case screws may be farther apart.

Figure 4-9
Softforms® throughout the interior create an effect of softened space. Photograph courtesy of Pittcon Industries, Inc.

A thorough inspection of the studs should be made before application of the gypsum wallboard to ensure that all warped studs are replaced. If this is not done, the final appearance of the wallboard will be rippled. Of course, this problem is not present when metal studs are used as in commercial construction.

After all the sheets have been installed, outside corners are protected by a metal corner or bead. The normal bead is right-angled but Softforms® extruded aluminum profiles come in 90° inside and outside corners and create an effect of softened space. This curve is shown in Figure 4–9. Trim strips are available for a reveal effect.

Joint cement, spackling compound—or as it is called in the trade, "mud"—is applied to all joints with a 5-inch wide spackling knife. Then the perforated tape is placed to cover the joint and is pressed into the mud. Another layer of compound is applied, **feathering** the outer edges. After drying, the compound is sanded and a second or even a third coat is applied, the feathering extending beyond the previous coat. All screw holes are filled with joint cement

and sanded smooth. Care must be taken to sand only the area that has been coated with joint cement, because sanding the paper layer will result in a roughness that will be visible, particularly when a painted semigloss or gloss finish is to be applied. In fact, the Gypsum Association suggests of a thin skim coat of joint compound be applied over the entire surface to provide a uniform surface for these paints. The dry-wall installer should be informed of the final finish so that attention can be paid to special finishing.

ALL seams or joints must be taped regardless of length because, if they are not taped, cracks will soon appear. The outside beads have joint cement feathered to meet the edge.

The surface of the wallboard may be left smooth, ready for painting or a wallcovering, or it may have some type of texture applied. The latter is done for several reasons. Aesthetically, a texture may be more desirable to eliminate glare and is also more likely to

Figure 4-10
FRESCO™ from Pittcon Industries is actually debossed 3/16 inch below the surrounding surface of a 5/8 inch thick gypsum wallboard to simulate paneling. Photograph courtesy of Pittcon Industries, Inc.

hide any surface discrepancies cause by warping studs and/or finishing of joints. The lightest texture available is called an *orange peel*, with the surface appearing just as the name suggests. Another finish is a skip-troweled surface where, after the texture has been sprayed on, a metal trowel is used to flatten some areas. The heaviest texture is a heavily stippled or troweled appearance similar to rough finished plaster. A texture is preferred whenever there is a **raking light** on the wall surface so that surface discrepancies are not quite so visible.

Gypsum wallboard may also be installed on a curved wall by qualified dry-wall installers. Only **simple** curves may be used. **Compound** curves cannot be fabricated.

A new product on the market, FRESCO™ from Pittcon Industries is actually debossed 3/16 inch below the surrounding surface of a 5/8 inch thick gypsum wallboard to simulate paneling. This product comes in two parts, a lower portion (32 inch high by 48 inch) for a wainscot effect, or by using the upper portion as well, a fully paneled wall can be achieved. The flat borders surrounding the "raised panel" areas provide space for attachment with drywall screws. All sheets have recessed edges for receiving tape and joint compound for finishing. FRESCO is very effective for a painted paneled appearance especially where fire codes prohibit the use of solid wood as shown in the close-up in Figure 4–10.

When water may be present, such as in bathrooms and kitchens, some building codes require the use of a water-resistant gypsum board. If a pliant wallcovering is to be used, all wallboard must be sealed or sized, as the paper of the gypsum board and the backing of the wallcovering would become bonded together and the wallcovering would be impossible to remove.

Another type of wallboard is prefinished vinyl plastic in a variety of simulated finishes, including wood grains and other textures. It can be applied directly by adhesive to the studs or as a finish layer over a preexisting wall. The edges may be square or beveled. Wood or metal trim must be applied at both floor and ceiling to create a finished edge.

WALLPAPER/ WALLCOVERING

The Chinese mounted painted rice paper on their walls as early as 200 B.C. Although mention of painted papers has been historically documented as early as 1507 in France, the oldest fragment of European wallpaper, from the year 1509, was found in Christ's College, Cambridge. This paper has a rather large scale pattern adapted from contemporary damask. Seventeenth century papers, whether painted or block printed, did not have a continuous pattern repeat and were printed on sheets rather than on a roll, as is the modern practice. The repetitive matching of today's papers is credited to Jean Papillon of France in the later 17th century. In the 18th century, England and France produced handprinted papers that were both expensive and heavily taxed.

Leather was one of the original materials to be used as a covering for walls. The earliest decorated and painted leathers were introduced to Europe in the 11th century by Arabs from Morocco and were popular in 17th-century Holland.

Flocked papers were used as early as 1620 in France. The design was printed with some kind of glue and then heavily sprinkled with finely chopped bits of silk and wool, creating a good imitation of damask or velvet. Flocked papers have been popular in recent decades, but are now falling from favor.

Scenic papers were used in the 18th century, many of them handpainted Chinese papers. Wallpapers used in this country were imported during the second quarter of the 18th century. Domestic manufacturing did not really start until around 1800 and even then the quality was not equal to the fine imported papers.

After the Industrial Revolution, wallpaper became available to people of more moderate means and the use of wallpaper became more widespread. In the late 19th and early 20th centuries, William Morris provided the stimulating interest in wallpapers and their designs. In the first half of the 20th century, papers imitating textures and having the appearance of wood, marble, tiles, relief plasterwork, paneling, and moire silk were in demand.

In the late 1930s and 1940s, wallpaper was in style, only to be replaced by painted walls in the 1960s and 1970s.

Today, designers are more discriminating with the use of wallpapers or, as they will be known from now on, "wallcoverings." This change of name is due to the fact that, while paper was the original material for wallcoverings, today these wallcoverings may be all paper, paper backed by cotton fabric, vinyl face with paper or cotton backing, or fabric with a paper backing. Foils or mylars have either paper or a nonwoven backing to ensure a smooth reflective surface.

The face of the paper wallcoverings is usually

treated with a protective vinyl finish and provides a washable surface. ''Washable'' means wiping the surface with a damp cloth. Solid vinyl wallcoverings backed by woven cotton are more durable and are scrubbable.

Patterns

There are many collections available which have been researched by the manufacturer. By using these collections, the designer will be able to create the desired atmosphere.

Many of the Early American designs were inspired by the valuable brocades and tapestries that adorned the homes of the wealthy. Katzenbach & Warren has done extensive research into New England homesteads and their early papers. Since many were created before the machine age, they were often painted entirely by hand or stenciled or printed by means of a wood block. The designs include small all-over floral patterns, floral vine patterns, and flowing arabesques. Stencils with pineapples, the symbol of hospitality, and small stylized designs were also used. Katzenbach & Warren's Williamsburg Wallpaper Reproductions are copies from existing documents in the Williamsburg collection.

Albert van Luit and Co., in their Winterthur Museum Collection, have meandering **chinoiserie** and the beautiful adaptation of an eight-panel scenic is the perfect background for English style furniture. The scenic murals are hung above the chair rail. Murals are large scale, nonrepeat, handscreened patterns done on a series of panels. They may be scenic, floral, architectural, or graphic in nature. Murals are sold in sets varying usually from two to six or more panels per set. Each panel is normally 28 inches in

Figure 4-11
The eight panel mural from Albert Van Luit is called "Cathay Chinois" and is typical of the imported handpainted wallpapers used in the Georgian era. (Photograph courtesy of Albert Van Luit.)

width and is printed on strips 10 to 12 feet in length. The height of the designs varies greatly, but most fall somewhere between 4 and 8 feet, although some graphics go from ceiling to floor (see Figure 4–11).

For a French ambience, wallcoverings with delicate scrolls or lacy patterns are suitable for a formal background, while toile-de-Jouy and checks are appropriate for the French Country look. Wallcoverings for a formal English feeling range from symmetrical damasks to copies of English chintzes and embroideries.

Geometrics include both subtle and bold stripes and checks, as well as polka dots and circles. The colors used will dictate where these geometrics can be used.

Trompe l'oeil patterns are three-dimensional designs on paper. Examples of realistic designs are a cupboard with an open door displaying some books, a view from a window, or a niche with a shell top containing a piece of sculpture. These trompe l'oeil patterns are sold in a set.

The pattern repeat is the distance between one point to the next repeated same point. This may vary from no repeat or match (as in a texture) to repeats as large as 48 inches. Therefore, for an exceptionally large repeat, additional paper should be ordered.

When a patterned wallcovering is hung, the left side of a strip will match or continue the design with the right side of the previous strip. If this match is directly across on a horizontal line, then it would be called a *straight match*. If the second strip has to be lowered in order to continue the design, this is called a *drop match*. A drop match does not necessarily mean that more wallcovering must be ordered, but must be taken into consideration when cutting the strips.[1]

Types

Textures include embossed papers, which hide any substrate unevenness, solid color fabrics, and grasscloths. Embossed papers have a texture rolled into them during the manufacturing process. Care should be taken not to flatten the texture of embossed papers when hanging them.

Anaglypta® is an embossed product imported from England. This wallcovering provides the textured appearance of sculptured plaster, hammered copper, or even hand-tooled Moroccan leather. These highly textured wallcoverings are applied to the wall like any other product. Once painted, the surface becomes hard and durable. The advantage of these

wallcoverings is that not only are they used on newly constructed walls in residential and commercial interiors, but they may also be applied after minimal surface preparation. In older dwellings and Victorian restoration projects, they provide the added advantage of actually stabilizing walls while covering moderate cracks and blemishes. Friezes, with ornate embossed designs, are part of the heavier Lincrusta® line.

Fabrics should be tightly woven, although burlap is frequently used as a texture. The walls are pasted with a non staining paste and the fabric, with the selvage removed, is brushed onto the paste (see Figure 4–12). Custom Laminations, Inc. paperbacks fabrics for wallcoverings.

Grasscloth is made of loosely woven vegetable fibers backed with paper. These fibers may be knotted at the ends and these knots are a decorative feature of the texture. Because these are vegetable fibers, width and color will vary, thus providing a highly textured surface. Due to the natural materials, it is impossible to obtain a straight-across match, so the seams will be obvious. Woven silk is frequently included in grasscloth collections, and this finer texture gives a more refined atmosphere to a room.

Flocked papers, as has been mentioned before, are one of the oldest papers on record. They are currently manufactured by more modern methods but still resemble pile fabrics. One problem with flocked papers is that through abrasion or constant contact with the face of the paper, the flocking may be removed and a worn area will appear. A seam roller should never be used to press down seams, as this also flattens the flocking.

Foils and mylars provide a mirrored effect with a pattern printed on the reflective surface. It is due to this high shine that the use of a lining paper is suggested to provide a smoother substrate. Foils conduct electricity if allowed to come in contact with exposed wires. In moist areas, some of the older foils had a tendency to show rust spots. This is why most ''metallic'' wallcoverings are presently made of mylar. To achieve the best effect from foils, there should be an abundance of light in the room in order to reflect off the foil surface.

Kraft papers are usually hand-printed on good quality kraft paper which is similar to the type used for wrapping packages. Unless specially treated these kraft papers absorb grease and oil stains, so care should be taken in placement of these types of wallcoverings.

For a cork-faced paper, razor-thin slices of cork are applied by hand to tinted or lacquered ground

Figure 4-12
Jack Lenor Larsen wall coverings and furniture fabric are used in this room setting at the Suzy Langlois showroom in Paris. The wall covering, entitled "Pantheon," was inspired by Piranesi's imaginary arches. The sofa is covered with "Loatian Ikat," a unique silk dyed in a painstaking process to produce a bold geometry of pinks and saffrons. (Photograph courtesy of Jack Lenor Larsen, Inc.)

papers. The base color shows through the natural texture of the cork and may blend or contrast with the cork itself. The sliced cork may also be cut into definite shapes for a repetitive pattern or it may printed with a design on top of the cork. Cork also comes in 12-inch square tiles varying in thickness from 1/8 to 5/8 of an inch. These solid cork tiles are of varying texture and provide good heat and sound insulation. Leather is cut into designs or blocks much like Spanish tiles because the limited size of the hide prohibits large pieces from being used. The color of the surface varies within one hide and from one hide to another; therefore, a shaded effect is to be expected.

Coordinated or companion fabrics are used to create an unbroken appearance where wallcovering and draperies adjoin. When using coordinated paper and fabric, the wallcovering should be hung first and then the draperies can be adjusted to line up with the pattern repeat of the wallcovering. The tendency is to call these companion fabrics "matching fabrics," but this is incorrect. It is extremely important to realize that paper or vinyl will absorb dyes in a different manner than will a fabric, and many problems will be resolved by the strict avoidance of the word "matching."

Lining paper is an inexpensive blank paper rec-ommended for use under foils and other fine quality papers. It absorbs excess moisture and makes a smoother finished wall surface. A heavier canvas liner is available for "bad walls."

Printing of Wallcoverings

Roller printing is used for the less expensive wall-coverings. The inks are transferred from a metal roller with raised design blocks to a large printing roller and then to the paper as it is fed through the press.

There are several means by which a wallcovering can be hand-printed. First of all, it may be silk screened. A separate screen must be made up for each color used and the screens must be meticulously positioned so that the patterns match at the edges. In silk screening, the wallcovering must be allowed to dry between application of the different colors (see Figure 4–13).

Block printing produces a similar effect to silk screening, only instead of the paint being squeezed through the open pores in the silk screen, the paint or color is rolled on a block where the negative or unwanted areas have been cut away. Block printing also requires positive positioning when printing.

Because silk screening and block printing are hand processes, a machine-like quality is not possible

Figure 4-13
Custom silk screening. (Photograph courtesy of Manuscreens, a Division of J. Josephson, Inc.)

or perhaps even desirable. The pattern does not always meet at the seams as positively as does the roller-printed one. Matching should be exact in the 3– to 5-foot area from the floor, where it is most noticeable.

Adhesives

There are several materials available to attach a wallcovering to the wall. The old standby is the wheat-base paste and this is used for many wallcoverings. However, certain wallcoverings such as wetlook vinyls, handprints, naturals, and foils require a special adhesive. The manufacturer will always specify which type of adhesive is to be used. If fabric or grasscloth is to be hung, a nonstaining cellulose paste should be used. Regular vinyls are hung using a vinyl adhesive that is not the same as the special adhesive mentioned above.

Prepasted papers come with a factory-applied dehydrated cellulose or wheat paste. To activate this paste, cut strips are soaked in water for a designated number of seconds and then applied the same as regular wallpaper. The prepasted papers are usually less expensive and are mainly for use by the homeowner in a do-it-yourself project. Strippable or peelable wallcoverings can be removed by simply prying up one corner and pulling off the whole strip. *Strippable* means that the base material used for the wallcovering is sufficiently strong to break away from the adhesive without shredding. *Peelable* means that the top layer of material will peel away from the substrate, leaving a suitable surface for repapering.

Most machine-printed wallcoverings are **pretrimmed** at the factory, but the majority of handprints and handmade textures are untrimmed.

Packaging

A single roll of an American wallcovering contains approximately 36 square feet of material regardless of the width, while a single roll of an European wallcovering contains 28 square feet. To make allowance for waste and matching patterns, it is advisable to calculate 30 usable square feet for a domestic wallcovering and 24 usable square feet for an imported one. This allowance is sufficient for a room with an average number of doors and windows, but for a room with window walls, more precise calculations should be made.

All wallcovering is priced by the single roll, but it is usually packaged in two- or three-roll bolts. A double-roll bolt is a continuous bolt containing the equivalent of two single rolls. The cost is twice the single roll price. The same applies to a triple-roll bolt. By packaging wallcovering in bolts rather than in single rolls, the paperhanger has more continuous lineal yardage with which to work and, therefore, less waste. When ordering handprints from a retail store, there are a few things one must know. There is a cutting charge if the wallcovering order requires a cut bolt. As the shading and even the positioning of the pattern on the roll may vary between dye lots or runs, SUFFICIENT BOLTS SHOULD ALWAYS BE ORDERED when the order is placed. The particular dye lot, which is stamped on the back of the roll, may not be still available if it is necessary to order more in the future. Opened or partially used bolts are not returnable, and unopened bolts may be subject to a restocking charge.

Commercial Wallcoverings

Commercial wallcoverings are the exception to the single roll containing 36 square feet. Commercial wallcoverings are usually 52- to 54-inches wide and are packaged in 30–yard or more bolts. These wider coverings require a highly skilled professional paperhanger and a helper. The final appearance of the walls depends on the ability of the paperhanger.

Commercial wallcoverings are classified according to federal minimum performance standards. Until 1983, the specifications for commercial wallcoverings were based on the number of ounces per square yard. Previously, 100 percent cotton was used as a backing, but today a blend of polyester and cotton is used. Polyester fibers are not as bulky as cotton fibers, and they do have more **tensile** strength. Tensile strength is the single most important performance feature in commercial wallcovering. Abrasion resistance is important but mainly in key areas such as outside corners.

A second major change is the inclusion of washability, scrubability, and stain resistance requirements. These qualities increase from Type I to the most durable Type III. The three types are further classified into Class 1, not mildew resistant, and Class 2, mildew resistant.

Mildew is a fungus that flourishes in a moist, dark environment. If mildew is present or even suspected, the walls should be washed with a mixture of equal parts of household bleach and water. The correct paste or adhesive will also help prevent mildew from forming under newly hung wallcovering. If proper precautions are not taken, any mildew that forms will permanently discolor the wallcovering.

From Numetal Surfaces comes a flexible metal wallcovering for use in contract and residential interiors. The patterns are abstract and are individually fabricated. The pattern continues from one 27 3/16-inch by 10-foot high panel to the adjacent one with as many as 22 panels in one order. This product was given the 1991 Roscoe award for wallcoverings.

Forbo-Vicrtex Inc. has two award-winning commercial wallcoverings. First, is Solitaire the First Place Winner in the 1990 ASID Product Design Award which has a fine horizontal texture, combined with a pleated symmetrical stripe creating interesting shadows and reflective highlights. Seurat, inspired by the pointillism artist, has been ingeniously designed to combine speckle prints with a polished angular texture. Seurat received the best of NEO-CON® 1990 Silver Award Winner.

With plain textures, grasscloths, and suedes, it is advisable to reverse the direction of every other strip. This will make a better finished appearance particularly if one side of the covering happens to be shaded a little more than the other.

As mentioned before, commercial wallcovering usually comes in 52- to 54-inch wide bolts. However, MDC Wallcoverings has a wallcovering, Quantum™, which is 106 inches wide and endless in length. The total width of all the walls is the length ordered. This woven textile has the best characteristics of olefins, such as durability and cleanability but due to its extreme width provides seamless installations and avoids panel shading. This wallcovering is made to be *railroaded*. In other words, instead of hanging Quantum vertically, it is hung horizontally.

Koroseal® vinyl wallcoverings (with the exception of Tiffany Suede, Surface, and Fresco patterns) contains the Early Warning Effect formulation which, when heated to about 300°, give off a harmless, odorless, and colorless vapor that will set off the alarm on an ionization smoke detector located in the same room. These vinyls are also UL approved to Class A federal standards, and contain antimicrobial and mildew resistant elements. Koroseal Wallcoverings also has Textiles for Walls in 54-inch widths. (Textile Wallcoverings do not include the Early Warning Effect formulation.)

Tassoglas wallcovering is a highly textured, 100 percent woven fiberglass wallcovering which is 39 inches wide and 54 yards long. This product combines the versatility of paint with the strength and benefits of woven glass fiber. Beneath the surface, Tasso reinforces the substrate. It easily bridges cracks, hides roughness or minor imperfections, and is ideal for use in both new construction and renovation. All Tasso textures come unpainted from the factory and may be painted up to 15 times depending on the texture.

For high-abuse areas, such as hospital corridors, hotels, malls, etc. Kydex® from Kleerdex Company may be used. This semi-rigid high-impact acrylic/polyvinyl chloride is very suitable for wainscoting in such areas.

If wood paneling is not permitted under the existing fire or building codes, a product called Flexwood® or Flexwood® + Plus may be specified. Flexwood is of two-ply construction (veneer and cloth backing), while the latter is four-ply construction (veneer, paper, foil, and paper). Both products are made of carefully selected wood veneers permanently laminated to a fiber backing. They can be applied to straight or curved walls and wrapped around columns. They are available in 50 domestic and imported woods, with the veneers so carefully matched that joints are practically invisible after installation. Every sheet is factory matched and numbered in sequence to ensure panoramic matching of the wall.

The recommended finish for Flexwood is a good alkyd varnish, which has a fast drying time and a low gloss matte finish. This material has a Class 1 flamespread rating of 15 when applied with the recommended adhesive. Flexwood + Plus, is prefinished with a urea sealer. Some installations may require no further finishing.

WILSONART Craftwood™ veneers, type 870, can be used for flat or curved surfaces. This veneer has an 8 mil. cloth backer.

A new concept in commercial wallcovering is the deeply embossed PVC or expanded vinyl wallcoverings which are not only attractive but offer acoustic values. They are packaged in full bolts, 29 inches wide by 55 yards in length.

All textile wallcoverings have good acoustic qualities and also good energy-saving insulation qualities. Textiles may be backed by paper and the fiber content may be 100 percent jute, or a combination of synthetics and wool, and jute and/or linen and cotton. These textiles usually have a flame spread rating of 25 or less.

Tretford Broadloom, a concentric ribbing in 38 colors from Eurotex, is, in Europe, mainly used for floors, but in this country it is usually used on walls. Face yarns are 80 percent wool/mohair, 20 percent nylon with a primary backing of poly vinyl chloride (PVC) and a secondary backing of jute. With a flame spread of 5, it is very suitable for contract work and absorbs sound, cushions impact, insulates to save energy, and is an excellent display surface that accepts Velcro® and push pins. Tretford can be installed on any dry, smooth surface such as concrete, dry wall, plaster, wood paneling, particle board etc. Installation on cinder or cement blocks or on surfaces covered with wallpaper or vinyl walcovering is *not* recommended. Tretford is installed with an adhesive applied with a notched trowel and maintenance involves brushing lightly in the direction of ribs and periodically vacuuming the surface.

Sisal is another wallcovering which has high sound absorption and is also static-free. Rolls are either 4 or 8 feet wide and 100 feet long. Sisal has an extremely prickly texture, as opposed to the other textiles, but this roughness can be an asset as in the following case: A school found that when students lined up outside the cafeteria, there was a tendency for the wall to get very dirty and be defaced by graffiti. Installation of sisal prevented both problems and also reduced the noise level.

One of the special surface treatments for wallcoverings is Tedlar®. This is a tough, transparent fluoride plastic sheet that is very flexible, chemically inert, and extremely resistant to stains, yellowing, corrosive chemicals, solvents, light, and oxygen. Most commercial wallcovering manufacturers have wallcovering products which are, or may be, surfaced with Tedlar. Another stain resistant product is PreFixx™, available on Essex 54 products which protects invisibly with no loss of texture as occurs with other products.

Some companies offer special-order printing, with minimums of 50 rolls or more. These may be designs already in their line or custom designs. Because these are handprints, they are expensive, but they may solve a particular design problem.

Installation. Before hanging any wallcovering, the walls must be sized. *Sizing* is a liquid applied to the wall surface which serves several purposes. First, it seals the surface against alkali, also known as hot spots; second, it reduces absorption of the paste or adhesive to be used; and third, it provides tooth for the wallcovering. The sizing must be compatible with the paste or adhesive to be used.

Wallcoverings are installed in either of the following manners:

1. Table trimmed with a straight edge. This means cutting the selvage from both edges so that the panels can be butted. This procedure reduces the amount of surface adhesive residue and facilitates clean up.

2. Panels are overlapped on the wall and seams are made by double cutting through both sheets. Care must be taken NOT to cut into the substrate surface. Various hooked knife-type cutting tools are available for this procedure. After the cut is made, the face strip may be removed and the adhesive cleaned off. Vicrtex® Wallcovering has the following extremely useful suggestions in its "Suggested Specification, Installation Instructions, Care and Maintenance" booklet: "Remove excess paste from a seam before making the next seam. Vertical joints should occur at least 6 inches from inside and outside corners." Vicrtex has also provided much of the information in this section.

Paste or adhesive is applied by means of a wide brush to the back of the wallcovering. Particular attention should be paid to the edges because this is where any curling will occur. The wallcovering is folded or **booked**, without creasing. This allows the moisture in the adhesive to be absorbed by the fabric substrate or backing, thus allowing for any shrinkage before being applied to the wall surface. Booking also makes an 8– or 9-foot strip easier to handle and transport from the pasting table.

The first strip is always hung parallel to the **plumbline**, which has been previously marked. A seam roller is used on most wallcoverings, except as noted before. As has been mentioned already, for some wallcoverings, the paste must be applied to the wall rather than to the backing. THE MANUFACTURER'S INSTRUCTIONS FOR INSTALLATION METHODS SHOULD ALWAYS BE FOLLOWED. Inspect each roll before cutting the first strip.

Maintenance. All stains or damage should be corrected immediately. Paper- faced wallcoverings should be tested to ascertain if the inks are permanent before cleaning fluids are applied. Vinyls may be scrubbed with a soft brush and water if they have been designated scrubbable. Foils are washed with warm water and wiped with a soft cloth to avoid any scratching. Hard water does have a tendency to leave a film on the reflective surfaces of foil.

Grasscloths, suedes, fabrics, sisal, and carpeting may be vacuumed to remove the dust. Again, always follow the manufacturer's instructions for maintenance.

It is suggested that vinyl-covered walls be washed at least once or twice a year. Grease and oils in particular should not be allowed to accumulate.

1. For routine dirt and grime, use a mild detergent dissolved in warm water.

2. For severe dirt conditions use a concentrated solution of a mild detergent applied with a stiff brush. Remove the grimy suds by padding with a damp sponge. The wall should then be rinsed with clean water to remove detergent residue.

3. For surface stains such as lipstick, ballpoint ink, heel marks, shoe polish, carbon smudges, and the like; use anhydrous isopropyl alcohol as an efficient cleaner for removal of such stains from vinyl wallcovering. Ethyl alcohol or denatured alcohols are also efficient. Do not use strong alkaline or abrasive cleaners.[2]

TAMBOURS

Tambours may be solid wood, wood veneer, metallic face laminate, or cork, laminated to a tempered hardboard core with brown fabric backing approximately 3/16 of an inch thick overall. Slats are cut 1/2 to 1 inch o.c. with the angle of the groove varying between 28° and 90°. Depending on the face material, dimensions may be 24-inch by 96-inch slat length or 48-inch by 96-inch slat length. A 120-inch length is available from some companies. Solid hardwood slats are also available in oak and maple (see Figure 4–14).

Flexible mirror may be clear, bronzed, or colored. This mirror is also bonded to a cloth back in square, rectangular, or diagonal pattern cuts and gives a multifaceted or broken reflection. Both the tambour and flexible mirror may be used on straight or curved walls.

Installation. The method of installation depends on the surface to which the tambour is to be attached. A special adhesive is usually required, but the man-

Figure 4-14
A bank reception area features curved walls of Chrome Mylar tambours from Flexible Materials. The durable backing joins the individual slats and allows easy application and flexibility. Photograph courtesy of Flexible Materials.

manufacturers' instructions should always be followed.

WOOD

Wood is a renewable resource and a good natural insulator due to the millions of tiny air cells within its cellular structure. For equal thickness, it is four times as efficient an insulator as cinder block, six times as efficient as brick, 15 times as efficient as stone, 400 times as efficient as steel, and 1,770 times as efficient as aluminum. The production of the final product is also energy efficient. One ton of wood requires 1,510 Kilowatt hours to manufacture, whereas one ton of rolled steel requires 12,000 Kilowatt hours, and one ton of aluminum requires 67,200 Kilowatt hours.

Wood for walls comes in two different forms: solid wood strips and plywoods.

Solid wood may be used on the walls of residences, but it is not usually used for commercial applications unless treated, due to the fire and building code restrictions. For residential use redwood, cedar, and knotty pine are the most commonly used woods, but walnut, pecan and many others may also be used.

There are several grades of redwood from which to choose. The Clear All Heart is unexcelled in **dimensional stability**, finish retention properties, and its well-known natural resistance to insects and decay. Clear All Heart gives a solid red color, whereas Clear redwood is also top quality but does contain some cream-colored sapwood and may also contain small knots and surface **checks**. This cream-colored sapwood may be attractive to some, but to others its random appearance is bothersome; therefore, the client needs to know the difference between the Clear All Heart and Clear.

Construction Heart is an economical all-purpose grade for decking and outdoor uses. The last two, Construction Common and Merchantable, are construction grades with knots and sapwood combined.

Redwood is available in vertical grain, equivalent to quarter sawn, and flat grain, cut at a tangent to the annual growth rings, exposing a face surface that appears highly figured or marbled.

For a stately atmosphere, Clear All Heart vertical-grained redwood enhances the effect. The smooth-faced redwood is referred to as surfaced; resawn has

Figure 4-15
Left is surfaced vertical grain redwood with a V-joint. Middle, saw-textured redwood gives a rough horizontally lined surface. Right, vertical grain produces these fairly even vertical stripes. The flat grain has a more uneven patterned appearance. (Photographs courtesy of California Redwood Association.)

one surface roughened by resawing during manufacture, which generates an extra dimension of shadow, contributing to a softened informal atmosphere. Boards range from 1/2 to 2 inches in thickness and 3 to 12 inches in width. (see Figures 4–15 and 4–16).

There are two types of cedar: aromatic cedar, which is used for mothproof closets, and regular cedar, which is used for both interior and exterior walls. Another soft wood frequently used for residential interiors is knotty pine where knots are part of the desired effect, unlike the top grade redwood.

Boards may be anywhere from 4 to 12 inches wide with tongue-and-groove for an interlocking joint, or **shiplap** for an overlapping joint. The tongue-and-groove may have the edges beveled for a V- joint or may be rounded or even elaborately molded for a more decorative effect. Shiplap boards come with their top edges beveled to form a V-joint, or with straight edges to form a narrow slot at the seams.

Square-edged boards are used in contemporary settings and may be board and batten, board on board, reverse board and batten, or contemporary vertical. Board and batten consists of wide boards spaced about one inch apart, and a narrow 1-by-2-inch strip of batten is nailed on top to cover the 1-inch gap. Board on board is similar to board and batten, except that both pieces of wood are the same width. Reverse board and batten has the narrow strip under the joint or gap. In contemporary vertical installations, the battens are placed on edge between the wider boards (see Figure 4–17).

Figure 4-16
Redwood installed diagonally gives a feeling of warmth to this restaurant. Photographer Richard Springgate.

For acoustical control, boards are often placed on edge and spaced about 2 to 3 inches apart on an acoustical substrate.

The National Oak Flooring Manufacturer's As-

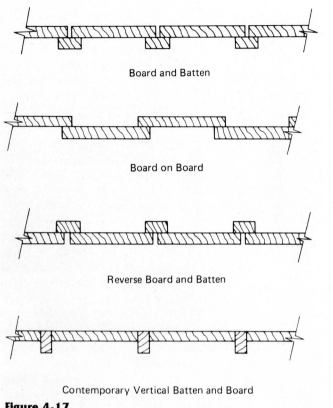

Board and Batten

Board on Board

Reverse Board and Batten

Contemporary Vertical Batten and Board

Figure 4-17
Boards and battens.

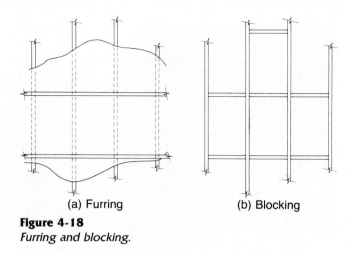

(a) Furring   (b) Blocking

Figure 4-18
Furring and blocking.

sociation suggests using oak flooring on the walls and ceiling. It is now possible to obtain a Class "A" 0–25 flamespread rating (often required in commercial structures) by job-site application of an intumescent coating. The NOFMA supplies literature showing that using Albert DS Clear by American Vameg meets this standard. A beveled oak strip flooring gives a three-dimensional effect when installed on a wall.

Several companies manufacture paneling that comes prepackaged in boxes containing approximately 64 square feet. The longest pieces are 8 feet and the shortest 2 feet, with the edges beveled and tongue-and-grooved sides and ends. This type of paneling, although more expensive than regular strips, eliminates waste in a conventional 8-foot-high room.

Installation. Siding, plank, or strips may be installed horizontally, vertically, or diagonally. Each type of installation will give a completely different feeling to the room. Horizontal planking will appear to lengthen a room and draw the ceiling down, while vertical adds height to a room and is more formal. Diagonal installations appear a little more active and should be used with discretion or as a focal point of a room.

Diagonal or herringbone patterns look best on walls with few doors or windows. Different application methods require different substrates.

If installed horizontally or diagonally over bare studs or gypsum board, no further preparation of the surface is needed. The strips are attached in the tongue area as with hard wood flooring, except that with wall applications, the nails penetrate each stud.

Vertical installations require the addition of nailing surfaces. The two types of nailing surfaces are blocking and furring. *Blocking* is the filling-in horizontally between the studs with a 2- to 4-inch piece of wood, in order to make a nailing surface. This blocking also acts as a fire stop. *Furring* is thin strips of wood nailed across the studs (see Figure 4–18).

When wood is to be used on an outside wall, a vapor barrier such as a polyethylene film is required. Also, wood should be stored for several days in the area in which it is to be installed so it may reach the correct moisture content. Some manufacturers suggest several applications of a water-repellent preservative to all sides, edges and especially the more porous ends. This is particularly important where high humidity persists.

There are several suggested finishes for wood walls: wax, which adds soft luster to the wood; or a sealer and a matte varnish, where cleaning is necessary. The paneling may also be stained, but it is important to remember that if solid wood is used, the natural beauty of the wood should be allowed to show through.

PLYWOOD PANELING

Plywood is produced from thin sheets of wood veneer, called *plies,* which are laminated together under heat and pressure with special adhesives. This produces a bond between plies that is as strong or stronger than the wood itself.

Plywood always has an odd number of layers which are assembled with their grains perpendicular to each other. Plywood may also have a lumber core or a particle board core. The lumber core is the most expensive plywood, but it is easily machined and has the most stable construction (see Figure 4–19).

The face veneer has the best quality veneer, and the back may be the same or of lesser quality, depending on its uses. The Hardwood Plywood Manufacturers Association (HPMA) sponsored plywood standard has six plywood veneer grade classifications. A grade (A), B grade (B), sound grade (2), industrial grade (3), backing grade (4) and specialty grade (SP). Designers will probably deal with (A), (B), and (SP).

A Grade (A). The veneer shall be smooth, tight-cut, and full-length. When used as a face and when it consists of more than one piece, the edges of the pieces shall appear parallel and be edge-matched. Edge joints shall be tight. The natural and other characteristics, the types of matching which will be permitted for each species, and the defects which will not be permitted are spelled out in the HPMA publication "American National Standard for Hardwood and Decorative Plywood."

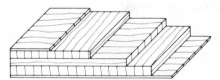

Veneer Core

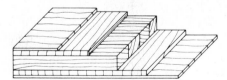

Lumber Core

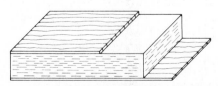

Particleboard Core

Figure 4-19
Types of plywood.

B Grade (B). The veneer shall be smooth, tight-cut, and full-length. When used as a face and when it consists of more than one piece, the edge joints shall be tight. Slip or **book matched** Grade B veneers are available if specified by the buyer. Otherwise, matching for uniform color or grain is not required, but sharp contrasts between adjacent pieces of veneer with respect to grain, figure, and natural character marking will not be permitted.

Specialty Grade (SP). This grade shall include veneer possessing characteristics unlike any of those described for the above-mentioned grades. Characteristics shall be as agreed upon between buyer and seller. Species such as wormy chestnut, birdseye maple, and English brown oak which have unusual decorative features are considered as Specialty Grade.

The manner in which the veneer is cut and the part of the tree from which it comes gives the different patterns—rotary, flat sliced, or quarter sliced. *Rotary cut* is used for all construction plywood (see Figure 4–20). The log is placed in a large lathe and, as the wood rotates against the sharp knife, the veneer peels off the log, in much the same manner as wrapping paper is pulled from a roll. The chief advantage to this method is that it produces wide, long sheets of veneer. Birch is one of the hardwoods cut by the rotary method, due to its uniformity of grain.

Flat slicing is the method of cutting veneer from wood the same way a potato is sliced. The veneer usually has a striped effect at the edges, with a larger, rather wide grain toward the center. Walnut is usually cut by this method.

Quarter slicing is the most costly method of veneer cutting. Quarter slicing is done for most fine imported woods where a definite striped effect is desirable. Mahogany is a good example.

Other decorative veneer patterns may be obtained by using the crotch, burl, or stump of the tree. The *crotch pattern* is always reversed so that the pointed part, or V, is up. *Burl* comes from an area of damage of the tree, where the tree has healed itself and grown over the injury. It is a very swirly pattern. *Olive burl* is frequently used in contemporary furniture.

Because rotary cutting provides large sheets, matching of pattern is not necessary. However, matching of veneers in flat and quarter slicing is very important. *Slip-matched veneers* are laid next to each other as the veneer comes from the cutter, giving a repetitive pattern, but also nonmatching joints. Slip-matched veneers result in maximum color conformity and are most commonly used with quartered and *rift-sliced veneers*. In *book-leaf matched veneers*, every

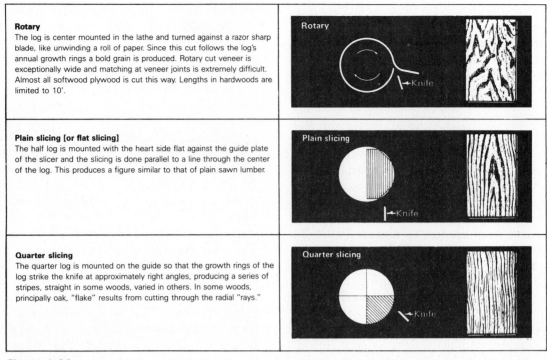

Rotary The log is center mounted in the lathe and turned against a razor sharp blade, like unwinding a roll of paper. Since this cut follows the log's annual growth rings a bold grain is produced. Rotary cut veneer is exceptionally wide and matching at veneer joints is extremely difficult. Almost all softwood plywood is cut this way. Lengths in hardwoods are limited to 10'.	
Plain slicing [or flat slicing] The half log is mounted with the heart side flat against the guide plate of the slicer and the slicing is done parallel to a line through the center of the log. This produces a figure similar to that of plain sawn lumber.	
Quarter slicing The quarter log is mounted on the guide so that the growth rings of the log strike the knife at approximately right angles, producing a series of stripes, straight in some woods, varied in others. In some woods, principally oak, "flake" results from cutting through the radial "rays."	

Figure 4-20

Veneer types. (Reprinted with permission of The Architectural Woodwork Institute.)

other piece of veneer is turned over, giving a more united feeling to the veneer. The meeting edges produce a matching joint and effect maximum continuity of grain. Book-matching is used with plain or quarter-sliced veneer. *End matching*, sometimes known as *butt matching*, is used when the panel height desired exceeds the veneer length, and is achieved by progressively book-matching lengthwise as well as horizontally, producing a uniform grain progression in both directions. A four-way center and butt match

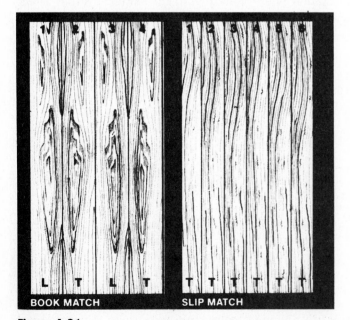

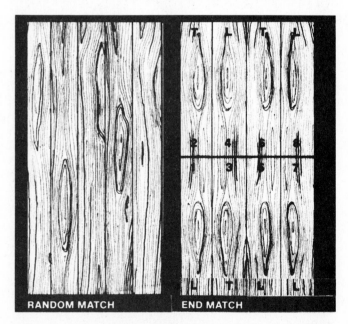

Figure 4-21

Book, slip, random, end matching. (Reproduced by permission of the Architectural Woodwork Institute.)

is used on table tops or wall paneling to give extremely interesting patterns (see Figure 4–21).

The following information is supplied by the Architectural Woodwork Institute, a not-for-profit organization representing the architectural woodwork manufacturers of the United States and Canada.

The individual leaves of veneer in a sliced flitch increase or decrease in width as the slicing progresses. Thus, if a number of panels are manufactured from a particular **flitch**, the number of veneer leaves per panel face will change as the flitch is utilized. The manner in which these leaves are "laid-up" within the panel requires book matching, and are classified as follows:

1. *Running Match.* Each panel face is assembled from as many veneer leaves as necessary. (Any portion left over from the last leaf may be used as the start of the next panel.)
2. *Balance Match.* Each panel face is assembled from leaves of uniform width. *Note:* Generally most aesthetically pleasing.

3. *Center Match.* Each panel has an even number of veneer leaves of uniform width. Thus, there is a veneer joint in the center of the panel, producing horizontal symmetry. Note: Increases waste and consequently cost. Available on special order (see Figure 4–22).

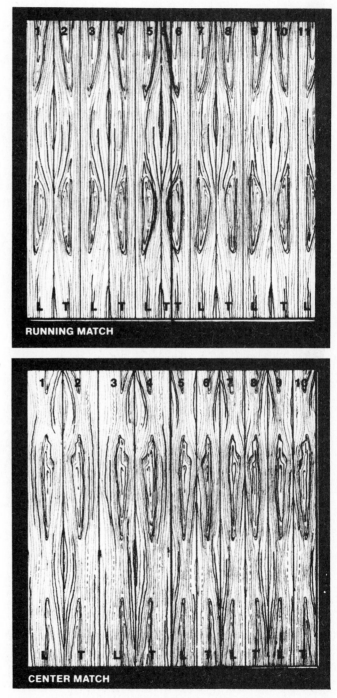

RUNNING MATCH

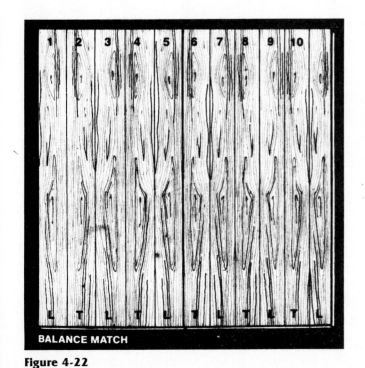

BALANCE MATCH

CENTER MATCH

Figure 4-22
Assembly of veneers within the panel face. (Reproduced by permission of the Architectural Woodwork Institute.)

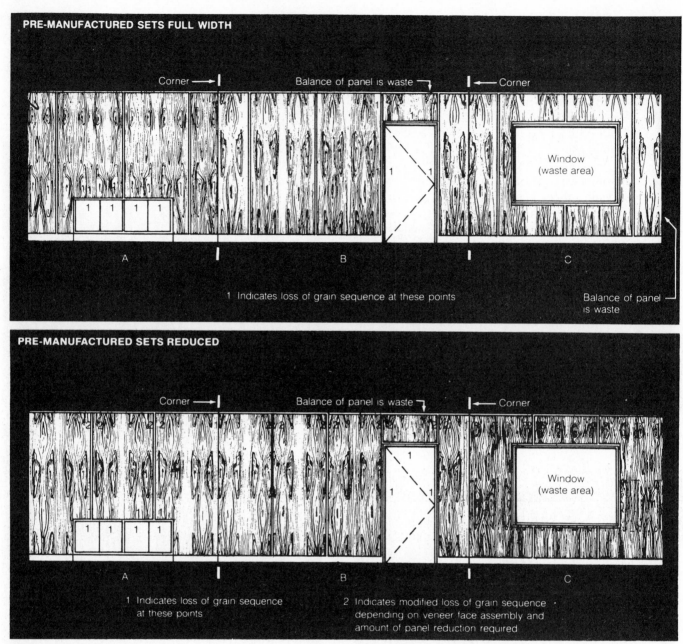

Figure 4-23
Matching panels. (Reproduced by permission of the Architectural Woodwork Institute.)

Methods of matching panels

1. *Pre-manufactured Sets.* These are pre-manufactured panel sets usually 48-by-96 inches or 48-by-120 inches, numbered in sequence. They may be the product of a single flitch or part thereof, usually varying in number from 6 to 12 panels. If more than one set is required, matching between the sets cannot be expected. Similarly, doors occurring within the wall cannot be matched to panels. Best utilization of these panels is achieved by using

them in near-full width, with necessary adjustments being made at wall ends or corners. A more aesthetically pleasing result can be accomplished by selectively reducing the width of the panels to achieve greater balance within each wall and in relation to doors and windows. This will result in a slight increase in cost.

2. *Sequence Matched Uniform Size Panel Sets.* These sets are usually manufactured for a specific installation to a uniform panel width and height. If more than one flitch is required to produce the necessary

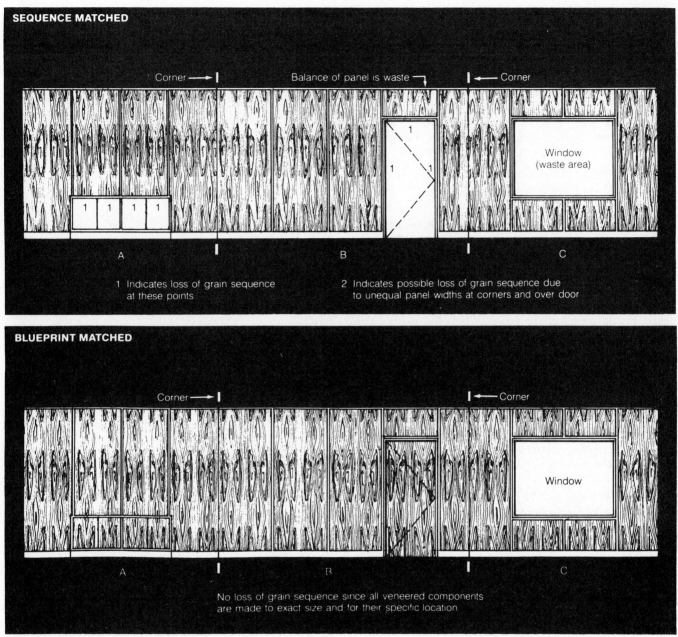

Figure 4-23 cont.

number of panels, similar flitches will be used. This type of panel matching is best used when panel layout is uninterrupted and when the design permits the use of near-equal width panels. Doors occurring within the wall cannot be matched to panel.

3. *Blueprint Matched Panel and Components.* This method of panel matching achieves maximum grain continuity, since all panels, doors, and other veneered components are made to the exact sizes required and in exact veneer sequence. If possible, flitches should be selected that will yield sufficient veneer

to complete a prescribed area or room; if more than one is required, flitch transition should be accomplished at the least noticeable predetermined location. This panel matching method is the more expensive, but does express veneering in its most impressive manner (see Figure 4–23).

Rooms treated with paneling always produce a feeling of permanency. Architectural paneling is as different from ready-made paneling as a custom-made Rolls Royce is from an inexpensive production car. The ready-made paneling will be discussed later.

There are three grades of architectural paneling as defined by AWI:

1. *Premium Grade:* The highest grade available in both material and workmanship is intended for the finest work. This is naturally the most expensive grade. It might be used throughout the entire building on rare occasions, but most often is used in selected spaces within a building or for selected items.
2. *Custom Grade:* The middle or normal grade in both material and workmanship, and is intended for high-quality conventional work.
3. *Economy Grade:* The lowest grade in both material and workmanship, and is intended for work where price outweighs quality considerations.

For a traditional type of paneling, **stile** and rail construction is used. This consists of a panel that may be flat, raised, or have a beveled edge. The vertical side strips are called stiles, and the horizontal strips are called rails. The rails, stiles and **mullions** may themselves be shaped into an **ovolo** or **ogee** moulding, or, to give a more intricate design, a separate moulding may be added. For raised panels under 10 inches in width, solid lumber may be used in custom grade, but for premium grade or wider panels, plywood is used with an attached edge of solid lumber which is then beveled (see Figure 4–24).

Since the detail and design options in this type of paneling are virtually unlimited, the AWI suggests that certain minimum information must be provided to properly estimate and detail this type of paneling:

1. Scale elevations of walls determining panel layout.
2. Determination by detail or instructions whether the panel mould is to be an applied moulding or a profiled portion of the stiles and rails. (Such profiles must be capable of being **coped.**)
3. Similar determination as to whether the panels are to be flat or raised.

Panels are assembled by means of mortise and tenon, or dowel joints. At the joining of the panel and the stiles and rails, a small space is left to allow for the natural expansion and contraction of the panel. This type of construction may sometimes be known as "floating panel construction." Panels that are glued have no allowance for this expansion and contraction, and may split if movement is excessive.

There are several methods of installing panels for acoustic control. The panels may be floated or raised, or batten mouldings of wood, metal, or plastic may also be used see Figure 4–25.

Finishing. The Architectural Woodwork Institute has specific standards for factory finishing of woodwork and its publications entitled Architectural Woodwork Quality Standards Guide Specifications and Quality Certification Program and Factory Finishing of Architectural Woodwork should be consulted.

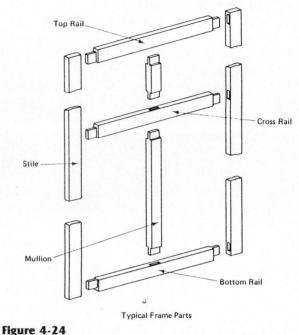

Typical Frame Parts

Figure 4-24
Frame parts.

PREFINISHED PLYWOOD

Prefinished plywood paneling varies from 1/4- to 1/2-inch thick, and standard panel size is 4-by-8 feet, but is also available in 7- and 10-foot heights. The face of the plywood is grooved in random widths to simulate wood strips. This also hides the joining where each panel is butted up to the next, as outside edges are beveled at the same angle as the grooves.

The finish on this type of paneling is clear acrylic over a stained surface.

Some plywood paneling has a woodgrain reproduction on lauan plywood or on a paper overlay applied to **lauan** plywood and then protected with an oven-baked topcoat.

Installation. As with all wood products, paneling should be stored in the room for 24 hours to condition for humidity and temperature. Paneling may be applied directly to the stud framing, but it is safer from a fire hazard point of view to install over gypsum board. A 1/4-inch sound-deadening board used as a backing decreases the sound transmission. Nails or adhesive may be used to install the panels. If nails are used, they may be color-coated when exposed fasteners are acceptable, or countersunk and filled with colored putty.

Maintenance. Prefinished plywood panels require frequent dusting in order to prevent a buildup of soil which dulls the finish. Each manufacturer supplies instruction for maintenance of its particular product, and these should be adhered to.

HARDBOARD

Sheets or planks of hardboard are manufactured of compressed wood fibers by means of heat and pressure. Hardboard sheets or planks consist of a hardboard base that is textured during the pressing process, usually in a wood grain pattern. A dark base coat is then placed on top. This layer gives the dark color to the V-joints. On top is the light precision coat that does not cover the V-joints. This precision coat is grained and coated with a melamine topcoat that is baked on and that is resistant to most household chemicals and such staining agents as cosmetics and crayons. Tape should not be applied to the panel surface because it may damage the surface).

Paneling is also available in 4-by-8-foot sheets and may utilize harmonizing mouldings between panels or may be butted. Pigmented vertical grooves simulate joints of lumber planks, and edges are also pigmented to match face grooves and to conceal butt joints. Hardboard panels are not to be used below grade, over masonry walls, in bathrooms, or in any area of high humidity.

When hardboard is covered with a photo-reproduction of wood, it does not have the depth or richness of real wood, and is probably best used for inexpensive installations where price and durability are more important than the appearance of real wood. Because this paneling is not wood-veneered but rather a reproduction, the same manufacturing methods may be used for solid colors or patterns. Fast food restaurants and many businesses requiring the same feature of durability and easy cleaning use Marlite plank. The plank may be used vertically, horizontally, and diagonally, provided furring strips have been installed over any sound, solid substrate.

Some hardboard is available in a stamped grille-type pattern or with holes (commonly known as Peg-Board®). The grille types are framed with wood and used for dividers. The perforated board is useful when hanging or storing items. Special hooks and supports are available for this purpose and are easily installed and removed for adjustment.

Installation. Thicknesses of hardboard vary from 1/8 and 3/16 of an inch to 1/4 of an inch. The 1/8-inch and 3/16-inch thicknesses must be installed over a solid backing, such as gypsum board. Panels are glued or nailed to the substrate.

Maintenance. A lint-free cloth should be used. To remove surface accumulation such as dust and grease, a soft cloth dampened with furniture polish containing no waxes or silicones may be used. More stubborn accumulations may require wiping with a soft cloth dampened in a solution of lukewarm water and a mild detergent. The hardboard must be wiped dry with a clean dry cloth immediately following this procedure. (An inconspicuous area or scrap paneling should be used for experimental cleaning.)

DECORATIVE LAMINATE

Decorative laminates are made from layers of kraft paper which have been impregnated with phenolic resins. The pattern layer is placed on top and covered by a translucent overlay of melamine. When all these layers are bonded with heat, 300°F, and pressure, 800 to 1,200 psi, the top translucent layer becomes transparent and forms the wearlayer. The pattern layer may be solid color, metal, or a photo reproduction of wood or fabric.

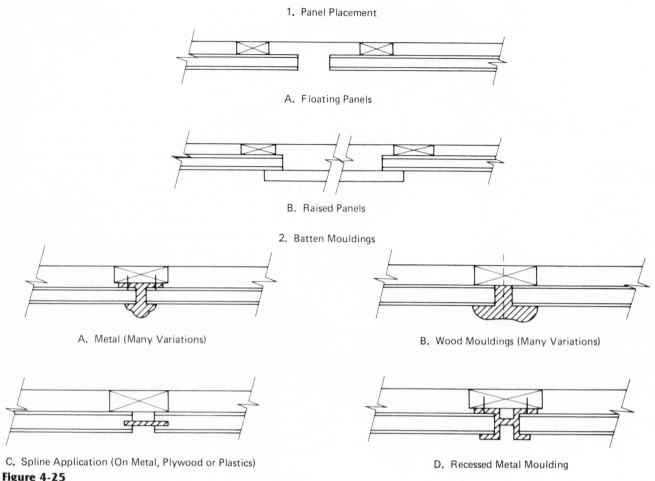

1. Panel Placement

A. Floating Panels

B. Raised Panels

2. Batten Mouldings

A. Metal (Many Variations)

B. Wood Mouldings (Many Variations)

C. Spline Application (On Metal, Plywood or Plastics)

D. Recessed Metal Moulding

Figure 4-25
Panel installation for acoustic control. (Courtesy of the Hardwood Plywood Manufacturers Association.)

The vertical surface may be .050 of an inch general purpose or .030-inch vertical surface. The .030-inch vertical surface type is not recommended on surfaces exceeding 24 inches in widths. Decorative laminate for walls are quite often installed on the job site.

Balancing or backing laminates are used to give structural balance and dimensional stability. They are placed on the reverse side of the substrate to inhibit moisture absorption through the back surface.

There are three types of decorative metals from WILSONART designed for vertical interior applications where special accent is required: anodized aluminum bonded to a phenolic backer for fabrication following **HPDL** techniques. They are available in three finishes: polished, satin brushed, and bright brushed. They are ideal for any area where a special accent is desired—in lobbies, theatres, restaurants and contemporary residential interiors. The second type is the solid polished brass, coated with a baked synthetic, transparent, protective coating with film

properties superior to regular lacquer. This material may be used for wainscoting, light troughs, planters, luggage trim, and even range backsplashes. The coating is highly resistant to oxidation, humidity, abrasion, and perspiration. The third type is a solid sheet of aluminum produced with a decorative, anodized finish and color on one side. The other side is prepared to facilitate bonding to a suitable substrate.

Where antistatic properties are required, a standard grade laminate is available. Several manufacturers of decorative laminate produce a laminate that does not have the usual dark edge associated with a square edge installation such as SOLICOR® and COLORCORE®.

Many manufacturers of HPDL produce a fire-resistant type which, when applied with approved adhesives to a fire-resistant core, results in wall paneling with Class 1 or "A" flamespread rating.

Many different textures are available ranging from high gloss to pebbled to simulated leather according to the use. The new #90 Crystal from WILSONART has a pearlescent texture which minimizes finger marks, and improves scratch resistance.

Installation. When decorative laminates are to be used on the wall, 3/4-inch hardwood-faced plywood or particle board should be used as a core. The use of an expansion type joint or reveal is suggested (see Figure 4–26). To permit free panel movement and to avoid visible fastenings, AWI recommends that panels be hung on the walls, utilizing metal panel clips or interlocking wood wall cleats, as shown in Figure 4–27.

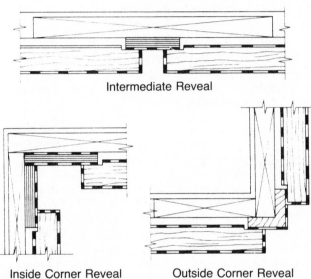

Intermediate Reveal

Inside Corner Reveal   Outside Corner Reveal

Figure 4-26
Reveals. (Reproduced with permission of the Architectural Woodwork Institute.)

Maintenance. Decorative laminates should be cleaned with warm water and mild soaps such as those used for hands or dishes. Use of abrasive cleansers or "special" cleansers should be avoided because they may contain abrasives, acids, or alkalines. Stubborn stains may be removed with organic solvents or two-minute exposure to a hypochlorite bleach such as Clorox, followed by a clean water rinse.

Metallic laminates other than solid polished brass may be cleaned as above. However, always wipe the surface of metallics completely dry with a clean soft cloth after washing. Stubborn smudges may be removed with a dry cloth and a thin, clean oil. For solid polished brass surfaces, use only glass cleaners free of petroleum products. The surface may be touched up with Fill 'n Glaze™ and a good grade of automobile wax. Follow the manufacturer's instructions carefully when applying.

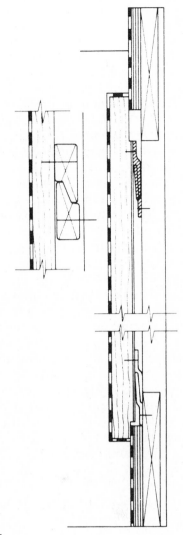

Figure 4-27
Hanging methods. (Reproduced with permission of the Architectural Woodwork Institute)

PORCELAIN ENAMEL

Porcelain enamel is baked on 28–gauge steel, laminated to 3/16 to 21/32 of an inch gypsum board or hardboard, and comes in many colors and finishes for use in high-abuse public areas, such as hospitals and food processing and preparation areas. It is also available with writing board surfaces that double as projection screens. Widths are from 2 to 4 feet, and lengths are from 6 to 12 feet. Weight varies from 1.60 to 2.75 pounds per square foot. This material is also used for toilet partitions in public rest rooms.

Maintenance. Same as for ceramic tile.

GLASS

Glass, one of our most useful products, is also one of the oldest (about 4,000 B.C). In ancient times, formed pieces of colored glass were considered as valuable as precious stones. In the past, glass was used mainly for windows, permitting light and sun to enter the interior of a home or building. Currently, due to modern construction methods, glass is used for interior walls or partitions. Of course, one disadvantage of glass is that it is breakable, but there are products specially made to reduce this problem.

There are three methods of manufacturing glass. The first is for sheet or *window glass*, where the molten glass is drawn out and both sides are subjected to open flame. This type, which is not treated after manufacture, can show distortions and waviness. *Plate glass* has both surfaces ground and polished, rendering its surfaces virtually plane and parallel. *Float glass* is a more recently developed and less expensive process of manufacturing; molten glass is floated over molten metal and is used interchangeably with plate glass.

Insulating glass consists of two or three sheets of glass separated by either a dehydrated air space or an inert gas-filled space, together with a **desiccant**. This insulating glass limits heat transference and, in some areas of the country, may be required by the building codes in all new construction for energy conservation purposes. It also helps to eliminate the problem of condensation caused by a wide difference in outside and inside temperatures.

There are various types of safety glass. The one with which we are most familiar is **tempered**, the kind used in entry doors or shower doors, where a heavy blow breaks the glass into small grains rather than sharp, jagged slivers. Another, which has a wire mesh incorporated into its construction, can break under a blow but does not shatter.

Laminated glass can control sound, glare, heat, and light transmission. It offers security and safety through high resistance to breakage and penetration. In interior areas where glass is desired, laminated acoustical glass is effective in reducing sound transmission. Where exterior sounds (traffic, airplanes, etc.) are present and distracting, laminated acoustical glass may be used. This glass may be clear or colored (see Figure 4–7 for custom etched panels). Another form of glass used for energy conservation is a laminated glass with a vinyl interlayer which, depending on the color of the interlayer, may absorb or transmit light in varying degrees. The tinted glass may have a bronze, gray, green, blue, silver or gold appearance, and these tints cut down on glare in a manner similar to sunglasses or the tinted glass in an automobile. Where 24–hour protection is required, such as in jewelry stores, banks, and detention areas, a security glass with a high-tensile polyvinyl butryal inner layer is highly effective. There are even bullet-resistant glasses on the market.

For those involved in historical restorations, there is Restoration Glass™ from Bendheim. This glass is handmade using the original cylinder method, yet the glass easily meets today's tougher building codes. It is available in two levels of distortion—"full," for thicker and more distortiing effects, and "light," for thinner and less distorting effects.

Taliq Varalite™ Vision Panels can, at the flip of a switch, change interior and exterior windows from clear to translucent. This option provides open vistas and a sense of spaciousness which can be converted to privacy and security.

MIRROR

The mirrors used two thousand years ago by the Egyptians, Romans, and Greeks were highly polished thin sheets of bronze. Today, many of these metal mirrors may be seen in museums. The method of backing glass with a metallic film was known to the Romans, but it was not until 1507 that the first glass mirrors were made in Italy. Plate glass was invented in France in 1691, enabling larger pieces of glass to be manufactured. The shape of mirrors used in various periods of design should be studied by interior designers, but mirrors are no longer just accessories hung on the wall for utilitarian or decorative purposes. Walls are often completely covered with these highly reflective surfaces (see Figure 4–28).

Quality mirrors are made of float glass and are silvered on the back to obtain the highly reflective quality. Also used under certain circumstances are the two-way mirrors, where from one side, the viewer can see out, but from the other side it appears to be an ordinary mirror. These two-way mirrors have many uses, such as in apartment doors, child observation areas, department stores, banks, and prison security areas.

Mirrors used on wall installations may be clear and brightly reflective or grayed or bronze hued. The latter are not as bright, but do not noticeably distort color values. The surface may also be antiqued, pro-

Figure 4-28
An entry way is enlarged by a wall-to-wall mirror. On the laminate shelf, a Frank Riggs sculpture, the reverse side of which is duplicated in the mirror. Oriental rug is a Bokhara.

Laminate from Wilsonart, ceramic tile from Dal Tile. Photographer Lyman Hafen.

ducing a smoky, shadowy effect. Mirrored walls always enlarge a room and may be used to correct a size deficiency or to duplicate a prized possession, such as a candelabra or chandelier. Mirrored walls may also display all sides of a piece of sculpture or double the light available in a room (see Figure 4–28).

Mirrors are available for wall installations in many sizes, ranging from large sheets to small mosaic mirrors on sheets similar to mosaic tile. Sometimes, a perfect reflection is not necessary and the mirrors may be in squares, **convex** or **concave**, acid etched, engraved, or beveled.

Mirror Terminology

The following terminology was provided by the National Association of Mirror Manufacturers.

Acid Etch A process of producing a specific design or lettering on glass, prior to silvering but cutting into the glass with a combination of acids. This process may involve either a frosted surface treatment or a deep etch. This process can also be done on regular glass as seen in Figure 4–7.

Antique Mirror A decorative mirror in which the silver has been treated to create a smokey or shadowy effect. The antique look is often heightened by applying a veining on the silvered side in any one of more of a variety of colors and designs.

Backing Paint The final protective coating applied on the back of the mirror, over copper, to protect the silver from deterioration.

Concave Mirror Surface is slightly curved inward and tends to magnify reflected items or images.

Convex Mirror Surface is slightly curved outward to increase the area that is reflected. Generally used for safety or security surveillance purposes.

Edge Work Among numerous terms and expressions defining types of edge finishing, the five in most common usage are listed here:

Clean-cut Edge Natural edge produced when glass is cut. It should not be left exposed in installation.

Ground Edge Grinding removes the raw cut of glass, leaving a smooth satin finish.

Seamed Edge Sharp edges are removed by an abrasive belt.

Polished Edge Polishing removes the raw cut of glass to give a smooth-surfaced edge. A polished edge is available in two basic contours.

Beveled Edge A tapered polished edge, varying from 1/4 of an inch to a maximum of 1 1/4 inches thick, produced by machine in a rectangular or circular shape. Other shapes or ovals may be beveled by hand, but the result is inferior to machine bevel. Standard width of bevel is generally 1/2 of an inch (see Figure 4–29).

Electro-Copper-Plating Process of copper-plating by electrolytic deposition of copper on the back of the silver film, to protect the silver and to assure good adherence of the backing paint.

Engraving The cutting of a design on the back or face of a mirror, usually accomplished by hand on an engraved lathe.

Finger Pull An elongated slot cut into the glass by

a wheel, so that a mirrored door or panel, for instance, may be moved to one side.

First-surface Mirror A mirror produced by deposition of reflective metal on front surface of glass, usually under vacuum. Its principal use is as an automobile rear-view mirror or transparent mirror.

Framed Mirror Mirror placed in a frame that is generally made of wood, metal, or composition material and equipped for hanging.

Hole Piercing of a mirror, usually 1/2 inch in diameter and generally accomplished by a drill. Generally employed in connection with installations involving rosettes.

Mitre Cutting The cutting of straight lines by use of a wheel on the back or face of a mirror for design purposes. Available in both satin and polished finishes.

Rosette Hardware used for affixing a mirror to a wall. A decorative rose-shaped button used in several places on the face of a mirror.

Sand Blasting Engraving or cutting designs on glass by a stream of sand, usually projected by air.

Shadowbox Mirror Mirror bordered or framed at an angle on some or all sides by other mirrors, creating multiple reflections of an image.

Stock-sheet Mirrors Mirrors of varying sizes over 10 square feet, and up to 75 square feet, from which all types of custom mirrors are cut. Normally packed 800 to 1,000 square feet to a case.

Transparent Mirror A first surface mirror with a thin film of reflective coating. To insure most efficient use, the light intensity on the viewer's side of the mirror must be significantly less than on the subject side. Under such a condition, the viewer can see through the mirror as through a transparent glass, while the subject looks into a mirror.

Installation. Both mastic and mechanical devices such as clips or rosettes should be used in order to install a mirror properly. Clips are usually of polished chrome, and are placed around the outside edges. Rosettes are clear plastic type fasteners and require a hole to be drilled several inches in from the edge, in order to accept the fastening screws and rosettes. Due to the fragile quality of mirror, use should be limited to areas where the likelihood of breakage is minimal.

Installation of Ceramic, Metal, and Mirror Tile. Due to the force of gravity, mortar cement cannot be troweled directly onto the wall without sagging. To prevent this sagging, a metal lath, similar to the one used for a plaster wall, is attached to the solid backing

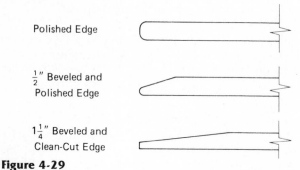

Polished Edge

$\frac{1}{2}$" Beveled and Polished Edge

$1\frac{1}{4}$" Beveled and Clean-Cut Edge

Figure 4-29
Mirror bevels.

Table 4-2
Wall Tiling Installation Guide.

WALL TILING INSTALLATION GUIDE

Simplest methods are indicated; those for heavier services are acceptable. Some very large or heavy tile may require special setting methods. Consult ceramic tile manufacturer.

SERVICE REQUIREMENTS	WALL TYPE (numbers refer to Handbook Method numbers)					
	Masonry or Concrete	Page	Wood Studs	Page	Metal Studs	Page
Commercial Construction — Dry or limited water exposure: dairies, breweries, kitchens.	W202 W221* W223	20 21 21	W223 W231 W243 W244	21 22 23 23	W223 W241 W242 W243, W244	21 22 22 23
Commercial Construction — Wet: gang showers, tubs, showers, laundries.	W211 W202 W221* B414	20 20 21 25	W231 W244 B411	22 23 24	W241 W244 B411 B414, B415	22 23 24 25
Residential & Light Construction — Dry or limited water exposure: kitchens and toilet rooms, commercial dry area interiors and decoration.	W221* W223	21 21	W222* W223 W243 W244	21 21 23 23	W222* W242 W243 W244	21 22 23 23
Residential & Light Construction — Wet: tub enclosures and showers.	W202 W211 W223	20 20 21	W222* W223 W244 B412, B413 B415, B416	21 21 23 24 25	W222* W241 W244 B412, B413 B415, B416	21 22 23 24 25
Exterior (see notes on page 22)	W201 W202	20 20	W231	22	W241 Refer to page 7	22

*Use these details where there may be dimensional instability, possible cracks developing in or foreign coating (paint, etc.) on structural wall which includes cleavage membrane (15 lb. felt or polyethylene) between wall surface and tile installation.

Source: 1991 Handbook for Ceramic Tile Installation. *Copyright © Tile Council of America, Inc. Reprinted with permission.*

and then troweled with mortar. The metal lath acts as a stabilizing force. The backing may be wood, plaster, masonry, or gypsum board. This is equivalent to the thick-set method of floor installation. For wall use over gypsum board, plaster, or other smooth surfaces, an organic adhesive may be used. This adhesive should be water-resistant for bath and shower areas.

CERAMIC TILE: The Installation Handbook is available from the Tile Council of America Inc., and also in Sweet's Catalogs, is the nationally accepted guide line for writing specifications, even for materials other than ceramic tile.

CERAMIC TILE

Ceramic tile is frequently used on walls when an easily cleaned, waterproof, and durable surface is desired. One use of ceramic tile is as a **backsplash** in the kitchen. When it is used for this purpose, the

grout may be sealed by use of a commercial sealer or by using a lemon oil furniture polish. Ceramic tile is also used for the surrounds of showers and bathtubs, and for bathroom walls in general. These three uses are probably the most common ones, but ceramic tile may also be used on the walls in foyers and hallways, either plain, patterned or in logos, and as a heat-resistant material around fireplaces and stoves. Ceramic tile for counter tops will be discussed later.

American Olean has a new series of 8 inch by 10 inch glazed wall tiles and coordinating floors that can be used with Kaleidostrips™, a 2 inch by 8 inch decorative strip. One of this series is Damask™ an oyster tile with bands of polished platinum luster alternating with matte glazed strips for a fine shadow-striped effect.

If the walls are completely covered with ceramic tile, there will be no need for trim pieces. However, in bathrooms or kitchens, or any place where tiling will not be continued from wall to wall or from ceiling to floor, trim pieces must be added to cover the unglazed and uncolored side of the tile. These trim pieces are different in appearance, depending on the type of installation, thick or thin set.

A bullnose for thick-set installations has an overhanging curve piece, whereas a bullnose for thin-set is the same thickness as the surrounding tiles, but has a curved finished edge. For bath and shower installations, angle trims for the top and inside edges are used, and for walls meeting the floor, a cove is used (see Figure 3–12).

METAL

In the latter part of the 19th century, during the Victorian era, stamped tin panels were used on ceilings and dadoes of rooms. The dadoes even had a molded chair rail incorporated into them. Today, Pinecrest manufacturers 26–gauge tin in 24 by 96 inch panels stamped with dies dating back to the Civil War. These panels are virtually indestructible and come with a silver tin finish. They may be painted with an oil base paint, if desired. Matching cornices are also available.

For a more contemporary metal surface the new FS3 panels from Forms + Surfaces may be used. These are a high-tech series of panels for interior surfaces that combine three important features: noncombustible material, deep relief patterns (grids, horizontal flutes, domes, and convex and concave pyramids) and are available prefinished in 10 automotive lacquers or unfinished for field painting after installation. The panels are bonded to a Class 1 rated substrate and the weight is approximately 2.5 pounds per square foot. Forms + Surfaces also supplies embossed metal with geometric patterns, textures and graphics or etched metals.

ACOUSTICAL PANELS

Several manufacturers produce a mineral fiberboard or fiberglass panel, which, when covered with fabric, absorbs sound and also provides an attractive and individually designed environment. Because of the textured, porous surface and the absorbent substrate, sound is absorbed rather than bounced back into the room. These panels may also be used as tack boards for lightweight pictures and graphics. In open plan areas, different colors can be used to direct the flow of traffic through an open office and to differentiate between work areas. In addition to the acoustical qualities of these panels, there are two other beneficial features. One is that the panels are fire retardant and the other is that, when installed on perimeter walls, there is an insulating factor that varies with the type of board used.

The panels may take the form of appliques in sizes of 2 by 4 feet, 2 by 6 feet, or they may cover the wall completely in panel sizes of 24 or 30 inches by 9 feet.

Vinyl or fabric faced acoustic panels may be designed for various types of installation. For use on an existing wall, only one side needs to be covered. For open-plan landscapes, both surfaces are covered to absorb sound from both sides. Some panels are covered on the two side edges for butted installation while another portable type is wrapped on all surfaces and edges. Sculptwall, with its rounded contour, provides an acoustical and aesthetic solution for sound absorbency. The surface area of the arc is 24 inches wide, which covers 18 inches of wall surface. The internal construction is either 1- or 2-inch molded fiberglass board, which is adhered with the fabric or perforated Vicrtex vinyl of your choice.

Installation. As there are numerous types of acoustic panels, no one installation method covers all panels. Depending on the type of panel, panels may be attached to the wall by means of an adhesive and/or may have moulding concealing the seams. Manufacturers recommended installation methods should be followed.

Maintenance. Surface dirt is removed by vacuuming or light brushing. Spots can be treated with drycleaning fluid or with carpet shampoo.

CORK

Cork tiles are available in 12 by 36 inches in 1/2-, 3/4-, 1-, and 1 1/2-inch thicknesses and may be used in residential, commercial, educational, and institutional buildings. Due to its porous nature, cork can breathe and therefore can be used on basement walls or on the inside surface of exterior support walls without the risk of moisture difficulties. Due to the millions of dead-air spaces in the cork particles themselves, cork also has good insulating properties.

Installation. Panels are applied by using 1/8 by 1/8 of an inch notched trowel and the recommended adhesive.

Maintenance. Dodge Cork Company recommends vacuuming periodically with the brush attachment. A light, dust-free sealing coat of silicone aerosol spray will give dust protection; a heavier spray protects against dust and gives the surface a glossier finish, providing more light reflection. However, a heavy spray tends to close the pores of the cork, thus decreasing its sound deadening and insulating qualities. An alternate to the silicone spray is a 50–50 blend of clear shellac and alcohol.

Surface Design and Technology Inc., has metal graphics which are materials for elevator door and cab facings, wall and ceiling panels, door claddings, column covers etc.

OTHER MATERIALS

Duroplex® coatings are very tough finishes applied exclusively by factory-trained installers who are in the painting trade. Depending upon the desired finish, Duroplex can be applied by spray or roller methods and cures to a surface hardness that is 80% as hard as mild steel. It is as tough as concrete and provides an improved performance dimension to drywall.

Paleo™ from Forms + Surfaces is a cementitious, glass-reinforced, mineral formulation which is formed into prefinished panels, bases, crown and corner mouldings, and column covers. Visually, it suggests the varying, surface textures of natural stone materials and is available in two textures, three moulding styles and five inherent colors. The panels are installed with any solvent-based commercial panel adhesive. (See Figure 4–30.)

VITRICOR® is a high-molecular acrylic from Nevamar and is very suitable for vertical surfaces which

Figure 4-30
Paleo™ from Forms + Surfaces covers the walls of this elevator lobby, providing a textural contrast to the highly polished floor. Inset shows a close-up of the surface texture. Photograph courtesy of Forms + Surfaces.

require a reflective gloss appearance with deep, rich, saturated color much like that of hand lacquered finishes. (See Figure 4–31.)

Forms + Surfaces also uses Avonite®, a patented, nonporous polymer that is a homogeneous blend of polyester alloys and fillers, as a wall surface treatment. Two ribbed patterns add a dimensional texture to the flat Avonite panels. (See Figure 4–32.)

BIBLIOGRAPHY

Ackerman, Phyllis. Wallpaper, Its History, Design and Use. New York: Frederick A. Stokes Company, 1923

Architectural Woodwork Institute. Architectural Woodwork Quality Standard, Guide Specifications and Quality Certification Program, Alexandria, VA: Architectural Woodwork Institute, 5th ed. 1989.

Entwisle, E.A. The Book of Wallpaper, A History and an Appreciation. Trowbridge, England: Redwood Press Ltd., 1970.

Kicklighter, Clois E. Modern Masonry. South Holland, IL: Goodheart-Wilcox Co., 1980

Landsmann, Leanne, Painting and Wallpapering. New York: Grosset & Dulap, 1975.

Schumacher. A Guide to Wallcoverings. New York: Schumacher.

Time-Life Books. Paint and Wallpaper. New York: Time-Life Books, 1981.

Time-Life Books. Walls and Ceilings. Alexandria, VA: Time-Life Books, 1980.

Wilson, Ralph Plastics Co., The ABC's of Easy Care for Wilsonart® Brand Decorative Laminate, Temple, TX: 1985.

ENDNOTES

[1] Schumacher, *A Guide to Wallcoverings.* (New York: Author, n.d.)

[2] Vicrtex Wallcoverings, "Suggested Specification, Installation Instructions, Care and Maitenance." (New Jersey: Author, n.d.)

GLOSSARY

Ashlar. Precut stone (see Figure 4–2).

Backsplash. The vertical wall area between the kitchen counter and the upper cabinets.

Booked. Folding back of pasted wallcovering so that pasted sides are touching.

Figure 4-31
Vitricor®, a high-molecular acrylic from Nevamar was used for the retail display case of a gift department. Design by Ruth Mellergaard, B.I.D., I.S.P. Fabrication Columbia Art and Photograph: Jack Neith JDN Photography. Photograph courtesy of Nevamar Corporation.

Book match. Every other leaf is turned over, so the right side of a leaf abuts a right side, and a left side abuts a left side.

Beads. Rounded formed pieces of metal used in finishing the edges of gypsum wallboard.

Casing. Exposed trim or moulding (see Figure 6–1).

Check. A small crack parallel to the grain of the wood.

Chinoiserie. (French) Refers to Chinese designs or manner.

Cobble. Similar in appearance to fieldstone.

Compound curves. Curving in two different directions at the same time.

Compressive strength. Amount of stress and pressure a material can withstand.

Concave. Hollow or inward curving shape.

Figure 4-32
Forms + Surfaces used Avonite® for an interesting textured wall treatment. Photograph courtesy of Forms + Surfaces.

Convex. Arched or outward curving shape.

Coped. Shaped or cut to fit an adjoining piece of moulding.

Cramps. U-shaped metal fastenings.

Desiccant. Substance capable of removing moisture from the air.

Dimensional stability. Ability to retain shape regardless of temperature and humidity.

Dry wall. Any interior covering that does not require the use of plaster or mortar.

Evacuated. Air is removed.

Feathering. Tapering off to nothing.

Fieldstone. Rounded stone.

Flitch. Portion of a log from which veneer is cut.

Header. End of a exposed brick (see Figure 4–4).

Header course. Headers used every sixth course (see Figure 4–4).

Heads. Horizontal cross member supported by the jambs.

HPDL. High pressure decorative laminate.

Jambs. Vertical member at the sides of a door.

Laminated glass. Breaks without shattering. Glass remains in place.

Lauan mahogany. A wood from the Phillipines which although not a true mahogany, does resemble mahogany in grain.

Mortar stain. Stain caused by excess mortar on face of brick or stone.

Mullions. Center vertical member of paneling (see Figure 4–24).

Nonferrous. Containing no iron.

Ogee. A concave and a convex curve in one moulding.

Ovolo. A convex shaped moulding.

Plumb line. True vertical line.

Pre-trimmed. Selvages or edges have been removed.

Raking light. Light shining obliquely down the length of the wall.

Rubble. Uncut stone (see Figure 4–2).

Scratch coat. In three coat plastering, it is the first coat.

Shiplap. An overlapping wood joint.

Simple curve. Curving in one direction only.

Stile. Outside vertical member of paneling (see Figure 4–24).

Stretcher. Long side of an exposed brick (see Figure 4–4).

Struck. Mortar joint where excess mortar is removed by a trowel.

Suction. Absorption of water by the gypsum board from the wet plaster.

Tambours. Thin strips of wood or other material materials attached to a flexible backing for use on curved surfaces. Similar in appearance to a roll-top desk.

Tensile strength. Resistance of a material to tearing apart when under tension.

Tempered glass. Glass toughened by heating and rapid cooling.

Toile-de-Jouy. Similar to the printed cottons made by Oberkampf in France during the 18th and 19th centuries.

Trompe l'oeil. French for fooling the eye. Also used on painted surfaces such as walls or furniture.

5

Ceilings

Early Greeks and Romans used lime stucco for ceilings, in which low, medium, and high **reliefs** were carried out. The Italians in the 15th century worked with plaster, and Henry VIII's Hampton Court has very highly decorative plasterwork ceilings. In the Tudor and Jacobean periods, the plasterwork for ceilings had a geometric basis in medium and high relief. This was followed by the classicism of Christopher Wren and Inigo Jones, an admirer of Palladio. In the latter part of the 18th century, the Adam brothers designed and used cast plaster ornaments with **arabesques**, **paterae**, and urns.

Stamped tin ceilings used in the 19th and 20th centuries disappeared from use in the 1930s but are now staging a come-back. In private residences, tin ceilings were occasionally used in halls and bathrooms. In commercial buildings, metal ceilings were used in order to comply with the early fire codes.

Today, the ceiling should not be considered as "just the flat surface over our heads, which is painted white." The ceiling is an integral part of a room, affecting space, light, heat, and sound, and consideration should be given to making it fit the environment. There are many ways of achieving this integration, such as beams for a country or Old World appearance, a stamped metal ceiling for Victorian, a wood ceiling for contemporary warmth, or acoustical for today's noisier environments. Ceiling treatments are limited only by the imagination.

PLASTER

There are times when the ceiling should be the unobtrusive surface in a room. When this is required, plastering is the answer. The surface may be smooth or highly textured or somewhere in between. A smooth surface will reflect more light than a heavily textured one of the same color.

The plaster for a ceiling is applied in the same manner as for walls, although it will require scaffolding so that the surface will be within working reach. It will take a longer period of time to plaster a ceiling when compared with a similar wall area, due to the overhead reach.

The ornately carved ceilings of the past are obtained today by using one of three means.

1. Precast plaster, either in pieces or tiles.
2. Molded polyurethane foam.
3. Wood mouldings, mainly used as **crown** mouldings.

The decorative ceiling shown in Figure 5–1, is an example of precast plaster ceiling tiles, which drop into any standard, commercial, 2 foot by 2 foot grid system with wires 4 feet on center. The relief varies from 1/4 inch to 2 1/2 inches according to the design.

Figure 5-1
Orlando's Restaurant in San Rosa, CA has suspended plaster ceiling tiles. Classic Panel from Above View, Inc. combines the look of an ornate plaster ceiling with easy installation and maintenance. Photograph courtesy of Above View, Inc.

The moulded urethane foam mouldings will be discussed in detail in the next chapter, under the heading "Mouldings."

GYPSUM WALLBOARD

The main difficulty with the installation of gypsum board for ceilings is the weight. It does require more labor and, again, scaffolding. Gypsum wallboard may be applied to a flat or curved surface. The seams and screw holes are filled in the same manner as gypsum board walls. The surface may be perfectly smooth, lightly or heavily textured, with the smooth surface reflecting not only the most light, but also showing any unevenness of the ceiling joists.

By using FRESCO ceiling sheets from Pittcon Industries, a paneled ceiling can be achieved. The 48-inch by 48-inch by 5/8-inch gypsum wallboard raised panel sheets consists of nine 12-inch square panels separated by 4-inch borders and surrounded by a 2-inch border. When joined to an adjacent sheet,

these combined borders continue the same 4-inch spacing throughout the installed surface.

BEAMS

This is probably the oldest of ceiling treatments. Originally, the ceiling beams of the lower floor were the floor joists of the room above. The old New England houses had hand-hewn timbers that ran the length of the room; the larger-sized **summer beam** ran across the width. The area between the beams was covered by the floor boards of the room above, or in the case of a sloped ceiling, the wood covering the outside of the roof timbers. Later these floorboards were covered with plaster and the timbers were left to darken naturally. The plaster in between the timbers had a rough or troweled surface. Today, instead of plaster, a plank ceiling is used in combination with beams.

Today, beamed ceilings are used for a country setting with an Old World or contemporary feeling. The original beams were made of one piece of wood,

12 inches or more square, but today beams of this size are very difficult to obtain.

If unavailable, there are several methods of imitating the solid heavy look of hand-hewn beams. A box beam may be built as part of the floor joists or as a surface addition. In order to make a box beam appear similar to a hand-hewn beam, the surface must be treated to avoid the perfectly smooth surface of modern lumber.

In contemporary homes, **laminated beams** are used. These consist of several pieces of lumber (depending on the width required) glued together on the wider flat surfaces. Because of the type of construction, laminated beams are very strong. Laminated beams are commonly referred to as "lam" beams.

WOOD

A natural outgrowth of the beamed ceiling is using wood planks or strips to cover the ceiling joists. With the many types of wood available on the market today, wood ceilings are used in many homes, particularly contemporary ones.

Almost all types of strip flooring and solid wood for walls may be used on the ceiling. Due to the darkness of wood, it is more suitable for a cathedral or shed ceiling as the color appears to lower the ceiling.

ACOUSTICAL CEILINGS

Residential

Due to the fact that the ceiling is the largest unobstructed area in a room, sound is bounced off the surface without very much absorption. Just as light is reflected from a smooth, high-gloss surface, so sound is reflected or bounced off the ceiling. This is the reason for the textured tiles on the market today, for both residential and commercial interiors. Uncontrolled reverberations transform sound into noise, muffling music and disrupting effective communication.

Acoustical ceilings, however, do not prevent the transmission of sound from one floor to another. The only answer to sound transmission is mass—the actual resistance of the material to vibrations caused by sound waves.

Sound absorption qualities may be obtained by using different materials and different methods. The

Figure 5-2
As can be seen in this photograph, not all acoustical ceilings are square or rectilinear. Intersections™ from USG Interiors combine 2-feet by 2-feet field modules with 5-inch by 5-inch accent modules in an oblique, zig-zag fashion. To accommodate lighting, sprinklers or speakers, the 5-inch by 5-inch accents are omitted. Photograph courtesy of USG Interiors.

most well-known is the acoustical **tile** (a 12-inch square) or **panel** (larger than 1 square foot) composed of mineral fiber board. Other materials such as fiberglass, metal, plastic-clad fiber, and fabric may also be used. Sound absorption properties are produced by mechanical dies perforating the mineral fiber board after curing. Metal may also be perforated to improve its acoustical qualities if backed with an absorptive medium.

The **Noise Reduction Coefficients (NRC)** is a measure of sound absorbed by a material and the NRC of different types of panels may be compared. The higher the number, the more sound reduction. When making a comparison, be sure tests are made at the same **Hertz (Hz)** range.

The **Sound Transmission Class (STC)** is a measure of the reduction of sound between two rooms due to transmission via the **plenum** path. The higher the STC value, the better the resistance to sound transmission. Another heading often found in acoustical mineral fiberboard charts is **Light Reflectance (LR)** which indicates the percentage of light reflected from a ceiling product's surface. This LR varies according to the amount of texture on the surface and the value of the color.

Some ceiling panels have a mineral fiber substrate with a needle-punched fabric surface.

Installation. In private residences, two or three methods of installation are used. If the tiles are to be used over an existing ceiling, they may be cemented to that ceiling provided the surface is solid and level. Tiles have interlocking edges that provide a solid joining method as well as an almost seamless installation. If the existing ceiling is not solid or level, furring strips are nailed up so that the edges of the tile may be glued and stapled to a solid surface.

The third type of installation is the suspended ceiling which consists of a metal spline suspended by wires from the ceiling or joists. The tiles are laid in the spline so that the edges of the panels are supported by the edge of the T-shaped spline.

The splines may be left exposed or they may be covered by the tile. There are several advantages to using a suspended ceiling:

1. Damaged panels are easily replaced.
2. The height of the ceiling may be varied according to the size of the room or other requirements.

With an exposed spline, it is easy to replace a single panel; the damaged panel is merely lifted out. However, if the spline is covered, the damaged panel or panels are removed and when replacing the last panel, the tongue is removed.

Maintenance. Celotex suggests that a soft gum eraser be used to remove small spots, dirt marks, and streaks. For larger areas, or larger smudges, a chemically treated sponge, rubber pad, or wallpaper cleaner is used. The sponge rubber pad or wallpaper cleaner must be in fresh condition. Nicks and scratches may be touched up with colored chalks. Dust is removed by brushing lightly with a soft brush, clean rag, or by vacuuming with the soft brush attachment.

Do not moisten tile excessively. Never soak tile with water. Wash by light application of sponge

Figure 5-3
In keeping with the ambiance of the Filling Station Restaurant, decorative metal ceiling panels from Chelsea Decorative Metal Company were used. Photograph courtesy of Chelsea Decorative Metal Company.

Figure 5-4
The combination of Vista, the linear strips, and the Cube Open Cell systems provide a contrast in the high ceilings of a shopping mall. Photography courtesy of Chicago Metallic Corporation.

dampened with a mild liquid detergent solution: about 1/2 cup in 1 gallon of water. After saturating the sponge, squeeze it nearly dry, and then lightly rub the surface to be cleaned. Use long, sweeping, gentle strokes. Clean in the same direction as the texture if tile is ribbed or embossed.

When painting, avoid clogging or bridging surface openings. Use a paint of high hiding power since it is desirable to keep the number of coats to a minimum on acoustical tile. Hiding character of paint is a particularly important consideration when a single coat is expected to cover stains or change the color of the tile. Some paint manufacturers provide specific formulations that have high hiding power, low combustibility, and are not likely to bridge opening in the tile. Wherever possible, apply paint of this type. In all cases, apply paint as thinly as possible.

Commercial

Acoustical ceiling products have become a mainstay of commercial installations. Due to the flexibility of the movable office partitions, audio privacy is very necessary. In this day of electronic word processors and data processing equipment, the noise of an office

has been somewhat reduced from the noisy typewriters of the past, but telephones and voices can still cause distracting sounds. Productivity is increased in a quieter environment, but a noiseless environment is easily disrupted.

The advantages of a residential suspended acoustical ceiling also apply in commercial installations, but the major reason for using a suspended ceiling in commercial work is the easy access to wiring, telephone lines, plumbing, and heating ducts.

The traditional approach is **luminaires** recessed at specific intervals into the acoustic ceiling. The fixtures are often covered by lenses or louvers to diffuse the light.

Today, not only lighting but also heating and cooling are incorporated into the installation. This is done in several ways. The heating and cooling duct may be spaced between the modules in one long continuous line or individual vents may be used. One interesting innovation is where the whole area between the suspended ceiling and the joists is used as a plenum area with the conditioned air entering the room below through orifices in the individual tiles.

One word of warning: If you are replacing a ceiling

which may contain asbestos, OSHA has some very stringent regulations and safety precautions which must be strictly adhered to.

METAL

Metal ceilings were originally introduced in the 1860s as a replacement for the ornamental plasterwork that decorated the walls and ceilings of the most fashionable rooms of the day. Once in place, it was discovered that these ceilings had other benefits. Unlike plaster, the metal could withstand rough use and could also be more easily maintained than plaster, which could flake, crack, and peel. Many of today's metal ceilings are actually steel.

Shanker uses a 665–ton press built in 1928 (completely rebuilt to modern manufacturing standards in 1986) to stamp its 2 foot by 4 foot panels which can be colored with oil-based paint or left steel gray, protected by a coat of clear polyurethane. Copper and brass plating are also available as are color coatings baked on to the metal.

Stamped metal ceilings now come in 1 foot squares, 1 foot by 2 foot, 2 foot by 4 foot, or 2 foot by 8 foot and are installed by tacking the units to furring strips nailed 12 inches apart. These stamped metal ceilings are very suitable for Victorian restoration work (see Figure 5–3).

A contemporary metal ceiling is made up of 3- to 7-inch wide strips of painted or polished aluminum, which clip to special carriers. The polished metals also include bronze and brass finishes and can provide an almost mirrored effect. These ceilings may be used in renovations over existing sound ceilings or for new construction.

The metal strips may be installed as separate strips with the area between the strips left open to the plenum or the open space may be covered with an acoustical pad. They may also be covered with a joining strip on the face to form a flush surface, or on the back for a board-on-batten effect.

Steel or aluminum panels, perforated or unperforated are available in 12-inch squares or as large as 24- by 48-inch panels.

OTHER CEILING MATERIALS

A vinyl-coated, embossed aluminum, bonded to the mineral fiber substrate, results in an easily main-tained, corrosion-resistant, durable product. Grease vapor concentrations may be wiped clean with a sponge or a mild detergent solution, thus providing a suitable ceiling for commercial kitchens, laboratories, and hospitals.

Mirrors are not recommended for ceilings, instead the Classique™ lay-in panels from Chicago Metallic Corporation can provide a reflective finish. These panels are all metal so there are no fibers to create dust or dirt. Typical applications for metal panels are in high traffic areas such as restaurants, retail outlets or lobbies, and in "clean room" areas such as hospitals, high-tech computer rooms, audio-video facilities, and laboratories. The noncombustible metal surface is easily cleaned with mild soap or window cleaner. (See Figure 5–5.)

Another product A-Look®, an unbreakable re-

Figure 5-5
The 2 inch by 2 inch Classique™ panels offer metal lay-in ceilings in a variety of colors and reflective metal finishes to provide a dramatic ceiling treatment. Since the panels and the grid are available from the same manufacturer, a perfect color match is assured. Photography courtesy of Chicago Metallic Corporation.

flective material from Mitsubishi Kasei America, Inc. may be used. These mirrored panels expand the visual impact of displays and may be a major deterrent to shoplifting and pilfering in shops and stores.

Now being manufactured in this country is Barrisol® Stretch Ceilings from France. The mirror-like finish of Barrisol will visually enlarge areas with a variety of colors and textures. The stretch material can be used for flat ceilings, inclined or vaulted. Barrisol is impermeable to moisture, is rated class I within the requirements of the ASTM E84 Flame Spread Test. When a blunt instrument makes a deep depression in this material, it will return to its original shape when slight heat is applied, and is so strong it will support a man's weight.

The use of an acoustical mineral fiberboard will also increase fire resistance. Custom-designed fiberglass core panels are used to upgrade existing ceilings as well as for new custom designed ceiling construction. This same material may be used for baffles constructed of 1-, 1 1/2-, or 2-inch thick panels. They are hung from the ceiling by means of wire attached to eyelets installed in the top edge.

Baffles are functional, decorative and may be used graphically for signage or by changing colors denote areas or departments within a larger space.

The Designers Series from Forbo-Vicracoustics, offers a more tailored and trendier look being wrapped in fabric, Vicrtextures, or perforated Forbo-Vicrtex vinyl of your choice and has two u-bolts attached for easy installation. The standard dimension is 11 inches high by 24 inches. Also available are 35 inches or 48 inches width with a thickness of 2 inches.

With the increasing awareness of making buildings earthquake proof, the Seismic Panel from Simplex Ceiling Products would fulfill that requirement. Seismic is an aluminum ceiling with a completely concealed suspension system that will resist failure due to the multi-directional movement during an earthquake. The panels will not disengage from the suspension regardless of what motion the earth's surface may make during an earthquake.

Not all acoustic ceilings are flat. Many are **coffered** in two to four foot square modules. These panels may or may not include luminaires. A cell system from Hunter Douglas dramatizes design, while masking plenum clutter.

The INTERSECTIONS™ from USG Interiors, Inc. combines 2 foot by 2 foot field modules with 5 inch by 5 inch accent modules in an oblique, zig-zag fashion. Integrated Ceilings™ specialty products include Pipe and Junction™, a component parts system

Figure 5-6
A contemporary bathroom in Milwaukee, Wisconsin shows the Dome It ceiling with silver trim and acrylic blades on the fan. The sink is from American Standard and the bathtub is Jacuzzi. The towel bars are from Arselux. Photograph courtesy of Dome It Ceilings.

of pipes that are snapped or bolted together from up to six different directions. A new radius pipe adds graceful curves and infinite design possibilities. Transparencies™ is a luminous ceiling system designed to give the same subtly refracted light play as traditional glass blocks but without the weight, cost, and installation difficulties of glass.

Dome It® gives a skylight effect to any area and utilizes the soffit above the cabinets and energy-efficient "daylight" fluorescent lighting. Effective circulation, the key to raising your thermostat in the summer and lowering it in winter, is provided by a white ceiling fan using as little as 35 watts. This product is very suitable for kitchens with no windows, such as is found in many attached condominiums (see Figure 5–6).

Ceramic Tile

For a ceiling that is easy to wipe clean, or in very moist areas such as bathrooms and showers, ceramic tile may be installed.

BIBLIOGRAPHY

Rothery, Guy Cadogan. Ceilings and Their Decoration. London England: T. Werner Laurie, 1978.

Time-Life Books. Walls and Ceilings, Alexandria, VA: Time-Life Books, 1980.

GLOSSARY

Arabesque. Elaborate scroll designs either carved or in low relief.

Coffered. Recessed panels in the ceiling. May or may not be decorated.

Crown moulding. The uppermost moulding next to the ceiling.

Hertz. Unit of frequency measurement. One unit per second. Abbreviation: Hz.

Laminated beam. Several pieces of lumber glued to form a structural timber.

LR. Light Reflectance. The amount of light reflected from the surface.

Luminaires. Lighting fixture, with all components needed to be connected to the electric power supply.

NRC. Noise Reduction Coefficient. The average percentage of sound reduction at various Hz levels.

Panel. A ceiling unit larger than one square foot.

Patera. A round or oval raised surface design.

Plenum. The space between the suspended ceiling and the floor above.

Reliefs. A design that is raised above the surrounding area.

STC. Sound Transmission Class. A number denoting the sound insulating value of a material.

Summer beam. A main supporting beam in old colonial homes, in the middle of the room resting on the fireplace at one end and a post at the other.

Tile. Ceiling tile (12-inch square).

Other Components

MOULDINGS

To an interior designer, trim and mouldings are what icing is to a cake; they cover, enhance, and decorate a plain surface. Basically, heavily carved or ornate trim is used in a traditional setting, whereas the simpler trim is used where a contemporary feeling is desired.

Materials for trim and mouldings should be constructed from easily shaped stock. Both pine and oak are used, providing details that are easily discernible and smooth. Trim should always be **mitered** at the corners; that is, the joint should be cut at a 45° angle.

Bases are universally used to finish the area where the wall and floor meet. There are several reasons for the use of a base or skirting. First, it covers any discrepancy or expansion space between the wall and the floor; second, it forms a protection for the wall from cleaning equipment; and third, it may also be a decorative feature. The word *base* is used to include all types of materials. *Baseboard* is the term used for wood bases only. When a plain baseboard is used, the wood should be smoothly sanded on the face and particularly on the top edge to facilitate cleaning. The exposed edge should be slightly beveled to prevent breaking or chipping. The more traditional baseboard usually has a shaped top edge with the lower part being flat. This may be achieved with one piece of wood 3 1/2 to 7 inches wide or may consist of separate parts, the top being a base moulding above a square-edged piece of lumber. A base shoe may be added to either type. Traditional one-piece baseboards are available as stock mouldings from the better woodworking manufacturers (see Figure 6–1).

For residential use, windows come prefabricated with the **brickmold** or exterior trim attached. The interior casing (the exposed trim) may be flat or molded and is applied after the window and walls have been installed and the windows **caulked**, the latter step being extremely necessary in these days of energy conservation. The interior casing usually matches the baseboard design, although the size may vary, as seen in Figure 6–1.

Doors, particularly for residential use, often come **prehung** and, after installation of the door frame, the space between the jamb and the wall is covered by a casing. This casing matches the profile of the one used around the windows, with the width of the casing being determined by the size, scale, and style of the room.

Crown and **bed** mouldings are used to soften the sharp line where ceiling and walls meet. Cove mouldings also serve the same purpose, the difference being that crown mouldings are more intricately shaped and cove mouldings have a simple curved face. Cove mouldings may be painted the same color

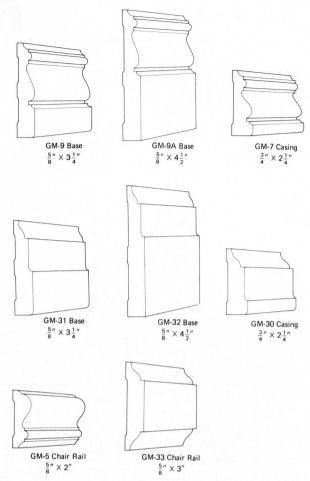

Figure 6-1
Wood bases, chair rails, and casings. (Courtesy of Granite Mill)

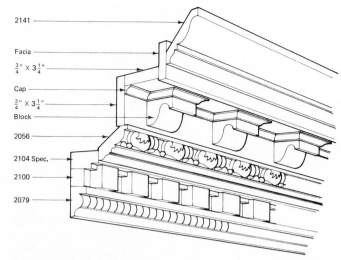

Figure 6-2
This enlargement of the cornice shown in Figure 6-2 shows the 11 individual pieces which go to make up this elaborate yet authentic moulding. (Drawing courtesy of Driwood Period Mouldings)

as the ceiling, thus giving a lowered appearance to the ceiling.

Cornice mouldings may be very ornate and made up of as many as ten separate pieces of wood, as seen in Figures 6–2 and 6–3.

Chair rails are used in traditional homes to protect the surface of the wall from damage caused by the backs of chairs. These rails may be simple strips of wood with rounded edges or have shaped top and bottom edges, depending upon the style of the room (see Figure 6–1). The installed height should be between 30 and 36 inches. When trim is to be painted, it should be made of a hard, close-grained wood. If it is to be left natural, it should be of the same material and should be finished in the same manner as the rest of the woodwork.

When plywood panels are used on the walls, the edges are sometimes covered with a square-edge batten. In more traditional surroundings, a molded batten is used.

Picture mouldings, as the name implies, were used to create a continuous projecting support around the walls of a room for picture hooks. The picture moulding has a curved top to receive the picture hook. Of course, when pictures are hung by this method the wires will show, but this method is used in older homes, museums, and art galleries where frequent rearranging is required. No damage is done to the walls, as with the more modern method of hanging paintings by means of concealed wires. The picture moulding is placed just below or several inches below the ceiling. Wherever the placement, the ceiling color is usually continued down to the top of the moulding.

An infinite variety of patterns may be used for mouldings. Some are stock shapes and sizes; others may be custom ordered; and a third may be shaped to the designer's specifications by the use of custom-formed shaper blades. This latter method is the most expensive, but does achieve a unique moulding.

Wood mouldings may also be covered with metal in many finishes, including bright chrome, brass, copper, or simulated metal finishes for use as picture frame moulding, interior trim, and displays.

All the mouldings discussed thus far have been constructed of wood. When a heavily carved cornice moulding is required, the material may be a **polymer**.

Figure 6-3
This Southern Colonial mansion has a very decorative 11-piece wooden ceiling cornice. (Photograph courtesy of Driwood Period Mouldings.)

Focal Point, Inc., makes a polymer moulding by direct impression from the original wood, metal, or plaster article. This direct process gives the reproduction all the personality, texture and spirit of the original, but with several plusses. The mouldings are much less expensive than the hand-carved originals. They are lighter weight and therefore easier to handle; they may be nailed, drilled, or screwed; and are receptive to sanding. Another feature is that, in many cases, the original moulding consisted of several pieces, but modern technology has produced these multiple mouldings in a one piece-strip, thus saving on installation costs. For contract installations where fire rated materials must be used, Specicast™ meets the ASTM E-84, Class A specifications.

Focal Point is a licensee for architectural details for the Victorian Society in America, Colonial Williamsburg Foundation, National Trust for Historic preservation and a licensee for the Historic Natchez Foundation.

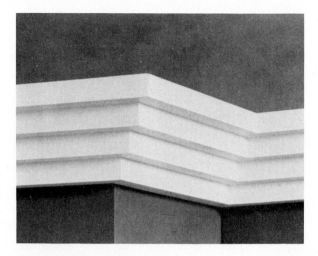

Figure 6-4
On the left, 01310 Stanton Hall moulding from the Natchez collection by Focal Point.

On the right, 11640 the Taos stepped moulding also from Focal Point.

Nor is the contemporary market being ignored, Focal Point has its new Santa Fe and Taos step moulding as shown in Figure 6–4.

Polymer mouldings are factory primed in white; however, if a stained effect is desired, the mouldings may be primed beige and stained with Mohawk non-penetrating stain. Careful brushstrokes will simulate grain and, when skillfully applied the effect is very convincing.

In Chapter 5, ceiling medallions were mentioned as a form of ceiling decoration. Originally, when these medallions were used as **backplates** for chandeliers, they were made from plaster, but again the polymer reproductions are lightweight and easy to ship. The medallions are primed white at the factory, ready to paint. The use of a medallion is not limited to chandeliers, but is also used as a backplate for ceiling fans (see Figure 6–5).

Other materials used in ornate ceiling cornices are gypsum with a polymer agent which is reinforced with glass fibers for added strength. A wood fiber combination may also be used.

Other reproductions from the past include the dome and the niche cap. When first designed, they were made of plaster or wood, which was then hand carved. These domes and niche caps can provide a touch of authenticity needed in renovations; in fact, many of Focal Point's designs have been used in restoration of national historical landmarks. Niche caps have a shell design and form the top of a curved recess that usually displays sculpture, vases, flowers, or any other prized possession.

Figure 6-5
The small D'Evereux Center Medallion and larger outside Medallion are the backplate for a glass chandelier. Around the cornice is the D'Evereux Cornice and D'Evereux Frieze, all part of the historic Natchez Collection from Focal Point. Photograph courtesy of Focal Point, Inc.

Stair brackets are another form of architectural detail and are placed on the finished stringer for a decorative effect.

DOORS

Doors for residential use are commonly constructed of wood, although metal may also be used. In commercial applications, however, doors are more likely to be made of metal or laminate due to fire codes and ease of maintenance.

Wood Doors

Flush doors are perfectly flat and smooth with no decoration whatsoever (see Figure 6–8). There are several methods of construction. A hollow core is used for some interior residential flush doors. The core of the door is made up of 2- to 3-inch wide solid wood for the rails and 1 to 2 inches of solid wood for the stiles, with an additional 20-inch long strip of wood called a *lock block* in the approximate hardware location. The area between the solid wood is filled with a honeycomb or ladder core. In less expensive doors, this is covered by the finish veneer. More expensive doors have one or two layers of veneer before the finish veneer is applied. Thus, a flush door may be of 3–, 5–, or 7–ply construction.

The better flush door is constructed with a lumber core, also known as *staved wood*, where wood blocks are used in place of the honeycomb or ladder core of the hollow core door. The staved or lumber core may or may not have the blocks bonded together. With staved core doors, the inside rails and stiles are narrower because this type of construction is more rigid (see Figure 6–6).

Another method of construction utilizes a particleboard or flakeboard core with a crossband veneer to which the face veneer is attached. A particleboard door core is warp resistant, solid, with no knots or voids and has good insulation values and sound resistance thereby limiting heat loss and transfer of sound waves.

Flush doors for commercial installations may have a high-pressure decorative laminate (HPDL) as the face veneer or, for low maintenance, a photogravure or vinyl covering similar to the paneling discussed in the chapter on walls may be used.

There are three methods of achieving the paneled look in doors. One is by using a solid ornate ogee

sticking; in other words, the stiles and rails are shaped so that the moulding and stile or rails are all one piece of wood. The second method is the same as above only using a simpler **ovolo** sticking. The third method uses a **dadoed** stile and rail and the joining of panel and stile is covered by a separate applied moulding. If the panel is large, it will be made of plywood and a moulding used; if under 10 inches in width, it may be of solid wood. Paneled doors reflect different periods, as do paneled walls. When period paneling is used, the doors should be of similar design (see Figure 6–7).

Dutch doors for residential use consist of an upper and a lower part. Special hardware joins the two parts to form a regular door or, with the hardware undone, the top part may be opened to ventilate or give light to a room, with the lower part remaining closed. Dutch doors are sometimes used commercially as a service opening. In this case, a shelf is attached to the top of the bottom half (see Figure 6–8).

Louvers are used in doors where ventilation is needed, such as in cleaning or storage closets or to aid in air circulation. Louvers are made of horizontal slats contained within stile-and-rail frames. Louvers may be set into wood or metal doors, with the louver being either at the top and/or bottom, or the center may be all louvered. Some louvers are vision-proof, some adjustable, and others may be lightproof or weatherproof (see Figure 6–8).

One of the most common residential uses for a louvered door is in a bifold door for a closet. Bifold doors consist of four panels, two on each side with a track at the top. The center panel of each pair is hung from the track, and the outer panels pivot at the jamb (see Figure 6–8).

A pocket door or recessed sliding door requires a special frame and track that is incorporated into the inside of the wall. The finished door is hung from the track before the casing is attached. The bottom of the door is held in place by guides which permit the door to slide while preventing sideways movement (see Figure 6–8).

For an Oriental ambience, fixed or sliding shoji panels are available; these are wood framed with vellum or synthetic vellum inserts.

Folding or accordion doors are used where space needs to be temporarily divided. These folding doors operate and stack compactly within their openings. The panels may be wood-veneered lumber core, or particleboard core with a wood-grained vinyl coating. Each panel is 3 5/8 inches or under in width, and the folding doors are available in heights up to 16 feet 1

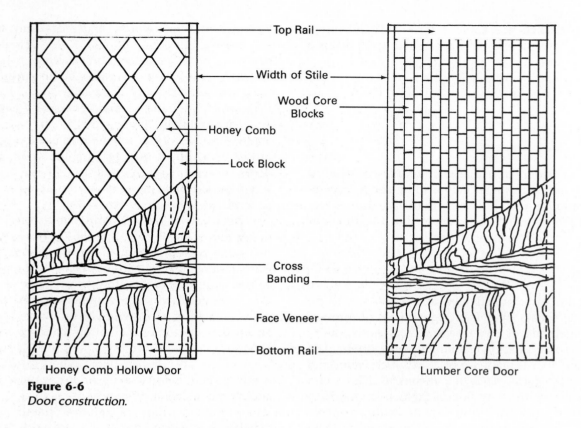

Figure 6-6
Door construction.

inch. Folding doors operate by means of a track at the top to which the panels are attached by wheels. The handle and locking mechanism is installed on the panel closest to the opening edge (see Figure 6–8).

Glass Doors

Sash doors are similar in construction and appearance to the panel door except that one or more panels are replaced with glass. French doors are often used

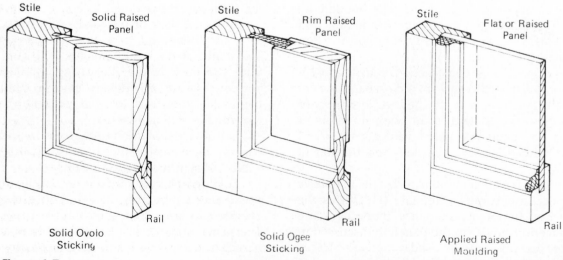

Figure 6-7
Paneled door construction. (Reprinted with permission from the Architectural Woodwork Institute)

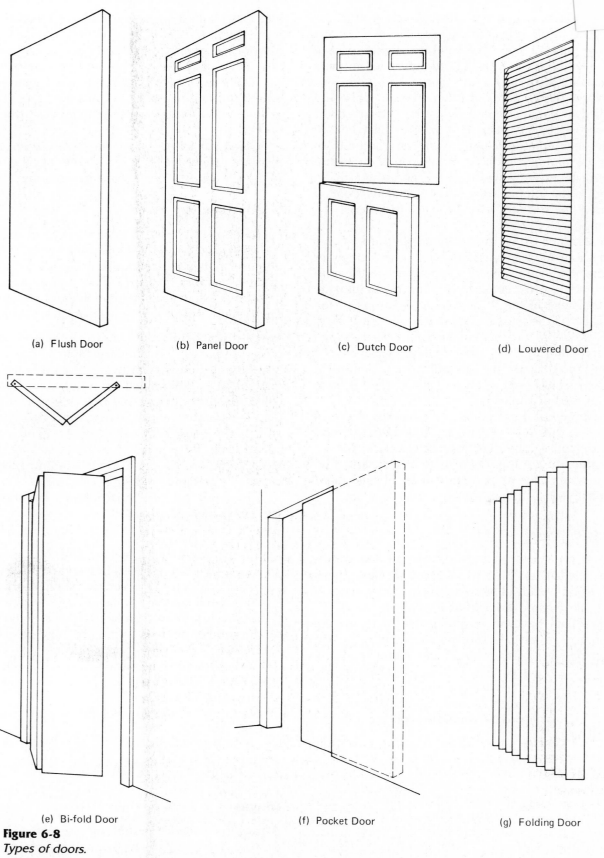

(a) Flush Door   (b) Panel Door   (c) Dutch Door   (d) Louvered Door

(e) Bi-fold Door   (f) Pocket Door   (g) Folding Door

Figure 6-8
Types of doors.

in residences to open out onto a balcony or patio. They have wood frames and may consist of one sheet of plate glass or may have multiple **lights** in each door. French doors are most often installed in pairs and usually open out.

When French doors or other styles of doors are installed in pairs, one is used as the primary door. The second one is stationary with a flush bolt or special lock holding it tight at top and bottom. To cover the joining crack between the pair of doors and to make them more weathertight, an **astragal** is attached to the interior edge of the stationary door. If required, both doors may be used to enlarge the opening.

Instead of using large sliding glass doors, the trend seems to be to use patio doors, either singly or in pairs. These are similar in appearance to the double French doors, except that they open into the house instead of out. If double doors are used, the astragal is on the exterior edge of the secondary door.

Glass doors for residential use may have a wood or metal frame and may pivot on hinges or have one sliding panel with the second panel stationary. Whenever full length glass is used, by law it must be tempered or laminated.

Commercial glass doors must also be made of tempered or laminated glass and are subject to local building codes. The door may be all glass, framed with metal at the top and/or bottom, or framed on all four sides. Due to the nature of an all glass door, the most visible design feature is the hardware.

Specialty Doors

When X-ray machines are used, special doors must be specified. These flush panel doors have two layers of plywood with lead between; then a face veneer of wood, hardboard, or laminate is applied.

Firedoors have an incombustible material core with fire-retardant rails and stiles covered by a wood veneer or high pressure decorative laminate. These doors are rated according to the time they take to burn. Depending on materials and construction, this time will vary between 20 minutes and 1 1/2 hours. Local building codes should be consulted before specifying.

Metal Doors

Most metal doors are made of steel, although some are available in aluminum. In the past, metal doors had a commercial or institutional connotation, but today many interior and exterior residential doors and many bifold doors are made of metal. Exterior metal doors were shunned in the past because wood exterior solid core doors had better insulating qualities. The use of polystyrene and polyurethane as a core has now provided a residential metal exterior door with similar insulating qualities, plus it is not as susceptible to temperature changes as is the wood door.

Metal doors are available coated with a rust-resistant primer for finishing on site, or they may be prefinished with a heavy baked-on coating.

Exterior Doors

For exterior use, a wood door must be of solid construction. Hand-carved doors are available for exterior use, but manufacturer's specifications must be studied carefully because a door that appears to be handcarved may actually be molded to imitate hand carving at less expense but with less aesthetic appeal.

Specifications for Doors. Most doors are available prehung that is, assembled complete with frames, trim, and sometimes hardware. For prehung doors, door hand is determined by noting hinge location when the door opens away from the viewer (i.e., if the hinge jamb is on his/her right, it is a right-hand door). In the case of a pair of doors, hand is determined from the active leaf in the same way. If prehung doors are specified, door handing should be included (see Figure 6–13).

The following additional information should be provided when specifying doors:

> *Manufacturer.*
> *Size* including width, height, and thickness.
> *Face description* —species of wood, type of veneer, rotary or sliced. If not veneer, laminate, photogravure, vinyl coating, or metal.
> *Construction* —crossbanding thickness, edge strips, top and bottom rails, stiles, and core construction.
> *Finishing*—prefinished or unfinished.
> *Special detailing* includes specifying **backset** for hardware and any mouldings. Special service such as glazing, firedoors.
> *Warranty*—differs whether for interior or exterior use.

DOOR HARDWARE

Hinges

A hinge is a device permitting one part to turn on another. The two parts consist of metal plates known as **leaves** and are joined by a pin that passes through the **knuckle** joints. These pins may be **loose**, **nonrising** loose, **nonremovable** loose pins, or **fast** pins. Hinges are available in brass, bronze, stainless steel, and carbon steel.

A loose pin hinge enables a door to be easily removed from the frame by merely pulling out the pin. A loose pin type of hinge is used for hanging less expensive residential doors. One problem with a loose pin is that the pin has a tendency to rise with use. If the pin of the loose pin hinge is visible, even a locked door can be removed from its frame by simply removing the pin. A nonrising loose pin has the same advantage as the loose pin but without the rising problem.

In a nonremovable loose pin hinge, however, a setscrew in the barrel fits into a groove in the pin, thereby preventing its removal. The setscrew is inaccessible when the door is closed. The fast (or tight) pin is permanently set in the barrel of the hinge at the time of manufacture.

The tips of the pins may be finished in different styles. Shapes include flat button, oval head, steeple, or ball tip. Hospital and fast riveted pin are other types of pin or tip styles. Flat button tips are standard for the majority of hinges. Oval head tips are used only on hinges with loose pins and no plugs. Steeple tips are used on colonial hinges. Ball tips are available by special order. On hospital types, the ends of the barrel are rounded for added safety as well as cleanliness. Fast riveted pins have both ends **spun** which makes the pin permanent.

Butt hinges are mortised into the edge of the door. A **gain** is cut in the jamb and also in the edge of the door, resulting in the leaves being flush with the surfaces of the door and jamb. Butt hinges are used on most doors. **Counter-sunk** holes are pre-drilled in the leaves. **Template** hardware has these holes drilled so accurately as to conform to standard drawings thus assuring a perfect fit. Template butt hinges have the holes drilled in a crescent shape. (See full mortise hinge in Figure 6–9.) The number of hinges per door depends on the size and weight of the door and, sometimes, on conditions of use. A general rule recommends two butt hinges on doors up to 60 inches high; three hinges on doors 60 to 90 inches high; and four hinges on doors 90 to 120 inches high.

With a full mortise hinge, the leaves are flush with the door and the frame and only the knuckles are visible when the door is closed. When a half mortise hinge is used, one leaf is mortised in the door edge and the other leaf is surface mounted on the jamb. A half surface hinge is the opposite with the surface mounted part being on the door and the mortise on the jamb. It is the type of installation on the door itself that provides the name. On full surface hinges, both leaves are surface mounted.

Swing-clear hinges are designed to swing doors completely clear of the opening when the door is opened 90° to 95°. This type is very expensive and is used almost exclusively in hospitals, institutions, or public buildings.

Bearings may be ball, oil impregnated, or anti-friction. Ball bearing hinges are packed with grease to assure a quiet, long life hinge. These types of bearings should always be specified for doors equipped with door closers.

Concealed hinges are used on doors when the design precludes the use of visible hinges. With concealed hinges, one side is mounted on the inside of the frame and the second side is mortised into the door. These hinges are available in 90 to 100° openings or 176° (see Soss hinge, Figure 6–10).

Concealed hinges for cabinets are different in construction. They are not visible from the outside of the cabinet, but are surface mounted on the inside of the cabinet door. (See Grass America, Figure 6–10.)

Spring hinges are used when automatic closing is required. The tension is adjustable.

Locks

The needs of the client and the expected usage of a lock will determine which lock will be selected. For residential uses, security is probably the foremost criterion, whereas for a commercial installation, heavy usage will necessitate not only a secure lock, but also one built to withstand constant use.

There are three weights or grades of locks. The most expensive is heavy duty; then standard duty. The least expensive is the light duty or builders grade. The first two types are made of solid metal with a polished, brushed, or antique finish; the light duty grade has a painted or plated finish that may be removed with wear.

The **Door & Hardware Institute** describes the types of locks and bolts as follows[1]:

Bored Type. These types of locks are installed in a door having two round holes at right angles to one another, one through the face of the door to hold the lock body and the other in the edge of the door to receive the latch mechanism. When the two are joined

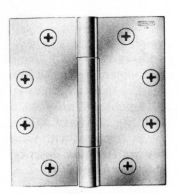

Full Mortise

Half Mortise

Half Mortise Swing Clear

Full Mortise Swing Clear

Full Surface

Half Surface

Full Surface Swing Clear   *Pivot Reinforced*

Half Surface Swing Clear

Figure 6-9
Types of hinges. (Photos courtesy of Stanley Hardware Division)

Figure 6-10
Top is a concealed cabinet hinge from Grass America which opens 176° and is self-closing. (Photograph courtesy of Grass America.) Shown on the bottom is the Soss Invisible Hinge which can only be seen when the door or lid is open. (Photograph courtesy of H. Soss & Co.)

together in the door they comprise a complete latching or locking mechanism.

Bored type locks have the keyway (cylinder) and/or locking device, such as push or turn buttons, in the knobs. They are made in three weights: heavy, standard and light duty.

The assembly must be tight on the door and without excessive play. Knobs should be held securely in place without screws, and a locked knob should not be removable. **Roses** should be threaded or secured firmly to the body mechanism. The trim has an important effect in this type of lock because working parts fit directly into the trim. Regular backset for a bored lock is 2 3/4 inches, but may vary from 2 3/8 to 42 inches (see Figure 6-11).

Preassembled Type. The preassembled lock is installed in a rectangular notch cut into the door edge. This lock is one that has all the parts assembled as a unit at the factory; when installed, little or no disassembly is required.

Preassembled type locks have the keyway (cylinder) in the knobs. Locking devices may be in the knob or in the inner case. Regular backset is 2 3/4 inches. The lock is available only in heavy duty weight (see Figure 6–11).

Mortise Lock. A mortise lock is installed in a prepared recess (mortise) in a door. The working mechanism is contained in a rectangular-shaped case with appropriate holes into which the required components, cylinder, knob, and turn-piece spindles are inserted to complete the working assembly. Regular backset is 2 3/4 inches. These locks are available in heavy duty and standard duty weights. **Armored** fronts are also available.

In order to provide a complete working unit, mortise locks, except for those with **deadlock** function only, must be installed with knobs, levers, and/or other items of trim as described in the section on door knobs and handles (see Figure 6–11). Regular backset is 2 3/4 inches. These locks are available only in heavy duty weight.

The lock achieves its function by means of various types of bolts. The bolt is a bar of metal that projects out of the lock into a strike prepared to receive it.

Latch Bolts. The function of a latch bolt is to hold the door in a closed position. A latch bolt is spring actuated and is used in all swinging door locks except those providing **deadbolt** function only. It has a beveled face and may be operated by a knob, handle or turn.

Auxiliary Dead Latch. An auxiliary dead latch is a security feature and should be required on all locks used for security purposes unless a deadbolt function is specified. This feature deadlocks the latch bolt automatically and makes it virtually impossible to depress the latch bolt when the door is closed.

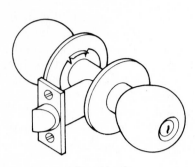

Bored Lock

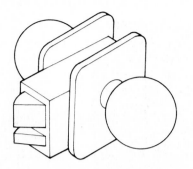

Pre-assembled Lock

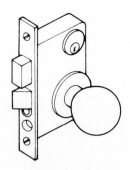

Mortise Lock

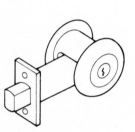

Bored Deadbolt

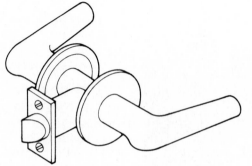

Bored Lever Handle Lock

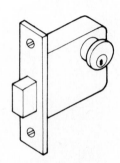

Mortised Deadbolt

Figure 6-11
Types of locks.

Deadbolts. A deadbolt is a bolt having no spring action and activated by a key or thumb turn. It must be manually operated. Deadbolts provide security. When hardened steel inserts are used, the security is greater. The minimum **throw** should be 1/2 inch, but today most throws are 1 inch.

Lock Strikes. A **lock strike** is a metal plate mortised into the door jamb to receive and to hold the projected latch bolt and, when specified, the deadbolt also, thus securing the door. It is sometimes called a *keeper.* The proper length lip should be specified so that the latch bolt will not hit the door jamb before the strike.

A wrought box should be installed in back of the strike in the jamb. This box will protect the bolt holes from the intrusion of plaster or other foreign material, which would prevent the bolt from projecting properly into the strike.[2]

Electric Strike. This is an electro-mechanical device that replaces an ordinary strike and makes possible remote electric locking and unlocking. When a control mechanism actuates the electric strike, this allows the door to be opened without a key and relocked when closed. Used in secured apartment buildings.

Rim Locks. Rim locks were first used at the beginning of the 18th century and are attached to the inside of the door stile. They are used today in restoration work or in new homes of medieval English, Salt Box, Cape Cod, or colonial styles. Because they are exposed to view, the case and other parts are finished brass.

The simplest type of door hardware is the passage set where both knobs are always free and there is no locking mechanism. An example would be the door between a living or dining room and a hallway. A **springlatch** holds this type of door closed.

Bathrooms doors require a privacy lock. This type locks from the inside in several ways. Some have a push-button located on the interior rose, some have a turn button in the interior knob, and still others

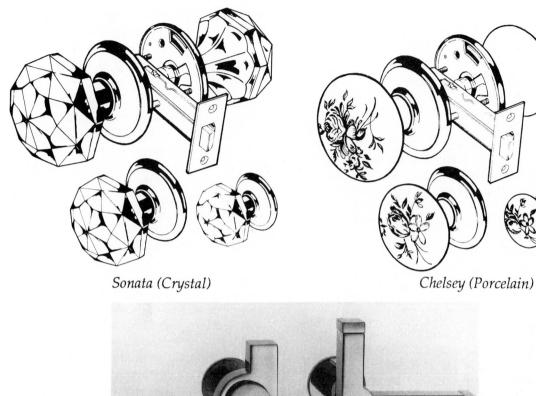

Sonata (Crystal)   Chelsey (Porcelain)

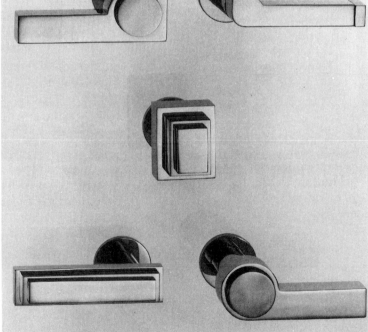

Figure 6-12
Handles and knobs. Left, Sonata (Crystal) knobs and right, Chelsey (Porcelain) showing door knobs, wardrobe knobs and cupboard knobs with gold accents from Gainsborough Hardware Industries Inc. Lower #560 series door knobs and levers made of solid brass in a variety of finishes. The design lends itself to combinations of brass and chrome finishes. Photograph courtesy of Paul Associates.

have a turnpiece that activates a bolt. In the case of an emergency entrance, all privacy locks have some means of opening from the outside, either with of an emergency release key or by using a screwdriver.

When the type of use has been decided upon, the style of handle, rose, and finish is selected. There are many shapes of knobs from ball, round with a semiflat face, to round with a concave face, which may even be decorated. Knobs may be made of metal, porcelain, or wood (see Figure 6–12). Grip handle entrance locks combine the convenience of button-in-the-knob locking with traditional grip handle elegance. Grip handles should be of cast brass or cast bronze. Interior colonial doors may have a thumb latch installed on the stile surface.

Natural finishes take the color of the base metal in the product and may be either high or low luster. Applied finishes result from the addition by plating of a second metal, a synthetic enamel, or other material.

Polished brass and bronze finishes are produced by buffing or polishing the metal to a high gloss before applying a synthetic coating. Satin brass and natural bronze finishes are obtained by dry buffing or scouring, and the resultant finish is then coated.

The most popular of the plated finishes are the chromiums, both polished and satin.

A lever handle must be specified when used by a handicapped person. When blind persons have access to areas that might be dangerous, such as a doorway leading to stairs, the knob must be knurled or ridged to provide a tactile warning.

Roses used to cover the bored hole in the door may be round or square and may also be decorated. Locks, which include all operating mechanisms, come with numerous finishes, including brass, bronze, chrome, and stainless steel in bright polish, satin, antique, or oil rubbed. Some locks, particularly the

mortise type, have **escutcheon** plates instead of roses. These are usually rectangular in shape.

Security, function, and handing are all factors to be considered with regard to mortise locks.

In the architectural hardware industry the position of the hinges on a door—in terms of right or left as viewed from the outside of the building, room or space to which the doorway leads-determines the hand.

The outside is the side from which security is necessary. In a series of connecting doors (as in a hotel suite) the outside will be the side of each successive door as one comes to it proceeding from the entrance. For two rooms of equal importance with a passage between, the outside is the passage side.

Strictly speaking, the door itself is only right or left hand; the locks and the latches may be reverse bevel. However, it is necessary to include the term *reverse* and to specify in accordance with the conventions shown here. This will prevent any confusion as to which side is the outside especially important when different finishes are desired on opposite side of the door.

Hardware in general may be:

1. *Universal.* Used in any position (Example: surface bolt).

2. *Reversible.* Hand can be changed by revolving from left to right, or by turning upside down or by reversing some part of the mechanism. (Example: many types of locks and latches).

3. *Handed* (Not reversible). Used only on doors of the hand for which designed. (Example: most rabbeted front door locks and latches.

Although the hardware item specified may be reversible, or even universal, it is good practice to identify the hand completely, in accordance with the convention stated here.[3]

While some locks are reversible and may be used on a right- or left-hand door, others must be ordered as right- or left-handed (see Figure 6–13).

Security has become an important feature of lockset selection. Schlage Interconnected locks are recommended by the experts. From the outside a key must be used. From the inside, one quick twist of the panic-proof knob or lever opens both the latch and deadbolt. Recommended by police and fire de-

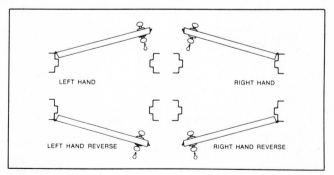

Figure 6-13
Door handing.

partments to provide compliance with many life safety and security codes.

Another security type lock is Key Optional™ lock from InteLock^R. Simply turn the knob right or left (as you would a combination lock), to enter the 3- or 4-digit secret access code. The numbers appear one by one in the bright, easy-to-read LED display. Once the correct sequence has been entered, the 1 inch thick deadbolt can be released simply by turning its outside ring. Without the right code, the ring spins freely, resisting attempts to wrench or pry it open. If an intruder doesn't enter the correct code within 30 seconds of trying to unlock the door, a tamper alarm will sound. Easily activated by a switch, a temporary code allows guests and tradespeople to enter without revealing the master code. This code can be erased in seconds.

A door should be controlled at the desired limit of its opening cycle in order to prevent damage to an adjacent wall, column, equipment, the door or to its hardware. This con-

trol is achieved by stops and holders, which may be located at the floor, wall or overhead.

Floor stops are available in varied heights, sizes, shapes and functions. They may have a mechanism such as a hook or friction device to hold the door open at the option of the user. Height of door from floor, shape of stops and location in relation to traffic are important considerations.

Wall stops or bumpers have the advantage of being located where they do not conflict with floor coverings or cleaning equipment and do not constitute a traffic hazard.

There are two commonly used types of floor holders; the spring- loaded "step-on" type and the lever of "flip-down" type. Neither type acts as a stop."[4]

Door controls used in commercial installations may be over head closers, either surface-mounted or

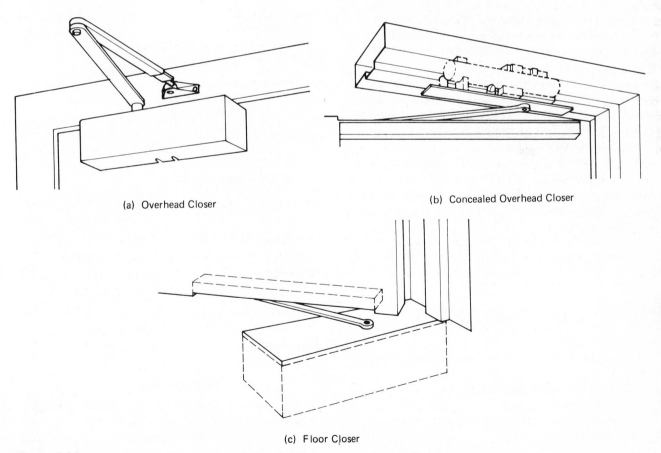

(a) Overhead Closer

(b) Concealed Overhead Closer

(c) Floor Closer

Figure 6-14
Door controls.

concealed, and floor-type closers. These devices are a combination of a spring and an oil-cushioned piston that dampens the closing action inside a cylinder. Surface-mounted closers are more accessible for maintenance but concealed closers are more aesthetically pleasing. Overhead installations are preferred because dirt and scrub water may harm the operation of a floor-type closer (see Figure 6–14). A 3- second delay is required to provide safe passage for a handicapped person.

In public buildings, all doors must open out for fire safety. A push plate is attached to the door or a fire exit bar or panic bar is used. Slight pressure of the bar releases the rod and latch. For handicapped use, this bar should be able to be operated with a maximum of 8 pounds of pressure.

Door opening may also be accomplished by the use of an electronic eye, when the beam is broken, the door opens. For areas requiring special security, doors can be opened by a specially coded plastic card, similar to a credit card, or a numbered combination may be punched in. The combination may be changed easily thus eliminating the need to reissue keys.

These security systems are being used more and more in restrooms of office buildings and other special areas where access is restricted to certain personnel.

To eliminate having to carry several keys for residential use, all the locksets for exterior doors, may be keyed the same. This may be done when the locks are ordered, or a locksmith can make the changes later but at a greater expense.

When specifying locksets, the following information must be provided: manufacturer's name and style number, finish, style of knob and rose, backset, wood or metal door, thickness of door, and door handing.

Installation should be performed by a professional locksmith or carpenter to insure correct fit,with no door rattles or other fitting problems.

HOSPITAL HARDWARE

Hardware for hospitals and health-related institutions includes items that might not be found in any other type of building. Because it may be used by aged, infirm, sick or handicapped persons, the hardware must meet all the requirements of safety, security and protection, and yet be operable with a minimum amount of effort.

Modifications of hinges may include hospital tips for added safety, special length and shape of leaves to swing doors clear of an opening, and hinges of special sizes and gauges to carry the weight of lead-lined doors.

Hospital pulls are designed to be mounted with the open end down allowing the door to be operated by the wrist, arm or forearm when the hands are occupied.[5]

BIBLIOGRAPHY

Ortho Books. Finish Carpentry Techniques. San Francisco: Chevron Chemical Company, 1983

National Particleboard Association. Builder Bulletin, Particleboard Shelf Systems, National Particleboard Association, Gaithersburg, MD 1988

Time-Life Books. Doors and Windows, Home Repairs & Improvement, Alexandria, VA: Time-Life Books, 1978

ENDNOTES

[1] *Butts and Hinges.* (McLean VA: Door and Hardware Institute, 1985) p. 1.

[2] *Basic Architectural Hardware.* (McLean, VA: Door and Hardware Institute, 1985), pp. 8–10.

[3] *Basic Architectural Hardware.* (McLean, VA: Door and Hardware Institute, 1985), p. 5.

[4] *Basic Architectural Hardware.* (McLean, VA: Door and Hardware Institute, 1985), p. 25.

[5] *Basic Architectural Hardware.* (McLean, VA: Door and Hardware Institute, 1985), p. 23.

GLOSSARY

Astragal. Vertical strip of wood with weatherstripping.

Armored. Two plates are used to cover the lock mechanism in order to prevent tampering.

Backplate. An applied decorative moulding used on ceilings above a chandelier or ceiling fan.

Backset. The horizontal distance from the center of the face-bored hole to the edge of the door.

Bed moulding. Cornice moulding.

Brickmold. Exterior wood moulding to cover gap between door or window frame.

Butt hinges. Two metal plates joined with a pin, one being fastened to the door jamb or frame and the other to the door (see Figure 6–9).

Caulk. Filling a joint with resilient mastic. Also spelled *calk.*

Chair rail. Strip of wood or moulding that is placed on the wall at the same height as the back of a chair to protect the wall from damage (see Figure 6–1).

Countersunk. Hole prepared with a bevel to enable the tapered head of a screw to be inserted flush with the surface.

Dado. A groove cut in wood to receive and position another member.

Deadbolt or deadlock. Hardened steel bolt with a square head operated by a key or turn piece (see Figure 6–11).

Door and Hardware Institute. DHI representing the industry.

Escutcheon. Plate which surrounds the keyhole and/ or handle.

Fast pin. Pin is permanently in place. Nonremovable.

Gain. Area cut away on door or jamb into which leaves of hinges are set.

Knuckle. Cylindrical area of hinge enclosing the pin.

Leaves. Flat plates of a pair of hinges (see Figure 6–9).

Lights. Small panes of glass. Usually rectangular in shape.

Lock strike. A plate fastened to the door frame into which the bolts project.

Loose. Able to be removed.

Mitered. Two cuts at a 45° angle to form a right angle. See Figure 7–2.

Nonrising. Pins that do not ride up with use.

Ogee. A double curved shape resembling an S-shape.

Ovolo. A convex moulding usually a quarter of a circle.

Polymer. A high-molecular weight compound from which mouldings are made.

Prehung. Frame and door are packaged as one unit.

Rose. The plate, usually round, that covers the bored hole on the face of the door.

Springlatch. Latch with a spring rather than a locking action.

Spun. Moving the metal by means of a spinning action and applied pressure which changes the shape of the metal.

Sticking. The shaping of moulding.

Template hardware. Hardware that exactly matches a master template drawing, as to spacing of all holes and dimensions (see Figure 6–9, full mortise hinge).

Throw. The distance a bolt penetrates when fully extended.

7

Cabinet Construction

To properly select or design well-made cabinet work, it is necessary to become familiar with furniture construction. By studying the casework joints, specifiers will be able to compare and contrast similar items and make an informed decision on which piece of furniture, or which group of cabinets, is the most value for the money.

When designing casework and specifying materials, several parts need definition. According to AWI, exposed surfaces include drawers and opaque doors

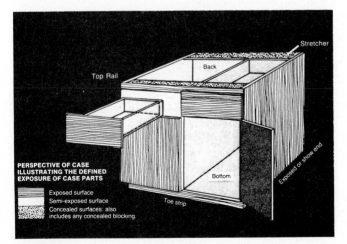

PERSPECTIVE OF CASE ILLUSTRATING THE DEFINED EXPOSURE OF CASE PARTS

- Exposed surface
- Semi-exposed surface
- Concealed surfaces: also includes any concealed blocking.

Stretcher, Top Rail, Back, Bottom, Toe strip, Exposed or show end

Figure 7-1
Casework Construction. (Reprinted with permission from the Architectural Woodwork Institute.)

(if any) when closed; behind clear glass doors; bottoms of cabinets 42 inches or more above finish floor; tops of cabinets below 78 inches above finish floor (see Figure 7–1).

Semi-exposed surfaces are surfaces which become visible when opaque doors are open or drawers are extended and bottoms of cabinets are more than 30 inches and less than 42 inches above finish floor. Concealed portions are surfaces not visible after installation; bottoms of cabinets less than 30 inches above finish floor; tops of cabinets over 78 inches above finish floor and not visible from an upper level; stretchers, blocking, and components concealed by drawers (see Figure 7–1).

JOINTS

The stile and rail joinery may use one of the following three methods: Mortise and tenon, where the stile has a mortise or hole and the rail has the tenon or tongue. Dowel joints consist of holes for the dowels being drilled in the stile and dowels being inserted in corresponding places on the rail. A stub tenon is similar to a tongue-and-groove joint, except that the rounded tongue-and-groove has been squared off. A spline joint is used for gluing plywood in width and length. Since the spline serves to align faces, this joint is also used for items requiring on-site assembly (see Figure 7–2).

French dovetail joints are used for joining drawer sides to fronts when fronts conceal metal extension slides or overlay the case faces. Conventional dovetail is the traditional joint for joining drawer sides to fronts and backs, and eliminates, due to its interlocking nature, any possibility of the drawer sides and front separating. Conventional dovetail joints are usually limited to **flush** or **lipped** drawers. A drawer lock joint also joins the drawer sides to the fronts and is usually used for flush installations, but can be adapted to lip or **overlay** drawers (see Figure 7–4).

Wood may also be joined together with a **butt joint**—merely placing the two pieces of wood at right angles to each other. This type of joint is found in cheap furniture. Another method of joining two pieces of wood at right angles is to miter the adjoining edges. A mitered joint is frequently used when constructing picture frames. It may also be used in furniture construction, sometimes in conjunction with a spline (see Figure 7–2).

Premium grade has some form of dovetail to attach the backs of the drawers to the sides. In custom grade, the shouldered lock joint may be used at the front and back.

A **dado** is a groove or square slot cut in the wood. All drawer bottoms should have a minimum thickness of 1/4 of an inch and should be inserted into dadoes on drawer sides, fronts and backs. This construction creates a bottom panel that is permanently locked into position.

Edge banding is required when materials other than solid wood are used. This edge treatment is used for case body members and shelves but varies according to the grade and finish of the work. When a transparent finish is used, for premium grade, the visible edge should be banded with same species as the face, and pressure-glued. In custom grade the banding should be a compatible species, pressure glued and for economy grade the compatible species may be nailed. When an opaque finish is used, premium grade requires close grain material, pressure glued, custom grade uses close grain material glued and nailed and economy grade edge is filled and sanded (see Figure 7–3).

DRAWERS/DOORS

Drawer or door fronts may be of one of the three following design categories.

1. Exposed face frame-flush
   Exposed face frame-lipped
2. Flush overlay
3. Reveal overlay

Exposed face frame—flush (also often known as *conventional flush construction*) is the design most basic to architectural woodwork. The drawer and door faces are flush with the face frame. This design is highly functional and allows the use of different thicknesses of wood for doors and drawer fronts. The exposed face frame has the advantage of providing a solid surround for the operating doors and drawers, which keeps them aligned. This type of construction is recommended for hard-service applications because of superior strength and rigidity. It

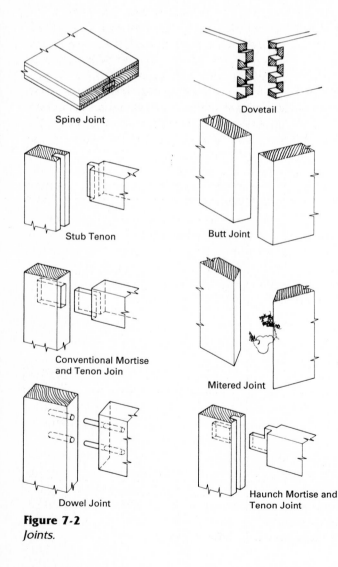

Spine Joint

Dovetail

Stub Tenon

Butt Joint

Conventional Mortise and Tenon Join

Mitered Joint

Dowel Joint

Haunch Mortise and Tenon Joint

Figure 7-2
Joints.

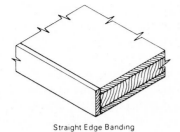

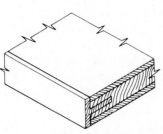

Figure 7-3
Edge banding.

is, however, a more expensive design, due to the necessity of careful fitting and alignment of the doors and drawers, and the close tolerances required by the exposed joinery in the face frame. For these reasons this design does not lend itself to the economical use of decorative laminate covering.

Exposed face frame—Lipped design has most of the advantages and is similar in construction to the flush design. Provided that edge banding is not required on the doors, the lipped design is a more economical style since the fitting tolerances of the doors and drawers are less critical.

Flush overlay is becoming increasingly popular. It offers a very clean, contemporary design since only the door and drawer fronts are visible on the face of the cabinet and a matched grain effect can be achieved, if specified, by having all the doors and drawer fronts cut from the same panel. It also lends itself ideally to the use of decorative laminate for the exposed surfaces. Heavy-duty hardware is required with a flush overlay design. The absence of a face frame requires careful site preparation and installation to maintain proper alignment of doors and/or drawers.

Reveal overlay, a variation of the flush overlay design, presents a "raised panel" effect. Although it requires a face frame, it is for the most part concealed and, as with a lipped design, requires less demanding fitting tolerances. The **reveal** between doors and drawer fronts reduces the problem of alignment. It incorporates most of the advantages of the flush overlay and exposed face frame designs. The architect or designer has the option of utilizing the reveals

vertically and/or horizontally, and the width of the reveal is variable (see Figure 7–4).

The thickness of the stock for cabinet doors is covered under Section 400A-S-5 of Architectural Woodwork Quality Standards, Guide Specifications and Quality Certification Program. It varies according to the grade, width, and height of the door.

When doors are covered with a high-pressure laminate, a **balancing** laminate must be used on the reverse side of the substrate.

For shelves, or when the case body is exposed, the following construction methods are used: Through dado is the conventional joint used for assembly of case body members and the dado is usually concealed by a case face frame. Blind dado has an applied edge "stopping" or concealing the dado groove and is used when case body edge is exposed. Stop dado is applicable when veneer edging or solid lumber is exposed (see Figure 7–5).

Drawer guides are an important feature of well-made casework. They may be constructed of wood or metal. If wood is selected, it should have both male and female parts made of wood. Wood drawer guides are usually centered under the drawer, but they may also be attached to the side of the case, with the drawer sides being dadoes to accommodate the wood guide. The reverse procedure may be used, with the guide attached to the drawer side and the

Exposed Face Frame—Flush

Exposed Face Frame—Lipped

Flush Overlay

Reveal Overlay

Figure 7-4
Cabinet door construction. Plan view.

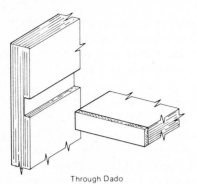

Through Dado

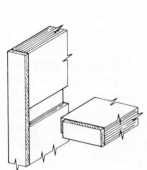

Blind Dado

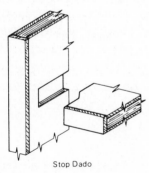

Stop Dado

Figure 7-5
Dados. (Reprinted with permission from the Architectural Woodwork Institute)

frame dadoes receiving the guide. Paste wax should be applied to the wood guides to facilitate movement.

When an exposed face frame with a flush drawer front is designed, a **stop** must be incorporated to prevent too much inward travel. As has been mentioned before, flush doors and drawers are the most expensive form of design because of the tolerances and hand-fitting of such extras as drawer stops.

Kitchen cabinets and some furniture use metal guides attached to the case and drawer sides. The drawers slide out on metal or nylon rollers running

in the guide track. Kitchen drawers often employ self-returning slides. In other words, when the drawer is pulled out to its fullest extent it remains open, but when pushed in approximately halfway, the rollers continue to close without more pressure being applied to the drawer front. This is a useful feature that prevents unsightly and unsafe half-open drawers in the kitchen. All drawer guides are installed with a very slight inward tilt.

A toe space is required for such items as kitchen cabinets and dressers, thus providing a recessed space for toes under the doors or drawers. This toe strip is usually 4 inches high and 2 1/2 inches deep. These measurements vary slightly with the European kitchen cabinets having a height of 5 7/8 inches.

CABINET HARDWARE

The type of hardware selected will depend upon the design category. With an exposed face frame and a flush door, heavy-duty **exposed hinges** may be used or they may be concealed. **Concealed** hinges are recessed into the door, attached to the side of the frame, and hidden from view when the cabinet door is closed (see Figure 6–10). A half-mortise or half-surface hinge with a decorative end to the pin may be used where a semi concealed hinge is desired. Lipped doors are hung by means of a semiconcealed hinge. Flush overlay and reveal overlay doors may be hung by using semiconcealed or concealed hinges. **Pivot hinges** are often used for fitting doors to cabinets without frames. Pivot hinges are particularly useful on plywood and particleboard doors. Only the pivot shows from the front when the door is closed (see Figure 6–9 for a pivot hinge). A piano hinge or continuous hinge is used on drop-leaf desks and on the doors of some fine furniture. Because they are installed the whole length of the edge, they support the weight of the door in an efficient manner.

Cabinet doors and drawers may be designed without pull hardware by having a finger pull either as part of the door or drawer construction or by the addition of a pieces of shaped wood, plastic, or metal to the front of the door. It is necessary to design these finger pulls in such a manner that the doors or drawers open easily, without breaking fingernails.

Cabinet pull hardware may be knobs, rounded or square, or handles ranging from simple metal strips to ornately designed ones. The material from which this hardware is constructed may be wood, porcelain, plastic, or metal. It is necessary to select hardware that is compatible with the design of the cabinets or furniture. For traditional or period cabinets, authentic hardware should be chosen.

In order to hold cabinet doors shut, some form of catch is needed. There are five different types: **friction**, roller, magnetic, **bullet** and touch catch. A friction catch, when engaged, is held in place by friction. The roller catch has a roller under tension, that engages a recess in the **strike plate**. The magnet is the holding mechanism of a magnetic catch and, in a bullet catch, a spring-actuated ball engages a depression in the plate. A touch catch releases automatically when the door is pushed. Many of these catches have elongated screw slots that enable the tension of the catch to be adjusted (see Figure 7–6). Some hinges are spring loaded, eliminating the need for a catch.

SHELVES

The span and thickness of shelves varies according to the purpose of the shelves. The AWI has the following specifications for shelves. For closet and utility shelving ends and back cleats to receive clothes rods or hooks shall be 3/4 by 3 1/2 inches. Ends and back cleats that do not receive clothes rods or hooks shall be 3/4 by 1 1/2 inches.

Shelves spanning less than 42 inches shall be 3/4 inch thick.

Three-quarter inch shelves spanning over 48 inches require intermediate support.

Shelves spanning 42 to 60 inches without an intermediate support shall be a minimum of 1 inch thick, or have an in-plant applied 3/4 by 1 1/2-inch **(apron)** edge. Where weight considerations are important, as with bookshelves, the span should be reduced.

The following information was used with permission of the National Particleboard Association (NPA).

Particleboard and **Medium-Density Fiber-board** (MDF) are often specified for shelves and designers should be aware of fairly specific applications. Kitchen cabinets, for example, normally will be designed for a uniform load of 15 pounds per square foot (psf), closets 25 psf; and books 40 psf. (See Table 7–1 for maximum shelf spans in inches for uniform loading.) This table has been abbreviated to only include information needed by designers. The use of underlayment and overhanging shelves has been omitted. The Builders Bulletin, Particleboard Shelf Systems, may be obtained from the NPA.

How to use the table:

1. *Design* The critical factor in shelf design is the span between supports and the load you expect to put on the shelf. Installation of extra support between the end supports will allow use of the *Multiple Support* values.

2. *Load Factor* This table is based on pounds per square foot loading (psf). Known weight that

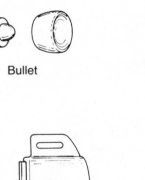

Bullet

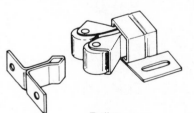

Roller

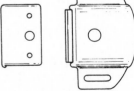

Magnetic

Figure 7-6
Cabinet catches.

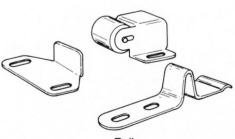

Roller

Table 7-1
Maximum shelf spans in inches for uniform loading

| Load* | End Supported Maximum Span | | | | | | Multiple Supports Maximum Span | | | | | |
| | Industrial Particleboard 1-M-2 | | | MDF | | | Industrial Particleboard 1-M-2 | | | MDF | | |
Inches	½	⅝	¾	½	⅝	¾	½	⅝	¾	½	⅝	¾
50.0	15	19	23	15	19	23	21	26	31	20	25	30
45.0	16	20	24	16	19	23	22	27	32	21	26	32
40.0	17	21	25	16	20	24	22	28	34	22	27	33
35.0	17	22	26	17	21	25	23	29	35	23	28	34
30.0	18	23	27	18	22	27	25	31	37	24	30	36
25.0	19	24	29	19	23	28	26	33	39	25	32	38
20.0	21	26	31	20	25	30	28	35	42	27	34	40
17.5	22	27	32	21	26	31	29	36	43	28	35	42
15.0	23	28	34	22	27	33	31	38	45	30	37	44
12.5	24	30	35	23	29	34	32	40	48	31	39	46
10.0	26	32	38	25	31	37	34	43	50	33	41	49
7.5	28	34	40	27	33	39	37	46	54	36	45	53
5.0	31	38	44	30	37	43	41	51	60	40	49	58

*Load in pounds per square foot.
Table courtesy of National Particleboard Association.

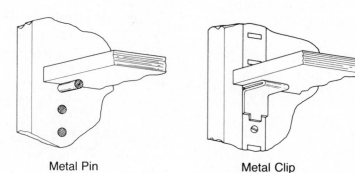

Metal Pin   Metal Clip

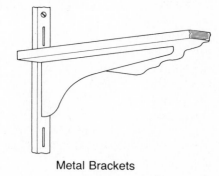

Metal Brackets

Figure 7-7
Shelf supports.

is not in the form of uniform loading psf will have to be converted before the Table may be used. To determine the uniform load in (psf), convert the inches of the shelf to square feet by dividing by 144 inches (one square foot); divide the expected load by the answer and you will get the uniform load. For example, a shelf is 9 inches by 36 inches or 324 square inches. To convert to square feet, divide by 144 inches and you get 2.25 square feet. If you have a 50-pound load, divide it by the square footage (2.25) and your uniform load is 22.2 psf.

3. *Continuous Support* The most efficient use of load bearing capacity involves using end supports with continuous support all along the rear edge of the shelf fastened at six inch intervals for shelves up to 12 inches wide you may double the span listed under the *End supported* heading when the same load is applied. For continuously supported shelves over 12 inches but less than 24 inches wide, first triple the load you are designing the shelf to hold. Then, find the span listed under the "End Supported" heading for that treble loading. Next, double that span for the original load. This analysis does not apply to shelves wider than 24 inches or longer than 6 feet.

When shelves are to be permanently installed, some form of dado may be used for positioning. The type used depends upon the frame construction. Another permanent installation uses a wood quarter round at the desired height.

If, however, the shelves are to be adjustable there are several methods of support. The type used in fine china cabinets is a metal shelf pin. A number of blind holes, usually in groups of three, are drilled 5/8 of an inch apart in two rows on each interior face of the sides. The metal shelf pins are then inserted at the desired shelf level.

Metal shelf standards have slots every inch, with two standards on each side running from top to bottom of the shelf unit. Four adjustable metal clips are inserted at the same level into these slots. The metal strips may be applied to the inside surface of the shelf unit or they may be dadoed into the interior face.

When metal brackets are used, the shelf stan-dards are attached to the back wall surface instead of to the sides.

BIBLIOGRAPHY

Architectural Woodwork Institute. Architectural Woodwork Quality Standard, Guide Specifications and Quality Certification Program, Alexandria, VA: Architectural Woodwork Institute, 5th ed. 1989.

GLOSSARY

Apron. A flat piece of wood attached vertically along the underside of the front edge of a horizontal surface, may be for support as in book shelves or decorative.

Balancing sheet. In decorative laminate doors, the lighter weight laminate on the interior face.

Bullet catch. A spring actuated ball engaging a depression in the plate (see Figure 7–6).

Concealed hinge. All parts are concealed when door is closed (see Figure 6–10).

Dowel joint. A joint usually right angle using dowels for positioning and strength (see Figure 6–9).

Exposed hinge. All parts are visible when door is closed (see Figure 6–9).

Flush. Door and frame are level and frame is completely visible when door is closed (see Figure 7–4).

Friction catch. When engaged, catch is held in place by friction (see Figure 7–6).

Lipped door. A door with an overlapping edge. Partially covers the frame (see Figure 7–4).

Overlay door. The door is on the outside of the frame and when closed, the door hides the frame from view (see Figure 6–4).

Pivot hinge. Hinge leaves are mortised into edge of door panel and set in frame at jamb and top of door. Some pivot hinges pivot on a single point (see Figure 6–9).

Reveal. The small area of the frame that is visible when door and/or drawer is closed (see Figure 7–4).

Stop. A metal, plastic, or wood block placed so as to position the flush drawer front to be level with the face frame.

Strike plate. Metal plate attached to the frame, designed to hold roller catch under tension.

8

Kitchens

The kitchen has undergone many changes over the years. In the Victorian era, the cast iron cookstove was the main source of cooking and heating and, although an improvement over the open fire of Colonial days, it still required much time and labor to keep it operating. The coal or wood had to be carried into the house and the stove itself required blacking to maintain its shiny appearance. In winter, the heat radiating from the cookstove heated the kitchen and made it a gathering place for the family. But, in summer, in order to use the top for cooking and the oven for baking, the fire had to be lit, causing the kitchen to resemble a furnace.

In the kitchens of the past, beside the cookstove, the only other pieces of furniture were tables and chairs and a sink. All food preparation was done on the table or on the draining board next to the sink. There were no such things as counters as we know them today and no such things as upper storage cabinets. All food was stored in the pantry or in a cold cellar. Today, the kitchen has once again become a gathering place for the family. Much family life is centered around the kitchen, not only for food preparation, but also for entertaining and socializing. In line with this, Joe Ruggiero, Publishing Director of *Home Magazine*, said, "The kitchen will have more upholstery as well as new types of furniture such as armoires, entertainment centers and custom dish-racks, instead of traditional cabinetry." He mentions the parade of gadgets such as wood-burning pizza ovens and built-in woks, to ice cream makers and sorbet freezers. "Many kitchens will be outfitted with canning centers, special preparation areas and doors opening up to herb and vegetable gardens. The trend will be to more wood in the kitchen."

Regardless of the type of kitchen desired, there are some basic requirements for all kitchens. The work areas or appliances most used in a kitchen are the refrigerator for food storage, stove for cooking, and the sink for the washing area. The **work triangle** connects these three areas and the total distance should not be over 22 feet and may be less than that in some smaller kitchens. The distance between the refrigerator and the sink should be 4 to 7 feet, with 4 to 6 feet between sink and stove, and 4 to 9 feet between stove and refrigerator.

The type of kitchen desired depends upon availability of space, life style, and ages and number of family members. Expense and space are the limiting factors in kitchen design. Best utilization of space will create a functional and enjoyable working area.

Life style involves several factors. One is the manner of entertaining. Formal dinners require a separate formal dining room, while informal entertaining may take place just outside the work triangle, with guest and host/hostess communicating while

135

Figure 8-1
A corridor kitchen appears larger with Wilsonart white laminate cabinets and a planter for herbs behind the Sculptura sink from Elkay. The faucet also from Elkay has a pull-out spray, used for watering the planter and washing vegetables in the small strainer sink on the right. The left side features a desk for meal planning and telephone calls, a Jenn-Air grill top stove and an appliance garage in which the doors open back against the walls to utilize the whole counter width. Counters are medium gray with an oak edging also from Wilsonart. Ceramic tile floor from Dal Tile. Dishwasher from In-sink-erator. Photographer Mark Breinholt.

meals are being prepared. If entertaining is done outside the home of a working host and/or hostess, then the kitchen may be minimal (see Figure 8–1).

A young couple with a beginning family, might require a family room within sight of the parents. Teenagers like to be near food preparation areas for easy access to refrigerator and snacks. All these factors need to be taken into consideration when planning a kitchen.

Some cooks prefer to work from a pantry and, therefore, do not need a lot of upper cabinets, others prefer to have a bake center and work from both the upper and lower cabinets.

Ellen Cheever, CKD, ASID, gives the following work simplification techniques for planning a kitchen:

1. Build the cabinets to fit the cook.
2. Build the shelves to fit the supplies.
3. Build the kitchen to fit the family.

FLOOR PLANS

Figure 8–2 shows some of the basic floor plans, but there are infinite variations on these plans, and this is where the customizing comes in. Many can have an island added for additional counter space.

The simplest of all kitchen floor plans is the one-wall, otherwise knows as **pullman**, **strip,** or **studio**. Here, all appliances and counter space are contained on one wall and, when required, folding doors or screens may be used to hide the kitchen completely from view. This is a minimal kitchen not designed for elaborate or family meals.

The **corridor** or two-wall plan utilizes two parallel walls and doubles the available space over the one-wall plan. The major problem with this design is through traffic. If possible, for safety's sake, one end should be closed off to avoid this traffic. The width of the corridor kitchen should be between 8 and 10 feet. A narrower width prevents two facing doors from being opened at the same time. For energy conservation, refrigerator and stove should not face each other directly (see Figure 8–1).

In an L-shaped kitchen, work areas are arranged on two adjacent walls rather than on two opposite walls, the advantages being there is no through traffic and all counter space is contiguous. The L-shaped kitchen may also include an island or a peninsula. This island may simply be an extra work surface, contain the sink or stove, and/or may also include an informal eating area (see Figure 8–5.)

The U-shaped kitchen is probably the most efficient design. There is no through traffic and three walls of counter space. Depending on location of the window, there are at least two walls or more of upper cabinets. The work triangle is the easiest to arrange with the sink usually at the top of the U, refrigerator on one side, and the range on the other. The refrigerator is always placed at the end of the U to avoid breaking up the counter space and also to be more easily accessible to the eating area. The stove, range, or cooktop is on the opposite side but more centered in the U. See Figure 8–2 for kitchen floor plans. When planning any kitchen, thought should be given to the activities of each area. The sink area serves a dual purpose. First, it is used for food preparation such as washing and cleaning fruits and vegetables. Second, after the meal it is used for cleanup. In the age of the electric dishwasher, the sink area is generally used only for preliminary cleaning, but in the

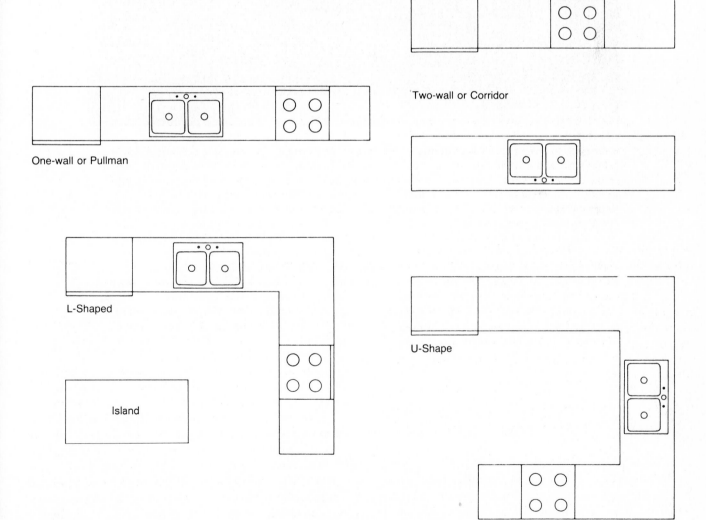

Two-wall or Corridor

One-wall or Pullman

L-Shaped

Island

U-Shape

Figure 8-2
Kitchen floor plans.

Figure 8-3

A farmhouse style kitchen has Monogram™ appliances from GE. On the right is a side-by-side refrigerator and a white double oven built into a wall of Allmilmo cabinets in a custom finish. Out of the picture to the right of the Monogram refrigerator is a walk-in pantry enclosed by ribbed glass doors. In the center is a butcher block table next to a slate counter which has a self-rimming stainless steel bar sink, under which are four slide-out bins for recycling cans and glass. The center background has a Monogram Component Cooktop installed parallel for easy access. Two two-burner gas units with a downdraft vent behind each cooking unit and to the right a downdraft grill unit, are set into a stainless steel counter and backsplash. The left wall features solid surface countertops and a custom fabricated deep marble sink with wrist blade faucet handles from The Chicago Faucet Company. The floor is 18-inch cast concrete squares custom colored surrounded by 12-inch concrete tiles. Kitchen designed by David Staskowski and Donna Warner and presented by GE Monogram and Metropolitan Home to the National Association of Homebuilders Women's Council. Photographer Scott Frances/ESTO. Photograph courtesy of GE Monogram™ and Metropolitan Home.

event of a large number of dishes, sufficient space should be provided next to the sink for a helper to dry the dishes.

The refrigerator or cold food storage should be at the end of one side of the counter near the entrance to the kitchen. Regardless of the type of design, there must be at least 16 inches of counter on the handle side of the refrigerator.

The refrigerator should be plugged into its own individual 115–volt electrical outlet on a circuit separate from those used for heating and cooking appliances. Place the refrigerator in an area that will not have direct sunlight or direct heat from the home heating system. Do not place it next to the range or dishwasher.

The cooking area is considered to be the cooktop

Figure 8-4
This raised panel kitchen combines cathedral-shaped panels with the same design glass doors. The same pattern with a squared top is used for the base cabinets. An appliance garage is behind the tambour on the right and a ceramic tile counter and backsplash provide a casual contrast. Photograph courtesy of Quaker Maid.

area. Many wall ovens are now located in separate areas from the cooktop. The cooktop may be gas or electric.

KITCHEN APPLIANCES

Only those appliances that are necessary to a kitchen floor plan will be discussed—in other words, what we consider major appliances: Mixers and toasters are outside the scope of this book.

Major appliance manufacturers must comply with a law enacted by Congress in 1975 (PL. 94–163). This law provides that energy costs for appliances must be calculated as so much per **kilowatt hour (kwh).** This information must be supplied on a tag attached to the front of the appliance. Consumers can then calculate their yearly energy cost by finding out their local kwh rate. It is important to bear in mind that

the higher the local rate the more important energy conservation features become. It is by using these figures that comparison shopping can be done.

Refrigerators

The most costly kitchen appliance to purchase and to operate is the refrigerator. For our purposes, the word refrigerator will be used instead of refrigerator/freezer combination since we assume that all refrigerators have some form of freezer section. This freezer section is commonly on top, but some refrigerators have the freezer section below the regular food storage area. Side-by-side refrigerators have separate vertical doors for the freezer and refrigerator sections and because of the narrower doors, they require less aisle space for opening. Other exterior features include panel adapter kits that are used on the the face of the refrigerator to match other appliances, the latest is stainless fronts for appliances. Doors that can be reversed are an important feature for those who move frequently.

For larger families, an ice water dispenser with cubed and/or crushed ice that is accessible without opening the door may conserve energy and justify the additional expense. One manufacturer even has a third door for access only to the ice cube compartment. Another has a storage unit in the door that can be opened for access to snack items without opening the full-length doors. The most common features found in refrigerators include meat keepers, vegetable storage, unwrapped food sections, and adjustable shelves and humidity controlled vegetable storage areas. Other interior features might include egg storage, handy cheese and spread storage, and glass shelves that prevent spilled liquids from dripping onto other shelves, although these solid glass shelves may prevent full air circulation. The shelves on the doors of both refrigerator and freezer may be fixed or adjustable. The latest feature are doors deep enough to hold gallon containers.

Some manufacturers specialize in energy conservation and there has been greatly improved efficiency over the past 15 years. A self-defrosting refrigerator consumes more energy than a manual defrost, but is much more convenient. Others have features such as frozen juice can dispensers, ice makers and, an ice cream maker within the freezer compartment.

Nylon rollers are provided for moving or rolling the refrigerator out from the wall. If the refrigerator is to be moved sideways, it should be moved by means of a **dolly** to avoid damaging the floor covering.

Refrigerators are sold by their storage capacity, in other words by cubic feet of space. It is interesting to note that while families and kitchens generally are getting smaller, the size of the refrigerator is staying around 16 to 17 cubic feet. This may be due to working parents with less time to shop or more frequent entertaining.

The average size for refrigerator/freezer combinations is 66 1/2 inches high, 35 3/4 inches wide (fits into a 36-inch space) and 30 1/2 inches deep. This depth measurement means that the door of the refrigerator extends beyond the counter for several inches. In order to design the refrigerator to be an integral part of the cabinetry, many manufacturers have recessed the coils or placed them above the refrigerator, which makes the refrigerator flush with the edge of the counter, however, this type is usually considerably higher in price (see Monogram™ from GE in Figure 8–3).

KitchenAid has refrigerators that are 36-inch, 42-inch and the new 48-inch wide. Marvel has a completely built-in 8 cubic foot under the counter refrigerator which can be custom painted for office or board room installations.

Traulsen manufacturers Ultra® wine refrigerators with Digitraul® exterior digital read-out for consistent temperature range of 53° to 57°. If other temperatures are required they can be set according to the need of the customer. The compressor mounting allows for the built-in look and the adjustable wine racks hold bottles tilted to keep the cork moist, and sedimentation controlled by minimizing vibration.

The Kohler Color Coordinates™ (KCC) program offers an easy way to color coordinate a kitchen with Kohler plumbing fixtures, major appliances from Amana Refrigeration, vinyl flooring from Armstrong World Industries, range hoods and trash compactors from Broan/Nautilus®, ceramic tile from Dal-Tile, laminates and solid surfacing materials from Nevamar Corporation and wallcoverings from Village® Wallcoverings.

Ranges

Old-fashioned stoves have been replaced by **drop-in** or **slide-in** units or **free-standing** units. Slide-in models can be converted to free-standing by addition of optional side panels and a backguard. Some ranges contain the cooking units, **microwave** and/or oven in one appliance, or the oven and cooktop may be in two separate units, often in two separate locations in the kitchen. Figures 8–1, 8–4, 8–7.

A free-standing range has finished sides and is usually slightly deeper than the 24-inch kitchen counter. This type of range may be considered if a change of residence will take place in the near future. The drop-in or slide-in units are designed for more permanent installation and are usually placed between two kitchen cabinets. The cooking medium may be gas or electricity. Some ranges have the cooking surface flush with the counter, while others are lowered an inch or so. The only difference being that, if several large or wide pans are used at the same time, such as during canning or for large parties, the lowered surface is more restricting. The flush surface permits the overhanging of the larger pans.

Electric Ranges. To obtain the most efficiency, all cooking utensils used on an electric range must be flat bottomed to allow full contact with the cooking unit.

There are now three different types of electric cooking surfaces. One is the conventional or coil element, the second is the European solid disk of cast iron sealed to the cooktop which some manufacturers refer to as **hobs**. The solid disks may also feature a pan sensor which maintains a constant preselected temperature. The third type is the **glass-ceramic** cooktop. When first introduced in 1966 these were white, but today most are black. All these above surfaces are heated primarily by conduction.

Some glass top cooktops have quick heating elements and, for safety's sake, the indicator lights will stay on as long as the surface is hot. DACOR with its five burner black Ceran® glass surface has three different types of elements for maximum cooking flexibility. The 8-inch Haloring has an infrared lamp encircling a radiant coil for extremely uniform heat distribution on the cooking surface. The Dual Circuit radiant element in effect is two elements in one. You can use the single inner coil of 6 inch (1,000 watts) alone or in combination with a larger diameter outer coil. The third is the Quick Star providing a visual heat response within three to five seconds.

Two new methods of heating are induction and halogen units, both of which have glass-ceramic cooktops. Magnetic cookware, such as cast iron, iron with porcelain enamel, or tri-ply must be used to activate the electromagnetic induction units. The halogen units from Gaggenau have vacuum-sealed quartz glass tubes filled with halogen gas which filters out the white light and uses infra-red as a heating source. This unit provides instant on and instant off with any type of cooking utensil, and as with the induction method, the surface unit itself does not get hot. The only heat the glass top may retain is absorbed from a hot pan.

Some cooktops are modular, with interchangeable coil elements, smooth top, **griddle, grille,** and **shish-kebab rotisserie** units, (see figure 8–4). Jenn-Air has introduced the new Expressions™ Collection which allows consumers to design their own cooktop. The cooktop is available in single, double, or triple sizes and three colors—black, white, and stainless steel. Each size features one grill assembly. With cleanability being the major consideration, Excalibur® was chosen for the grill grates and Duracoat for the Savorizer™ liner pan. The grill grates are so stick resistant that hamburgers need two spatulas to remove from the grill. The Savorizer liner pan transforms dripping juices into smoke giving food great grilled flavor. The basin pan under the liner pan never gets hot, so cleanup is easy. Options include electronic controls.

Cooktop cartridges include Halogen cartridge with Haloring™ elements, Quick-Start™ radiant, solid elements, or conventional coils to accompany the grill assembly. The wok accessory includes a heating element which replaces the large element in the optional conventional coil cartridge. The Big Pot canning element is a raised 2100–watt element which replaces the large coil of the conventional coil cartridge. The new PerimaVent™ downdraft ventilation system removes smoke through the air grille and whiffs of smoke from around the cooktop perimeter.

The Monogram Component Cooktop system from GE, is available in gas, solid disk, or electric grill with a downdraft ventilation system that can be installed parallel or perpendicular to counters to maximize design flexibility (see Figure 8–3).

Controls for ranges are usually at the back along with timer controls. On separate cooktops, controls are in the front or at the side of the cooktop. Controls on the latest cooktops are electronic touch pads.

Many 30-inch ranges now come with a second oven above the cooktop surface. This may be another **conventional oven** or a microwave. An exhaust fan is incorporated beneath some of the microwave ovens.

Free standing ranges vary from 20, 30, 40 inches wide, with slide-in ranges usually measuring 30 inches.

The cooktops now have concealed or visible hinges that make it easy to clean under the cooktop, where the overflow from drip bowls ends up. Porcelain drip bowls are much easier to clean than the shiny metal bowls, and can be cleaned in the oven during the self-cleaning cycle.

Gas Ranges. One advantage of using gas is that it is easier to moderate the temperature changes and the required temperature is reached more rapidly (see Figures 8–7). Formerly, glass cooktops were electric, but now they are available in gas models.

Most gas cooktops and ovens have a pilotless ignition that will relight any flame which has accidentally gone out. Many gas ranges and cooktops have sealed burners for cleaning convenience.

DACOR Quintessence gas glass 36-inch cooktop features the fifth Epicure™ burner which is perfect for melting butter, cheese or chocolate without scorching, sauces, and keeping coffee at the right temperature for pouring.

One of the trends of the 1990s is the use of the multiburner restaurant gas range with six or even eight burners in home kitchens. These ranges are free-standing and are very useful when catering for a large crowd, but the floor should be reinforced to support the extra weight. This problem can be over-

Figure 8-5
The cabinets are Amera's Karis door style, available on frameless (European style) laminate cabinets with a 90° radiused edge at the top and bottom of all doors and drawer fronts. The restaurant style cooktop is from Thermador and the counters are Formica with beveled edges. Photograph courtesy of Amera Custom Cabinetry.

come by using restaurant ranges designed for residential use which are made to be installed touching the adjacent cabinet. Most are stainless steel, but Russell Range may be obtained in a solid brass edition (see Figure 8–5).

The convenience of DACOR 46-inch six-burner cooktop provides more cooking elements for large scale entertaining. One of the elements is two sizes in one. For small pans the inner element is turned on and for large pans, the inner and outer are used.

Ovens

Electric ovens come in two types, self-cleaning **(pyrolytic)**, or continuous cleaning **(catalytic)**. Self-cleaning ovens have a special cleaning setting that is activated by the timer for the required length of time. This cleaning cycle runs at an extremely high temperature and actually incinerates any oven spills, leaving an ash residue. One of the excellent by-products of a self-cleaning oven is that, due to the

high temperatures required to operate the cleaning cycle, the oven is more heavily insulated than is customary, and so retains the heat longer and uses less energy when baking. There are now some gas ovens that are self-cleaning.

The continuous-cleaning oven features a special porous ceramic finish that disperses and partially absorbs food spatters to keep the oven presentably clean. Running the oven at the highest temperature for a while will help clean up remaining spatters. Oven-cleaning products available at the grocery store may *not* be used on the continuous-cleaning surface.

Ovens cook by one of three methods: The first is the conventional radiant baking method that is used in most ovens. The second is by convection where streams of heated air flow round the food, resulting in less cooking time and more natural juiciness. The last method is microwave which is treated below.

Most **convection ovens** have three shelves allowing three batches of cookies to be baked at the same time. The moving air causes even cooking on all three shelves. Therefore, it is possible to cook a greater quantity of food in a small convection oven cavity than in a larger conventional one. On low heat settings, foods can also be dehydrated for long term storage. The defrosting setting works on the same principle.

Built-in ovens are required when using a separate cooktop. These may be single conventional oven units, double oven units with one a conventional type and the other a microwave.

Electric ovens may have a solid door, a porcelain enamel door with a window, or a full black glass window door. The porcelain enamel is available in many colors. A glass door may be seen in Figures 8–3 and 8–7. Controls may be knobs or electronic touch pads.

Modern Maid has a new gas self-cleaning oven which is a major breakthrough in technology as previously this feature was only available in electric ovens.

Microwave Ovens

This method of cooking activates the molecules in the food about 2 1/2 billion times per second. It is the friction between molecules that produces the heat. Today, most microwave ovens are operated by means of touch controls that electronically monitor the amount of energy from full power to a warming setting or defrost cycle. Some microwaves have rotating glass dishes to spread out the microwaves and avoid hot spots. Others use microwave and/or convection to provide the speed of a microwave with the browning of a convection oven.

Microwave ovens may be programmed to cook whole meals on a delayed time basis. Some have recipes that are available at a touch, others use a meat probe to produce meat that is rare, medium, or well done.

Microwave ovens may be counter models, under-the-cabinet (UTC) without a vent, or the latest models over-the-range (OTR) with built-in exhaust fans. Spacemaker Plus™ from GE features higher wattage and a bottom-feed microwave distribution system. Some new features in 1991 were Auto Cook, Auto Popcorn, and Auto Reheat. They rely on a humidity sensor to precisely determine when the food has been properly cooked.

Exhaust Fans

Most exhaust fans are used above the cooking surface. They may be vertical or horizontal discharge, or be ductless. Vertical discharge takes up some of the space in the cabinet above the range. Horizontal discharges are usually used only on an outside wall. Ductless hoods have a **charcoal filter** that filters out odors with the filter being washable.

Jenn-Air manufactures cooktops and grill ranges with a built-in downdraft ventilation that removes smoke and odors to the outside, thereby eliminating the need for an overhead hood. Downdraft cooking is ideal for peninsula and island installation and eliminates bulky overhead fans. For conventional ranges, pullout slim line hoods are available which are only about 2 to 3 inches thick allowing them to be retracted when not in use. They have several speeds allowing the user to easily select a desired fan speed, also a light with different intensities. The blower will shut off automatically when the canopy is pushed in.

Dishwashers

Dishwashers are 24 inches wide and are usually, built-in adjacent to the sink so that the plumbing connections are easily made. Dishwashers discharge the dirty water through the sink containing the garbage disposal. For older-style kitchens with no under counter space for a dishwasher, movable models are available that connect directly to the faucet in the sink and discharge directly into the sink. An undersink model is made by GE for small kitchens.

Available features in dishwashers include a heavy-duty cycle for cleaning heavily soiled pots and pans, a regular cycle for normal soil, rinse and hold for a small number of dishes requiring rinsing, and low-energy wash cycles.

If your utility offers lower off-peak rates, the delay-start feature may be desirable. Some models will display an alert message, such as "blocked wash arm" or "PF" should a power failure occur.

Dishes may be dried by the heated cycle or for energy efficiency, a no-heat drying cycle may be programmed. Most dishwashers require little or no rinsing of soiled dishes as a soft food disposer is built-in to newer dishwashers. Racks and even dividers are now adjustable, allowing for large size dishes or wider items that do not fit over the fixed dividers. Some dishwashers have a separate rack on top for silverware, making them easier to get at, easier to clean and more scratch resistant. Water-saver dishwashers are now available.

Trash Compactors

Trash compactors reduce trash volume by 80 percent in less than one minute. Most have some form of odor control and use a compacting ram with the force of approximately 3,000 pounds. In today's society, where trash disposal has become a very expensive service, trash compactors do reduce the volume of trash considerably but may make trash less biodegradable due to its compacted volume. Trash compactors vary in width from 12 to 18 inches.

Due to recycling laws, trash compactors are becoming obsolete as far as some designers are concerned.

KITCHEN SINKS

Kitchen sinks are constructed of stainless steel, enameled cast iron, or man-made materials. Each material has its own pros and cons. Stainless steel sinks give a very contemporary look to a kitchen and are less likely to break dishes that are accidentally dropped into them. However, any drop of water will leave a spot on the shiny surface. Also, heat from the hot water dissipates more rapidly with a metal sink than with a porcelain enamel one. When selecting a stainless steel sink, the lower the number of the gauge, the thicker the metal.

Porcelain enamel sinks do show stains more easily, and a scouring powder is usually required to remove such stains. The porcelain may become chipped when hit with a heavy object. However, enameled cast iron sinks do provide a colorful touch in the kitchen.

Some kitchen sinks, such as the stainless steel ones and those designed to be used with a metal rim, are flush with the counter. Any water spilled on the counter may be swept back into the sink. However, the self-rimming type are raised above the surface of the counter and any water spilled, must be mopped up (see a self-rimming sink in Figures 8–1 and 8–4). Kohler has introduced the Madrigal triple basin kitchen sink with wide 18–gauge stainless basins bonded to decks that come in eight colors. The Black Black™ deck looks very sophisticated with the black marble or granite solid surface materials.

Kitchen sinks come bored with three holes standard or four holes for a spray or soap dispenser.

American Standard has Americast, a structural composite porcelained enamel surface which is quiet. Sculptura® from Elkay also has a "quiet" sink (see Figure 8–1). There are several options as to size and shape in selection of kitchen sinks. Both stainless steel and porcelain enamel sinks are available with one, two, or three bowls. Single compartment models should be installed only where there is minimum space. One bowl models do not provide a second disposal area if the bowl is in use. Two-bowl models may be the same size and depth, or one bowl may be smaller and shallower. For corner installations there are even L-shaped double ones.

In triple sinks one of the bowls is usually shallower and smaller than the other two and may contain the garbage disposal unit. Some sinks with small bowls have a strainer to fit for draining pastas or cleaning off vegetables (see Figure 8–1).

Corian, when used as a material for kitchen sinks, may or may not be an integral part of the counter and is discussed on page 149 under Counters.

The width of a kitchen sink varies between 25 and 43 inches. Some with attached drainboards are almost 50 inches wide.

Accessories for sinks may include a fitted cutting board where waste material may be pushed off one corner into the sink. Also wire or plastic baskets for holding food or vegetables that require rinsing (see Figure 8–1).

Kitchen Faucets

Faucets constructed of chrome-plated steel should be all chrome-plated steel with no parts chrome-plated plastic as plating will gradually peel off with use. A mixing type of valve, where hot and cold may be blended with one handle, allows one-handed operation, which is useful when holding something in the other hand. One problem is that the handle may be accidentally turned on when in the hot position and a burn can occur.

Kohler has introduced the Epicure™ European style-kitchen faucet. The convenient high-arc swivel spout has an integral pull-out spray with retractable hose. Volume and temperature are controlled by a single-lever cartridge. It is available in chrome but also white, black, and almond. Also from Kohler is Finesse™, with blade handles and a MultiSwivel™ spout that directs water wherever desired; it may be used in kitchens or bathrooms (see Figure 8–6). Moen makes a chrome plated solid brass faucet called the Riser® Simply lift and the spout locks into its high-rise position more than 10 inches above the top of the sink. This extra height is useful for filling tall buckets, tall vases, and hair washing (see Figure 8–6).

A gooseneck faucet is also higher than normal and may be used for the kitchen, but is more frequently used in a bar sink (see Figure 8–6).

Several hot water dispensers on the market provide very hot water (about 190°) for use in making hot drinks and instant soups.

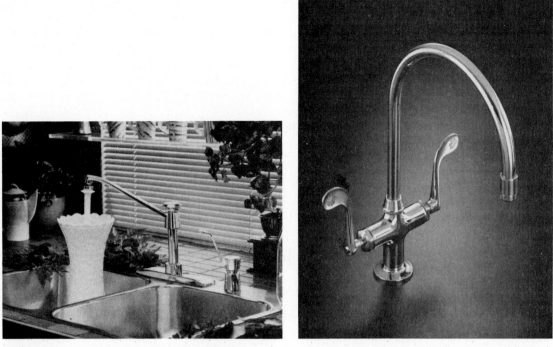

Figure 8-6
Kitchen faucets On the left the Riser® from Moen, which provides extra convenience with its adjustable heights. (Photograph courtesy of Moen, Inc.) On the right the Essex kitchen sink faucet with a 9-inch gooseneck swivel spout and easy-to-operate blade handles. Photograph courtesy of Kohler Co.

The extra hole in the sink may be used for filtered water when desired.

KITCHEN CABINETS

Kitchen cabinets come in 3-inch increments usually starting at 15 inches wide, and may be as wide as 48 inches. The depth of lower cabinets is 24 inches and the depth of upper cabinets is 12 inches. Filler strips are used between individual cabinets to make up any difference in measurements.

Kitchen cabinets are usually made of all wood or wood with decorative laminate doors. Some use a high density particleboard for the case and shelves; the edges are banded with a wood veneer that matches the door and drawer fronts. The color for the 1990s seems to be white in all types of cabinets. Under-cabinet appliances are also popular and clear the counter of clutter.

One of the many products available from the St. Charles Companies is the steel cabinet. Due to the strength of steel, the cabinets are thinner, taller, and feature an added shelf, hence more storage. They are resistant to temperature and humidity changes and won't twist, warp, swell, or absorb odors. The steel

cabinets are also available in hypo-allergenic material, which is important for those clients who need a chemical-free environment.

The kitchen is a very personal room and the style of cabinets selected should reflect the clients lifestyle. At one extreme are kitchens which have everything hidden from sight, in other words, behind solid doors and empty counters as seen in Figures 8–1, 8–5 and 8–7. The other extreme is the kitchen with raised panel doors, often shaped at the top, and shelves where personal collections and/or kitchen utensils are displayed. Glass doors should have glass shelves if displaying decorative items or the impact to the viewer is lost (see Figure 8–4). Glass doors also require some thought as to what is going to be visible. Another style of kitchen is where open shelves are used for the storage of dishes and glasses and a pantry is used for food storage. Most kitchens fall somewhere between these extremes but should be personalized for the client.

Wood cabinets may have flush overlay, reveal overlay or, for more traditional styles, an exposed frame with a lipped door. The face surface of the door may be plane, have a flat or raised panel, or have mouldings applied for a traditional approach. Contemporary kitchens have not only flush overlay

Figure 8-7
Kitchen Designer, Donna Bent, ASID, won First Place—Residential, in the 1990 ASID DU PONT "Corian" National Design Competition. The creative applications of Cameo White CORIAN in an all-white kitchen include custom-crafted wine rack, backlit valance above range, and a triple-depth eating bar with radius edges evocative of cabinetry. On the left, the counter was integrally seamed to the double-bowl sink. Architect Interior Designer: Michael J. Macaluso, ASID; Kitchen Interior: Donna Bent, ASID. Photograph courtesy of the Du Pont Company.

doors, but flush overlay in combination with linear metal or wood decorative strips that also function as drawer and door pulls. The traditional front frame construction and the European-style frameless construction are both popular. Shelves in all cabinets should be fully adjustable to accommodate the needs of the user.

Many special features may be ordered for the custom-designed kitchen. These will add to the cost of the installation but may be ordered to fit the personal and budgetary needs of the client. Base sliding shelves make all items visible, which eliminates getting down on hands and knees to see what is at the bottom of a base unit. A bread box may be contained within a drawer with a lid to help maintain

freshness. A cutting board, usually made of maple, that slides out from the upper part of a base unit is convenient and will help protect the surface of the counter from damage.

Lazy susans in corner units or doors with attached swing-out shelves both utilize the storage area of a corner unit. Another use for the corner unit is to install a 20 gallon water heater, thus providing instant hot water for the kitchen sink and the electric dishwasher, and prevent waste of water. A second water heater can then be installed close to the bathrooms for energy conservation and to avoid those long waits for the hot water to reach the bathroom lavatory.

Dividers in drawers aid in drawer organization

and vertical dividers in upper or base units utilize space by arranging larger and flat items in easily visible slots, thus avoiding nesting.

Bottle storage units have frames to contain bottles. Spice storage may be attached to the back of an upper door, built into a double-door unit or utilize a special spice drawer insert allowing seasonings to be easily visible. Hot pads may be stored in a narrow drawer under a built-in cooktop. A tilt-down sink front may hold sponges, scouring pads, etc. Wire or plastic-coated baskets for fruit and vegetable storage provide easily visible storage. A wastebasket, either attached to a swing-out door, a tilt-down door or sliding out from under the sink, also provides a neat and out-of-sight trash container.

Appliance garages are built-in to the back of the counter and enclose mixers, blenders, etc. The garage may have tambour doors or may match the cabinets (see Figures 8–1 and 8–7).

Portable recycling units have been on the market for some time, but some states and cities have comprehensive recycling laws, and cabinet makers, both custom and even stock cabinetry now have multibasket units, with the four-unit being most popular.

The recommendation is to put one single unit near the sink for compostables and then away from the food preparation area two others, one for aluminum cans and the other for bottles.

Check local building codes as to whether some type of venting is necessary for the cabinet under the sink.

COUNTER MATERIALS

Counters may be of the following materials: decorative laminate, wood, ceramic tile, marble, travertine, solid surface materials, stainless steel, granite, or slate.

Decorative Laminate

Decorative laminate is the most commonly used counter material. The construction is exactly the same as the material used for walls. For counter top use, two thicknesses are available; a choice of one or the other depends on the type of counter construction. For square-edged counters, the general purpose grade is used. If it is necessary to roll the laminate on a simple radius over the edges of the substrate, a **post-forming** type is specified. The post-forming method eliminates a seam, or brown line at the edge of the counter. Another method of eliminating the brown line is to use one of the "colorthrough" laminates.

Installation. Postformed counter tops must be constructed at the plant rather than at the job site, as heat and special forming fixtures are used to create the curved edge. The counter may be manufactured as a single unit, or each postformed side may be manufactured separately. By manufacturing each side separately, any discrepancy in the alignment of the walls can be adjusted at the corner joints.

Self-edged counters may be constructed on the job site in the following manner: a particleboard, plywood, or flake board substrate is cut to cover the countertop area. An equal thickness strip is glued to the underside of the front edge of the countertop to build up the counter thickness. Narrow strips of laminate are then cut slightly wider than the edge. An adhesive (contact cement) is spread on both the counter edge and the back of the strips and allowed to dry according to instructions on the adhesive container. The strips are then carefully positioned so that the lower edge is flush with the bottom and the top edge extends slightly above the edge of the counter. As bonding is immediate, it is important that the two surfaces do not touch until properly aligned. A router is then used to cut away the excess laminate. The color of the laminate may be the same as the top surface or contrasting.

Another method of finishing off the edge of the counter is by using the Wood Profiles or the Perma-Edge® bevel mouldings from Wilsonart. (See Figure 8–1 for wood profile and Figure 8–8 for edge treatments.) Perma-Tiers® is a sandwich edging that gives a pin stripe look.

Because the surface of the counter is very large, a slightly different method of application is used. The counter area and the back of the laminate are covered with the recommended adhesive. When the adhesive is dry, dowels are placed on top of the counter area, and the laminate is carefully positioned on top of the dowels. When properly placed with the front edge extending over the previously installed edge, the dowels are carefully removed, the counter and laminate become bonded. A secure bond is established by applying firm pressure with roller or hard wood blocks and hammer. The excess at the front is then trimmed with the router.

A decorative laminate surface is durable, but it is not a cutting surface and will chip if heavy objects are dropped onto it.

For areas where chemical spills or other destructive or staining substances may be used, a chemical

Perma-Edge Laminate Clad Moldings

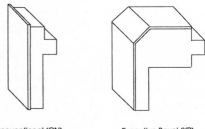

Conventional (CN)   Executive Bevel (XP)

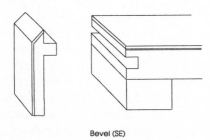

Bevel (SE)

Perma-Edge Wood Profiles

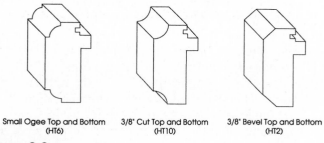

Small Ogee Top and Bottom (HT6)   3/8" Cut Top and Bottom (HT10)   3/8" Bevel Top and Bottom (HT2)

Wood Profiles With Laminate Or Metal Inserts Grooves

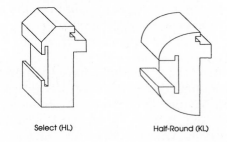

Select (HL)   Half-Round (KL)

Figure 8-8
Wilsonart Edge treatments.

and stain resistant laminate may be specified. Specific uses are chemistry laboratory tops, photographic lab tops, medical and pathology labs and clinics.

For high use, and heavy wear areas such as fast food counter tops, supermarket check-out stands or bank service areas, a .125-inch thickness of decorative laminate is available.

Maintenance. Decorative laminate may be cleaned with warm water and mild dish soaps. Use of abrasives or "special" cleansers should be avoided because they may contain abrasives, acids, or alkalines. Stubborn stains may be removed with organic solvents or two minutes exposure to a hypochlorite bleach such as Clorox, followed by a clean water rinse. Consult manufacturers for specific instructions and recommendations.

Wood

Wood counters are usually made of a hard wood such as birch or maple and are constructed of glued up strips of wood that are then usually sealed and coated with a varnish. Unsealed wood will permanently absorb stains. Wood counters should not be used as a cutting surface because the finish will become marred. Any water accumulating around the sink should be mopped up immediately; the surface can become damaged from prolonged contact with moisture.

Wood counters may be installed in a curved shape by successively adding a strip of wood, gluing, and clamping it. When dry, another piece is added.

Ceramic Tile

Ceramic tile has become a very popular material with which to cover kitchen counters. To facilitate cleaning, the **backsplash** may also be covered with tile. Ceramic tile is a very durable surface, but the most vulnerable part is the grout, which will absorb stains, unless a stain-proof grout is specified. A grout sealer or lemon furniture oil will also seal the surface of the grout so that stains will not penetrate.

Due to the hard surface of the tile, fragile items that are dropped on the counter will break and, if heavy objects are dropped, the tile may be cracked or broken. Always order sufficient tile for replacements (see Figures 8–4 for ceramic tile counter).

Installation. When installing a ceramic tile counter, it is recommended that an exterior grade plywood be used as the substrate. The remaining installation procedure is the same as for floors and walls.

Maintenance. Same as for ceramic tile floors.

Marble

In the past, marble was used as a material for portions of the countertop. Today in some expensive installations, marble may be used for the whole counter area. Some people like to use a marble surface for rolling out of pastry or making hand dipped chocolates. As was seen in the marble floor section, marble may absorb stains, and cause unsightly blemishes on the counter. Heavy items dropped on a marble surface will crack it.

Maintenance. Stain removal is the same as for marble floors.

Travertine

When travertine is used as a counter material, it must be filled. Maintenance is the same as for marble.

Solid Surface Materials

"Corian" is a one-of-a-kind material invented by Du Pont that combines the smoothness of marble, the solid feel of granite and the workability of wood. "Corian" is available in sheets of 1/4–, 1/2–, and 3/4-inch thicknesses and in a wide variety of double and single-bowl kitchen sinks and lavatory styles. Nonporous, highly resistant to abuse; even cigarette burns, stains and scratches can be removed with household cleanser or a Scotch-Brite® pad.

Thicker, built-up edges, made using joint adhesive, can be routed into a variety of decorative treatments, including bull-nose edges and 'sandwich' inserts. Figure 8–9 shows some of the ways in which "Corian" counters may be finished. Solid surface manufacturers may be able to supply custom colors for large projects.

GIBRALTAR® from Wilsonart is the latest addition to the solid surface market. This company has made their colored GIBRALTAR to exactly match their laminates so a co-ordinated look can be obtained although different materials are being used.

The edges of solid surface materials may be shaped like wood. Figure 8–9 shows some of the many ways in which the edge of a Corian counter may be finished.

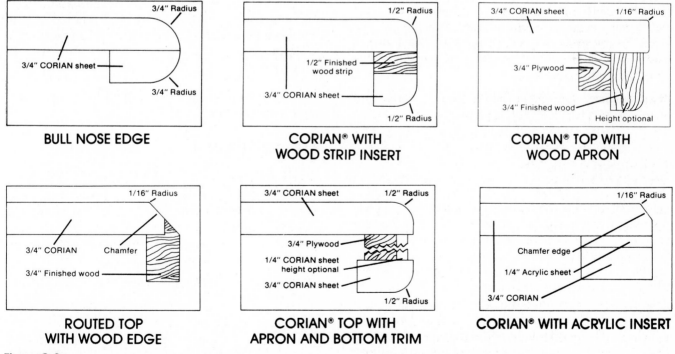

BULL NOSE EDGE

CORIAN® WITH WOOD STRIP INSERT

CORIAN® TOP WITH WOOD APRON

ROUTED TOP WITH WOOD EDGE

CORIAN® TOP WITH APRON AND BOTTOM TRIM

CORIAN® WITH ACRYLIC INSERT

Figure 8-9
Edge treatments for Corian® countertops. (Photograph courtesy of E. I. DuPont de Nemours & Company.)

Maintenance. Most stains just wipe right off with a regular household detergent. Due to the solid composition of these materials, most stains stay on the surface and may be removed with any household abrasive cleanser or Scotch-Brite® pad gently rubbed in a circular motion. Cigarette burns and cuts may be removed with very fine sandpaper, 120–140 grit; then use the Scotch-Brite pad as above. If the surface was highly polished it may need repolishing to blend the damaged area.

Stainless Steel

All commercial kitchens have stainless steel counters because they can withstand scouring, boiling water, and hot pans. Stainless steel counters can be installed in private residences, if desired, providing a high-tech look.

Maintenance. One of the problems with stainless steel is that the surface shows water spots and may scratch. However, scratches gradually blend into a patina and water spots may be removed by rubbing the damp surface with a towel. Apart from the spots and possible scratches, stainless steel is extremely easy to maintain.

Granite and Slate

Both these stones may be used as counter materials if desired, although construction of the cabinets must be strong enough to support the extra weight. As noted in the floor chapter, these stones vary in porosity, and care should be taken to prevent stains from penetrating the surface.

Maintenance. The same as for granite walls and slate floors.

Floors

Kitchen floors may be ceramic tile, quarry tile, wood, or any of the resilient floorings. The choice of flooring will depend on the client's needs and personal wishes. Some people find a hard-surfaced floor to be tiring to the feet, while others are not bothered at all. Ceramic tile on the floor is shown in Figures 8–1, 8–5, and 8–7. Wood floors need to be finished with a very durable finish that will withstand any moisture which may be accidentally spilled. Resilient flooring may be vinyl, cushioned or not, or the new rubber sheet flooring.

Walls

Walls should be painted with an enamel that is easily cleansed of any grease residue. The backsplash may be covered with the same decorative laminate used on the counter, either with a cove or a square joint (see Figure 8–7). Ceramic tile may be used in conjunction with a ceramic tile counter (see Figure 8–4), or it may be used with a decorative laminate. Mirror may also be selected for walls which provides reflected light and visually enlarges the appearance of the counter space. A completely scrubbable wallcovering may also be used for the backsplash.

Certified Kitchen Designers

A **certified kitchen designer (CKD)** is a professional who has proved knowledge and technical understanding through a very stringent examination process conducted by the Society of Certified Kitchen Designers, the licensing and certification agency of the American Institute of Kitchen Dealers. A CKD has technical knowledge of construction techniques and systems regarding new construction and light exterior and interior remodeling which includes plumbing, heating, and electrical.

A CKD will provide a functional and aesthetically pleasing arrangement of space with floor plans and interpretive renderings and drawings. In addition to designing and planning the kitchen, the CKD also supervises the installations of residential-style kitchens.

An interior designer would be well advised to work with a CKD.

BIBLIOGRAPHY

Jen-Air Company. *Four types of Electric Cooktops*. Indianapolis IN 1985

Jen-Air Company. *Solid Element Cooktops*. Indianapolis IN 1985

General Electric Company. *How to buy a Dishwasher*. Louisville KY 1984

General Electric Company. *How to buy a Microwave*. Louisville KY 1984

General Electric Company. *How to buy a Range*. Louisville KY 1984

General Electric Company. *How to buy a Refrigerator*. Louisville KY 1984

GLOSSARY

Catalytic. A porous ceramic finish that accelerates the dispersion of food spatters.

Charcoal filter. A frame that contains charcoal particles that filter the grease from the moving air.

Convection oven. Heated air flows around the food.

Conventional oven. Food is cooked by radiation.

Corridor kitchen. Two parallel walls with no contiguous area. See Figures 8–1 and 8–2.

Dolly. Two- or four-wheeled cart used for moving heavy appliances.

Drop-in range. Ranges designed to be built-in to the base units.

Free-standing range. Ranges having finished sides.

Glass-ceramic. A smooth ceramic top used as a cooking surface in electric ranges.

Griddle. A unit with a flat cooking surface used for cooking pancakes.

Grille. A unit specially for broiling food.

Hob. Sealed solid element providing a larger contact area with the bottom of the pan and better control at low-heat settings.

Kilowatthour. A unit of energy equal to 1,000 watt hours. Abbreviation: kwh.

Microwave oven. Heat is generated by the activation of the molecules within the food by the microwaves.

Post-forming. Heating a laminate to take the shape of a form.

Pullman kitchen. A one-wall kitchen plan. See Figure 8–2.

Pyrolytic action. An oven that cleans by extremely high heat, incinerating any residue to an ash.

Rotisserie. An electrical accessory that rotates the food on a spit or skewer.

Shish-Kebab. A rotisserie accessory combining alternate small pieces of meat and vegetables on a skewer or spit.

Slide-in range. Similar in construction to a drop-in range except that the top edges may overhang the sides and therefore, this type must be slid in rather than dropped-in.

Strip kitchen. One-wall kitchen plan (see Figure 8–2).

Studio kitchen. Also a one-wall kitchen plan (see Figure 8–2).

Work triangle. An imaginary triangle drawn between the sink, refrigerator, and cooking area.

9

Bathrooms

The Greeks had many large public baths where one could take a hot and cold bath and then get a rubdown with olive oil. Public bathing was also practiced by the Romans. The Romans used aqueducts to bring the water to the people of Rome. After the influence of the Romans was lost, very few people bathed in the Dark Ages. In the 1800s and early 1900s, one often reads of the ritual of the Saturday night bath, where a metal tub was brought into the heated kitchen and hot water was poured in by hand. The last 25 years have produced almost 90 percent of all the progress in bathrooms.

It was the American hotels that started the idea of bathing rooms, and the first one was built at the Tremont House in Boston in 1829. The idea proved very popular and spread to other hotels and private homes throughout the country. As a nation, Americans take more baths and showers than any other people in the world. The realities of the 1990s, however, include both energy and water conservation.

As all bathrooms have the same three basic fixtures, it is the designer's challenge to create a bathroom that is not only unique but functional. A knowledge of the different materials used in these fixtures and the variety of shapes, sizes, and colors will help solve this challenge.

PLANNING A BATHROOM

Eljer has the following suggestions for planning a better bathroom. First, the size of the family needs to be considered. The more people who will use a bathroom, the larger it should be. There should also be more storage, more electrical outlets and, perhaps, more fixtures. If the bathroom is to be used by several people at the same time, compartmenting can often add to utility.

The family schedule should also be considered. Where several people depart for work or school at the same time, multiple or **compartmented** bathrooms should be considered. Two lavatories will allow a working couple to get ready for work at the same time.

The most economical arrangement of fixtures is against a single **wet wall**. Economy, however, is not the only factor to be considered. Plumbing codes, human comfort, and convenient use require certain minimum separation between, and space around, fixtures. The minimum size for a bathroom is approximately 5 feet by 7 feet, although if absolutely necessary, a few inches may be shaved off these

153

Figure 9-1

Jack Lowery, FASID, New York, has created a soothing solarium bath of mirror and marble. The black 'ribs' of the shower enclosure are echoed in the armature of the glass roof. Fixtures used include: Arabesque™ pedestal lavatory, San Raphael™ Water-Guard toilet and San Tropez™ bidet. Deck mounted Cygnet™ bath spout, shower faucet, lavatory faucet and bidet faucet, all with cylindrical handles in black. Photograph courtesy of Kohler Co.

measurements. De luxe bathrooms may be very large and incorporate an exercise room and/or **spa** (Figure 9–1).

In a corridor-type bathroom, there should be 30 inches of aisle space between the bathtub and the edge of the counter or fixture opposite. The bathtub should never be placed under the window because this will create too many problems—lack of privacy, drafts, condensation on the window, and possible damage to the wall when using a shower. There should be a minimum of 24 inches in front of a toilet to provide knee room. When there are walls on either side of the toilet, they should be 36 inches apart. If the **lavatory** or bathtub is adjacent to the toilet, then 30 inches is sufficient.

The lavatory requires elbow space. Five feet is the recommended minimum length of a counter top with two lavatories. The lavatories should be centered in the respective halves of the counter top. For a sit-down **vanity**, make the counter 7 feet long and allow 24 inches between the edges of the lavatories for greatest comfort. Six inches minimum should be allowed between the edge of a lavatory and any side wall.

All bathroom fixtures, whether tubs, lavatories, toilets, or **bidets**, come in white, and also in standard colors which are 20 percent more expensive. High-fashion colors—even black—are 40 percent more expensive than white. Care should be taken not to select fad colors that will become dated because bathroom fixtures are both difficult and expensive to replace when remodeling. In order to obtain a perfect match, all fixtures should be ordered from the same manufacturer. Colors, even white, vary from one manufacturer to another.

Some manufacturers are working together to produce a color-coordinated look in the bathroom. The Kohler Color Coordinates (KCC) program is easy to use. Once the color family has been selected, the KCC literature provides the key decorating elements

Figure 9-2
The bold geometric design of Kohler's "Cactus Cutter™" Artist Editions fixtures, combined with the designer's memories of a trip to Japan determined the theme for this room in the Kohler Design Center. Joe Hamm, ASID, repeated the geometric design of the fixtures in the half kimona rug and the Oriental "lanterns" which frame the mirrors. Kohler's Finesse™ faucet in polished chrome accent the lavatory. Photograph courtesy of Kohler Co.

for the bathroom. Vinyl flooring from Armstrong World Industries; Broan/Nautilus bath cabinets; ceramic tile from Dal-Tile, Kohler plumbing fixtures; laminates and solid surfacing materials from Nevamar Corporation; and wallcoverings from Village Wallcovering.

The location of the door is extremely important. The door should be located in such a manner that it will not hit a fixture because it will eventually cause damage both to the door and the fixture. A sliding pocket door may have to be used to prevent this from happening.

Floors

Bathroom floors should be of a type that can be easily cleaned, particularly in the area of the bathtub, shower,

and toilet. Ceramic tile may be used but should not be highly glazed because glazed tiles when used on a floor, can be very slippery when wet. Other types of flooring material for the tub area can be wood with a good finish or any of the resilient flooring materials.

Carpeting may be used in the master bath, but is not suggested for a family bath because of a likelihood of excessive moisture, causing possible mold and mildew.

Walls

The bathroom is an area in the house where wallcoverings are often used. Vinyls or vinyl-coated wallcoverings are suggested because they are easy to wipe dry and maintain. Again, due to the moisture problem, the walls should be treated for possible mildew (see Chapter 4 page 77).

Only semigloss paints or enamels that can withstand moisture should be used on bathroom walls.

If an acrylic shower and tub surround is not used, ceramic tile is installed because of its vitreous quality.

Bathtubs

The average bathtub is 5 feet long, 30 inches wide and, in less expensive styles, only 14 inches deep. However, 6-foot long tubs are available for those who like to soak and the height, measured from the floor, may also be 15, 16, or even 22 inches. When bathing children the lower height is more convenient. However, the depth figures are the outside measurements and, making allowance for the **overflow** pipe, the 14 inches does not permit the drawing of a very deep bath. Many state laws require that all bathtubs installed today have a **slip resistant** bottom. Many tubs also come with a handle on one or both sides, which is extremely useful for the elderly or infirm. See Figure 9–3.

The straight end of the bathtub contains the drain and the plumbing, such as faucets or **fittings** as they are sometimes called, and the overflow pipe; therefore, location of the bathtub must be decided before the order is placed. Bathtubs may be ordered with left or right drain, all four sides enclosed, enclosed on the front and two sides, front and one side, or for a completely built-in look, a drop-in model may be specified.

The drop-in model is sometimes installed as a sunken tub. While this may present a luxurious appearance, thought must be given to the problem of getting into and out of a tub that low. Thought must also be given to maintenance. Cleaning a sunken tub means lying flat on the floor to reach the interior. Another danger of a sunken or partially recessed tubs is that small children may crawl into the bathtub and hurt themselves or, at the worst, drown.

Construction. Bathtubs are manufactured of several materials. The old standby is the porcelain enameled cast-iron tub. This was originally a high-sided bathtub raised from the floor on ball-and-claw feet with the underside exposed. This style is still available today in a slightly modernized version. The porcelain enamel, gives better color than other materials and

Figure 9-3
The Impromptu whirlpool offers comfortable seating for two in a compact five-foot length. The Twist Grab Bar and deck-mounted filler spout add a sculptured elegance. Ceramic tile is from Walker & Zanger Inc. Photograph courtesy of American Standard.

is approximately 1/16 of an inch thick, but this finish can be chipped if a heavy object is dropped onto it. Therefore, bathtubs should be kept covered with a blanket, or a special plastic liner may be used until construction has been completed.

A cast-iron bathtub is the most durable bathtub available but it is expensive and heavy; it weighs about 500 pounds. Therefore, the floor should be strong enough to bear the combined weight of the tub, a tub full of water, and the bather.

Formed steel tubs with a porcelain enamel finish were developed to provide a lightweight (about 100 pounds) tub that would be less expensive than cast iron. They are ideally suited for upper story installations or for remodeling because they are easier to move into place. A formed steel tub is noisier than the cast iron, but a sound-deadening coating may be applied to the underside at extra cost. Or, if the bathtub does not come with an insulated coating on the outside, a roll of fiberglass insulation can be wrapped around the tub. It not only helps the fixture retain the heat longer, but also helps reduce noise. Due to the properties of the steel, formed steel bathtubs may flex, and, therefore, they do not have such a thick layer of porcelain enamel as do cast-iron tubs.

One of the newer materials for bathtubs is heavy-duty polyester reinforced with fiberglass and surfaced with a **gel** coat. In specifying this type of tub, it is important to select a name brand. As there are currently many poor quality units on the market produced by a process that does not require a large investment, this field has many manufacturers, not all of whom are conscious of quality. Consequently, the tubs can crack easily and lose their surface fairly rapidly. Good maintenance practices and avoidance of abrasive cleansers is mandatory. Should the gel coat surface become dull in appearance, some manufacturers suggest using a coat of marine wax or a good automotive wax to restore the shine.

Another type of lightweight bathtub is acrylic reinforced with fiberglass with the color throughout. This type of bathtub does not have such a high gloss as the gel coated ones, but, it is easier to maintain and the color does not fade.

There are several advantages to this new material. First, it is much lighter weight than steel or cast iron, though maybe not as durable. Second, the tub **surround** can be cast as an integral part of the bathtub and can include such features as a built-in seat, soap ledges, and grab bars. This latter type can be installed only in new construction because the tub and surround are too large to be placed in a remodeled bathroom. For remodeling, there are molded tub units with wall surrounds in two, three, or four pieces that pass easily through doorways and join together in the recessed bathtub area to form a one-piece unit.

Soaking tubs are also made from reinforced fiberglass. Instead of sitting or laying in the tub, one sits on a molded, built-in seat and the tub is filled to the requisite depth. Some soaking tubs are recessed into the floor and one steps over the edge and down into the tub; others are placed at floor level and require several steps to reach the top. Soaking tubs should not be installed in every bathroom in the house, as bathing small children is impossible and the elderly or infirm will find entering and leaving a soaking tub too dangerous. A regular bathtub should be installed in at least one bathroom in the house.

Whirlpool baths are generally bathroom fixtures; they must be drained after each use. Jacuzzi® whirlpool bath has a high-gloss acrylic, fiberglass reinforced whirlpool bathtub with built-in patented jets. These whirlpool jets create a circular pattern of bubbles as the air/water mixture flows into the tub providing luxurious, deeply penetrating massage. Jacuzzi whirl pool baths come in one-person sizes (60 to 72 inches long by 30 to 42 inches wide and 18 to 20 inches high) and two-person or family sizes (60 to 72 inches long by 48 to 66 inches wide by 20 to 23–1/2 inches high. Most major manufacturers produce similar whirlpool-type tubs (see Figures 9–1 and 9–3).

Spas are similar to whirlpool baths but need not be drained after each use. They are equipped with heat and filtration systems. Since the same water is recirculated, daily testing and maintenance of the proper water chemistry is required. Spas may be installed outside in warmer climates or in an area other than the bathroom. They have many of the same features of the whirlpool baths but are larger, being 64 to 84 inches long 66 to 84 inches wide and 28 to 37 inches high. Spas come with factory installed redwood skirts and rigid covers.

Tub surrounds and shower enclosures may also be of reinforced fiberglass, as mentioned previously, or they may be of decorative laminate, ceramic tile, solid ABS, or solid acrylic. Many of these have integrated tubs with built-in whirlpool systems. The all-in-one type eliminates the need to caulk around the area where the tub and surround meet. Failure to install and caulk tub surround properly is the major cause of leaks in the tub area. When designing a bathroom, the bathtub should be placed where an access panel can be installed to facilitate future plumbing repairs. Access must also be provided to any whirlpool equipment to facilitate future maintenance.

Ceramic tile is installed as described in the chapter on walls. The substrate must be exterior grade plywood or a special water-resistant grade of gypsum board. The backer board mentioned in Chapter 3 also makes a suitable substrate. Particular attention must be paid to the application of the grout, as it is the grout that makes ceramic tile a waterproof material. Sometimes, particularly when a cast-iron tub is used, the extra weight may cause a slight sagging of the floor. Any space caused by this settling should be filled immediately.

Showers

Showers may be installed for use in a bathtub or they may be in a separate shower stall. There should always be at least one bathtub in a house, but stall showers may be used in the remaining bathrooms. When used in conjunction with a bathtub, the tub spout contains a **diverter** that closes off the spout and diverts the water to the shower head. A bathroom with a shower instead of a tub is designated as a three-quarter bath.

The standard height of a shower head is 66 inches for men and 60 inches for women, which puts the spray below the hairline. These measurements also mean that the plumbing for the shower head must break through the tub or shower surround. Therefore, it is recommended that the shower **feed-in** be at 74 inches above the floor. When placed at this height, the shower head should be adjustable so that it can be used for hairwashing or hit below the hairline.

A hand-held shower can easily be installed in any bathtub, provided the walls are covered with a waterproof material. These showers come with a special diversion spout and the water reaches the shower head by means of a flexible metal line. One type of shower head is hung on a hook at the required height. The second type is mounted on a 5-foot vertical rod and attached to the water outlet by means of a flexible hose. This full-range sliding spray holder or grab bar locks at any desired height. The spray holder is both adjustable and removable.

There are several positive attributes of the hand-held shower. One is that it can be hung at a lower level for use by children, and the hand-held unit can be used to rinse the hair of young children without the complaint of "the soap is getting in my eyes." A second factor is that the hand unit may be used to clean and rinse the interior of the bathtub.

Stall showers are 34 by 32 inches wide; a slightly larger 36 inch square is recommended if space is available. These are the minimum requirements and of course, the deluxe shower may be 48 inches or even 60 by 36 inches wide and usually has a seat. Stall showers may be constructed entirely of ceramic tile; in other words, the slightly sloping base and walls are all made of tile. When installing a shower area made from ceramic tile, particular attention should be paid to the waterproof base and installation procedures supplied by the manufacturer or the Tile Council of America. Other stall showers have a **preformed base** with the surround touching the top of the 5 to 6-inch deep base. This preformed base is less slippery than a base of tile but not quite as aesthetically pleasing. Shower walls may also be constructed of any of the solid surface materials.

Water is kept within the shower area by several means. One is the shower curtain which is hung from rings at the front of the shower. A shower curtain is a decorative feature but, unless care is taken to ensure the placement of the shower curtain inside the base when using the shower, water may spill over onto the floor and cause a slippery area. Glass shower doors are also used, the type depending upon the local building codes (see Figure 9–1). All have tempered glass, but some codes require the addition of a wire mesh. These glass doors may pivot, hinge, slide, or fold. The major maintenance problem with glass doors is removing the soap and hard water residue from the glass surface and cleaning the water channel at the base of the door.

A water softener does greatly reduce or even eliminate this residue. Some bathtub/shower units are designed with close fitting doors that completely enclose the front of the unit and become steam systems with a **sauna** effect.

Masterbath showers often are designed so that no door or curtain is required. These shower stalls have walls so placed that the water is contained within the wet area.

The Freewill™ line of barrier-free bathing products from Kohler are designed to meet the strict ANSI standards, with slip-resistant bottom for safety and grab bars fabricated of rigid nylon to provide a firm grip even when wet. It features a removable transfer seat so that bathers can sit down and swing legs over the edge of the tub, instead of stepping into it. The fold-up seats make them ideal for installation in a residence where one family member may have limited mobility, but the others need no special assistance (see Figure 9–4).

Wheelchair accessible stall showers are available

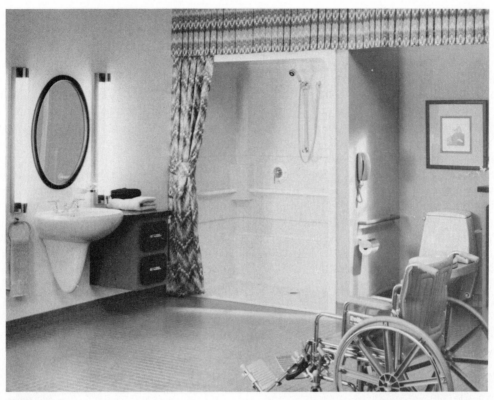

Figure 9-4
Wheelchair-accessible shower Kohler's Freewill™ line of barrier-free bathing units. On the left is a wall-hung Chablis™ lavatory and Wellesley™ toilet. Both can be installed at the height most convenient for the user. The easy-to-use lever-handled faucets are from the Kohler's IV Georges collection. Photograph courtesy of Kohler Co.

varying in size from 42 inch by 36 inch to the 65 inch by 36 inch unit with an interior threshold height of only 1/2 inch (see Figure 9–4). Units with integral seats have the seat placed toward the front of the enclosure for easier access.

Kohler produces a Masterbath Series, personal and programmable retreats that combine the soothing elements of sun, sauna, steam, shower, and warm breezes with the added relaxation of a spacious whirlpool bath. The size of the unit itself measures 91 by 52 by 82 inches with the whirlpool bath measuring 66 by 19 1/2 by 33 inches. However, the recess area must be 96 by 106 by 94 inches in order to accommodate the necessary equipment. The luxury Environment™ features an upholstered deck, 24–carat gold trim, and genuine teakwood interior-the ultimate in sybaritic pleasure. The Habitat™ Masterbath has the same functional features as the Environment Masterbath, but the interior is acrylic instead of teak, has chrome interior trim, and comes in 16 Kohler colors. The padded deck is optional.

Tub and Shower Faucets

The old-fashioned type of faucet is ledge mounted: the fitting is mounted on the edge of the tub or tub enclosure, usually with an 8- to 18-inch **spread**.

Tub/shower combinations may be of five different types. Two of them are wall mounted, including the single control which is operated by pulling to turn on, pushing to turn off, and twisting to regulate the temperature. The single control may be operated with one hand. The other wall mounted type has separate handles for hot and cold water. An 8-inch spread is standard.

Diverters include the diverter-on-spout where, when the water temperature is balanced, the diverter is pulled up to start the shower. To stop the flow of water to the shower head, the diverter is pushed down. The handle diverter design has three handles and, by twisting the middle handle, the water is diverted to the shower head. The two other handles control the hot and cold water. This handle diverter has 8-inch **centers**. The button diverter is often found on single control faucets where, by merely pushing the button, water is diverted.

Epic has created a new fast flowing Roman tub valve that features 27 gallons per minute at 40 pounds per square inch (psi), using 1/2-inch supply lines. This enable whirlpool baths to be filled rapidly provided a large capacity water tank is used.

For stall showers, the controls may be single control similar in action to the single control bath type. The second design has two separate hot and cold handles with a standard 8-inch spread.

Jacuzzi Whirlpool Bath has the new "J-Dream" a multifunctional whirlpool shower, with 16 multi-level jets, a cascading waterfall, an adjustable-height shower with three power levels and a shower seat. The fixture can also be used as a steam bath.

Most shower heads are adjustable and change the flow of water to drenching, normal, or fine spray. Some shower heads have a pulsating flow that provides a massaging action. Conventional shower heads use from 6 to 8 gallons per minute. With conservation of water in mind, the plumbing codes are being amended to make 2.7 gallons of water per minute at 60 psi. the maximum amount of water that can be used.

For a children's bathroom, Grohe America has shower heads featuring Disney characters.

Lavatories

Lavatories come in many sizes, shapes and materials according to personal and space requirements. Some are **pedestal** lavatories and may be as streamlined or decorative as desired (see Figures 9–1 and 9–5). Most are made of vitreous china, but some pedestals are even sculpted out of marble. Besides being made out of china, lavatories may be made from enameled cast iron, enameled formed steel, polished brass (see Figure 9–6) or some of the solid surface materials.

Lavatories are usually round or oval, but they may also be rectangular, or even triangular for corner

Figure 9-5
Left, inspired by the Victorian era, Sherle Wagner imparts a treasured old world feeling to a porcelain washstand. The graceful shaping of the top and its generous dimensions leave ample room for very special accessories. Pictured with rodocrosite spread-fit fixtures. (Photograph courtesy of Sherle Wagner International Inc.) Right, "Washmobil P" a colorful washbasin which is wall-hang with arched mirror, utility shelf, towel bars, and soap and tumbler holders. (Photograph courtesy of Hastings Tile and Il Bagno Collection.)

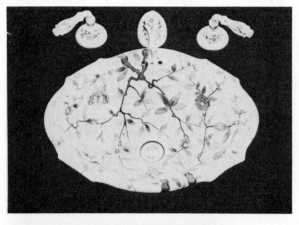

Figure 9-6

Top left is Summer Garden, a handpainted over edge porcelain bowl and top right is Ming Blossom showing the contrast of white ming blossoms on vibrant blue, an under edge china bowl set into a marble counter. Photographs courtesy of Sherle Wagner International Inc. Bottom, the Terragon™ lavatory a 20 inches by 16 inches hexagon with self-rimming design and five sculpted tiers leading to a flat bottom. Cast in solid red brass and polished to a high glass, shown with the Cygnet™ lavatory faucet by Kohler. (Photograph courtesy of Kohler Company.)

installations. Sizes range from 11 by 11 inches for powder rooms, to 38 by 28 inches for hair washing and other washing chores.

The pedestal lavatories are the latest style of lavatory to be used, but are probably more suitable in a master bathroom because there is no adjacent counter area usually needed in family bathrooms. To overcome this lack, some pedestal lavatories come as large as 44 by 22 inches, with a wide ledge surrounding the bowl area (see Figure 9–5).

Built-in lavatories may be one of five types. First, they may be self-rimming, where a hole is cut into the counter smaller than the size of the lavatory and the bowl is placed in such a manner that the edge is raised above the level of the counter. With a self-rimming sink, water cannot be swept back into the bowl but must be mopped up (see Figure 9–6).

Second, for a flush counter and bowl installation, the lavatory may be installed with a flush metal rim. This is a popular and inexpensive style but does cause a cleaning problem at the junctures of the rim with the countertop.

Third is the integral bowl and counter such as those made of the solid surface materials. With this type, which may be placed virtually anywhere on the vanity top, the countertop and bowl are integrally seamed for a one-piece look.

A fourth type is the more old-fashioned wall-hung installation that is quite often used in powder rooms or for wheelchair users (see Figure 9–2). The fifth type is installed under-the-counter and is generally used with a tile, marble, or synthetic counter top. With more types of solid surface materials being available, the under the counter installation is becoming very popular. Under-the-counter installations require that the fittings be deck mounted.

A specialty item in the way of a lavatory is the solid brass self rimming bowl, which adds a special elegant look to a bathroom. For a unique lavatory, a self-rimming painted ceramic washbasin may be used (see Figure 9–6).

All lavatories come punched with at least three holes. With single control fittings and 4 inch centerset fittings, the third hole is for the **pop-up** rod. However, in wide-spread fittings, the third hole is used for the mixed water.

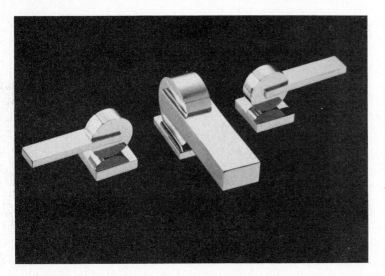

Figure 9-7
Top. The Antares Lavatory set from the Greenwich Collection by Paul Associates. The Antares design comes with one-quarter turn ceramic disc cartridges and Paul Associates' new "Quik-Prep" valving system for simplified installation. (Photograph courtesy Paul Associates.)

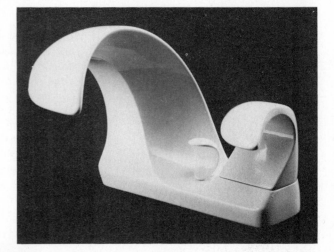

Middle. The sculptural form of the Wave faucet from Moen, Inc. (Photograph courtesy of Moen, Inc.)

Bottom. Kohler Company's Garland™ textured floral pattern from the Tapestries™ line of textured vitreous china products featuring bell-shaped ceramic bases and elongated oval handles with matching insets. (Photograph courtesy of the Kohler Company.)

Some lavatories are punched with one or two extra holes. These are for use as a shampoo lavatory and have a retractable spray unit. The second extra hole is used for a soap or shampoo dispenser. These shampoo lavatories are extremely useful for a family with children as the bowl is usually installed in a 32-inch high vanity as compared to the 36 inches of a kitchen sink. Some styles even have spouts that swing away.

Lavatory Faucets

There is also a wide choice of lavatory faucets. For the past few decades, **center-fit** faucet fittings have been used. With this unit, the two handles and spout are in one piece, with the spread being 4 inches. The single control unit with a 4-inch spread has a central control that regulates both temperature and rate of flow. This single control unit may also work by means of a lever which, when pulled up, increases the flow of water and, when pushed down, decreases the flow. Temperature is controlled by moving the lever to the right for cold and to the left for warmer or hot water. The lever is easier to operate for arthritis victims who cannot grasp and turn the knob type.

The popularity of center-fit faucets is declining, and the use of the spread-fit fittings now comprise 80 percent of the market and growing. Spread-fit faucets have the hot and cold handles and the spout independent of each other. In order to make installation and choice of faucet sets easier, the fittings should be joined by means of flexible connectors. If these flexible connectors are not used, selection of faucets may be limited to the spread of the holes that come in the selected lavatory. When the center-fit fittings are used, the plate covers the center hole. When a spread-fit fitting is used the center hole accommodates the spout.

The Sensorflo™ faucet from Speakman Company, is ergonomically designed as a barrier-free product and is primarily concerned with water conservation. When the electronic beam is broken by the hands, the water flows at the preset temperature. Savings of up to 85 percent of normal water usage are not unusual. Additional energy savings are realized by conserving hot water (see Figure 9–8).

Moen also produces a Riser for lavatories. This spout lifts 7 inches above the sink for washing hair or watering plants. The spout tip swivels to convert to a water fountain.

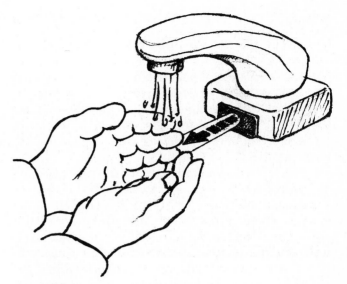

Figure 9-8
The Speakman SENSORFLO™ faucet requires no handles to turn on the flow of water. Drawing courtesy of Speakman Co.

Faucets may be polished chrome, black chrome, polished brass, or even gold plated. One of the current trends is using two different finishes in the same faucet such as black chrome with polished chrome and/or polished brass, wood and brass, and brushed nickel with brass. Two finishes are often used on what is known as the *ring handle* (see Figure 9–1). Delta Faucet Company has ring handles suitable for retrofit, so a new appearance can be given the bathroom without great cost. Translucent and metal handles have slight indentations in order to provide a nonslipping surface. Other handles may be of the lever type. The traditional shape for spouts is being replaced by the more delicately curved shape which is popular in Europe The Roman-style faucets previously used for bathtubs are now being used for lavatories (see Figure 9–1).

What has previously been a feature of kitchen faucets has now come to the bathroom. Delta has a 4-inch centerset faucet with a new pull-out spout which can extend to 21 inches and may be used for washing hair, bathing infants, filling containers, and even washing the family pet (in the utility room, of course).

For use by the handicapped are the **wrist control** handles that do not require turning or pulling but are activated by a push or pull with the wrist rather than the fingers (see Figure 8–6).

Toilets

In Europe, the toilet is often called the *water closet* and the plumbing trade frequently uses the term *water closet* or *closet* when referring to what the lay- man calls a toilet. In some areas of the country, it may also be referred to as a commode. We will use the word "toilet" in the text as this is the more common word, but when talking to a plumber, "closet" is more correct.

Toilet bowls are constructed of vitreous china and in most instances, so are the tanks. However, some tanks may be made of other materials. Only vitreous china can withstand the acids to which a toilet is subjected. Most toilets are designed with water-saving devices that are important considera- tions, both economically and environmentally.

There are two basic shapes to a toilet: the regular or round-bowl and the elongated bowl (see Figure 9–1). Toilets do not come with a toilet seat and, therefore, it is important to know the shape of the toilet before ordering a seat. Another design feature of the elongated bowl is that more space, usually 2 inches, is required for installation. Consult local building codes.

Toilets may be *wall hung*, which leaves the floor unobstructed for easy cleaning, or *floor mounted*. Wall hung toilets have a wall outlet; in other words, they flush through a drain in the wall. In order to support the weight of a wall-hung toilet, 6-inch studs must be used and an L-shaped unit called a *chair carrier* must be installed.

Floor-mounted toilets flush through the floor or the wall. For concrete floor construction, wall outlets are suggested to eliminate the extra cost of slab piercing.

Another choice in the design of toilets is whether tank and bowl should be a **low profile**, one-piece integral unit, or whether the tank and bowl should be in two pieces (see Figure 9–1 for a one-piece toilet). For space saving in powder rooms or bathrooms, a corner toilet, an Eljer exclusive, is available. The nostalgia of the past can be created by using an overhead wall-hung tank with the traditional pull chain. In areas where condensation on the toilet tank is a problem, an insulated tank may be ordered.

All toilets are required to have a visible water turn off down near the bowl on the back wall in case of a faulty valve in the tank.

Toilets for the elderly and infirm have an 18-inch high seat, while regular toilets have 15 1/2-inch high seats. This higher toilet may also have a set of metal rails or armrests for extra support. The height of the seat on the one piece toilets may be even lower.

Toilets have different flushing actions. The wash- down is the least expensive but is also the least efficient and the noisiest. The least inexpensive of the siphon-action toilets is the reverse trap, where the rush of water when flushed creates a siphon action in the trapway, assisted by a small water jet at the trapway outlet. More of the bowl is covered by water, so it stays cleaner. The siphon-jet that is used on almost all newer toilets is much quieter and more efficient but usually more expensive. However, most of the interior of the bowl is covered by water, thus aiding in cleaning.

Where 3.5 gallons per flush used to be the code, 1.6 gals is now the code in many cities, a savings that could add up substantially for an average family of four in these days of critical water shortages. A European import even has double handed flushers to vary the amount of water in each flush.

Bidets

While common in Europe, bidets are only now be- coming an accepted fixture in American bathrooms and then only in the more sophisticated types of installations. A bidet is generally installed as a com- panion and adjacent to the water closet or toilet and is used for cleansing the perineal area. Bidets do not have seats. The user sits astride the bowl, facing the controls that regulate water temperature and operate the pop-up drain and transfer valve. Water enters the bidet via the spray rinse in the bottom of the bowl; or the water can be diverted by the transfer valve to the flushing rim. A bidet may also be used as a foot bath when the pop-up drain is closed (see Figure 9–1).

When, as in a bidet, the fresh water supply is below or directly involved with piping, a **vacuum breaker** must be installed.

Countertops

The term *vanity cabinet* is not technically used in the architectural profession, but ready-made bathroom cabinets containing the lavatory are so often called and sold by this name that this term will be used for the prefinished cabinet with doors underneath the countertop. Vanity cabinets may be ordered with or without the finished countertop and, with this de- sign, the lavatory is purchased separately. Other types of vanities may come with the countertop and bowl molded in one.

A ready-made vanity is between 29 and 30 inches in height. For a master bathroom in a custom-designed house, the counter can be raised to suit personal requirements; however, at least one of the vanities in the house must be at the lower height.

Most custom-designed bathrooms have specially designed cabinets containing the lavatory with a storage area beneath. A bathroom countertop may be made of the same materials as a kitchen counter, though marble is more frequently used in bathrooms than kitchens.

Accessories

There should be 22 inches of towel storage for each person. Towels should be located within convenient reach of the bath, shower, and lavatory. Soap containers may be recessed into the wall, such as those used the the tub area. For the lavatory with a counter, a soap dish can be a colorful accessory. A toilet tissue dispenser should be conveniently located adjacent to the toilet.

Ground frequency interrupters (GFI) electrical outlets should also be provided for the myriad of electrical gadgets used in the bathroom. All switches should be located so that they cannot be reached from a tub or shower area. This is usually required by local codes.

Mirrors may be on the door of a built-in medicine cabinet or they may be installed to cover the whole wall over the counter area. When used in the latter manner, they visibly enlarge the bathroom. The top of the mirror should be at least 72 inches above the floor.

Broan has a wall-mounted hair dryer with two-speed control. The flexible hose reaches 72 inches to allow ample freedom of movement while drying hair.

The materials selected for floors, walls and ceilings should be compatible with the moist conditions that prevail in most bathrooms.

PUBLIC RESTROOMS

The bathrooms previously discussed were designed to accommodate one or two people at the most. However, in public restrooms, conditions and location may mean designing an area to be used by many people at the same time. This includes not only people who can walk, but also those using wheel chairs.

Public restrooms receive much physical abuse, most of which is not premeditated, but occurs through normal wear and tear. Unfortunately, vandalism is a major problem and, therefore, fixtures and materials must be selected for durability. Naturally, the two-stall restroom in a small restaurant and the multistall restrooms in a huge recreational facility will have to be designed differently with this factor in mind.

Another factor in the selection of materials and fixtures is maintenance. Floors are almost always made of ceramic tile or similar material and require a floor drain not only for an emergency flooding problem, but also to facilitate the cleaning and disinfecting of the floor.

Lavatories

To aid in cleaning the counter areas of public restrooms, vitreous china lavatories with flush metal rims are most frequently specified. This provides quick cleaning of any excess water on the counter. White sinks are usually selected in rest rooms for two reasons: first, they are cheaper and, second, cleanliness is more easily visible.

Lavatories come with the normal three holes punched in the top, but soft or liquid soap dispensers may be installed in a four hole sink. Or, the soap dispenser may be attached to the wall above each lavatory or between two adjacent ones.

For free-standing applications, wall-hung vitreous china lavatories may be specified.

For those who are confined to wheelchairs, a specially designed lavatory must be installed that enables the seated person to reach the faucet handles. Again, a wrist control handle or a push button that requires five pounds or less pressure should be specified. Because some wheelchair occupants are paraplegic, it is necessary to take safety precautions that include either turning down the temperature of the water to 110° or wrapping the waste pipe with some form of insulation. These measures will prevent inadvertent burns (see Figure 9–4).

Faucets

Some companies specialize in faucets designed to be used in public restrooms. These faucets are available with **metering devices**, usually of the push-button type, that can be adjusted to flow for 5 to 15 seconds.

This, of course, conserves both energy and water and prevents accidental flooding.

Toilets

Wall-hung toilets are quite often used in public restrooms to facilitate cleaning. Toilet seats do not have lids and must have an open front. To aid in quicker maintenance and to avoid vandalism, toilets in public restrooms do not usually use the conventional tank, but have a **flushometer** valve. This valve requires greater **water pressure** to operate but uses less water and is easier to maintain. This type of valve is not used in private residences because it is too noisy.

Several different types of **urinals** may be used in the men's room. All are constructed of vitreous china and all have integral flushing rims. One is the stall urinal mounted on the floor. Others may be wall hung, with a wall-hung unit with an elongated front for use by those who are physically disabled.

Stall Partitions

There are many different styles of stall dividers and many different materials from which to select. The **pilasters** may be floor mounted with overhead bracing, floor supported, or ceiling hung. The latter type minimizes maintenance but also requires structural steel support in the ceiling. Doors for regular stalls are 24 inches are wide and open into the stall. The actual width of the stall is determined by the width of the pilasters.

Figure 9-9
Marblstal® made of Georgia Marble® is perfect for toilet compartments and urinal screens as shown in this photograph. Marblstall is prefabricated, ready to install with rugged chrome plated hardware included. Photograph courtesy of The Georgia Marble Company.

Stalls for the handicapped have wider, outswinging doors, which must meet applicable codes. The handicapped stall is usually placed at the end so that a passer-by is not hit when the door is opened from the inside (see Figure 9–10).

The materials used for partitions may be galvanized steel that has been primed and finished with two coats of baked, stainless steel, seamless high-pressure decorative laminate, or even marble (see Figures 9–9 and 9–10). All of these come in a variety of colors and may be coordinated with the colors used for washroom accessories, vanity centers, shelves, and countertops.

When the design of restrooms dictates, entrance screens for privacy should be used. It is important to consider the direction the door opens and placement of mirrors to ensure privacy.

Another screen used in men's rooms is the urinal screen. These may also be wall hung, floor anchored, ceiling hung, or supported by a narrow stile going from floor to ceiling, in a similar manner to the stall partitions. They are placed between each urinal or between the urinal area and other parts of the rest room (see Figure 9–9).

Accessories

As was mentioned previously, soap dispensers may be installed on the lavatory rim itself. This type is probably preferable as any droppings from the dispenser are washed away in the bowl; the dry powder type usually leave a mess on the counter area. Paper towel dispensers should be within easy reach of the lavatory, together with towel disposal containers. Sometimes both these accessories come in one wall-hung or wall-recessed unit. Another method of hand drying is the heated air blower. At the push of a button, heated air is blown out and the hands are rubbed briskly. This type of hand dryer eliminates the necessity of having the mess of paper towel disposal, but is a problem if the dryer breaks down.

Each toilet compartment requires a toilet tissue dispenser; an optional accessory is the toilet seat cover dispenser. Necessary in each toilet stall in a ladies room is a feminine napkin disposal and outside, near the toilet stalls, a napkin and tampon vending machine. Optional in a toilet stall is a hook for hanging pocketbooks and jackets. The preferred location is on the handle side of the door so that no personal items are left behind. Another optional accessory in the ladies toilet stalls is a flip-down shelf that holds packages off the floor area.

Figure 9-10
Interior of handicapped stall. Note handrail and outswinging doors. Photograph courtesy of The Georgia Marble Company.

In handicapped stalls, stainless steel grab bars are required by law to be mounted on the wall nearest the toilet. They are 1 1/2 inches in diameter and 1 1/2 inches from the wall and 33 inches from the floor. Local codes vary from city to city and state to state, so it is important to consult these codes for exact measurements.

There are two methods of transfer for the wheel-chair-bound people, depending upon their abilities. Those who are able to stand with support can pull themselves upright by means of the grab bars. Others have to use the side transfer method, where the arm of the wheelchair is removed and the person leans across the toilet and pulls themselves onto the seat. The side transfer method requires a larger stall, as the chair must be placed alongside the toilet; the front transfer requires only the depth of the chair, plus standing room in front of the toilet.

BIBLIOGRAPHY

Mazzurco, Philip. Bath Design, New York: Whitney Library of Design, and imprint of Watson-Guptil Publications, 1986.

GLOSSARY

Bidet. A sanitary fixture for cleansing the genito-urinary area of the body (see Figure 9–1).

Center-fit. Two handles and one spout mounted on a single plate.

Centers. Another way of saying on centers; in other words, the measurement is from the center of one hole to the center of the second hole.

Compartmented. Bathroom divided into separate areas according to function and fixtures.

Diverter. Changes flow of water from one area to another.

Feed-in. Where the rough plumbing is attached to the fittings.

Fittings. Another word for the faucet assembly; a term used by the plumbing industry.

Flushometer. A valve designed to supply a fixed quantity of water for flushing purposes (see Figure 9–10).

Gel coat. A thin, outer layer of resin, sometimes containing pigment, applied to a reinforced plastic moulding to improve its appearance.

GFI Ground Frequency Interrupters. A special electrical outlet for areas where water is present.

Lavatory. The plumbing industry's name for a bathroom sink.

Low profile. A one-piece toilet with almost silent flushing action having almost no dry surfaces on the bowl interior.

Metering device. A preset measured amount of water is released when activated.

Overflow. A pipe in bathtubs and lavatories used to prevent flooding. The pipe is located just below the rim or top edge of these fixtures.

Pedestal. A lavatory on a base attached to the floor rather than set into a counter surface. Base hides all the waste pipes that are usually visible.

Pilaster. Vertical support member, varying in width.

Pop-up rod. The rod that controls the raising and lowering of the drain in the bottom of the lavatory.

Pre-formed base. Shower pans or bases of terrazzo or acrylic.

Sauna. A steam bath of Finnish origin.

Slip-resistant. Special material on the bottom of the tub to prevent falls.

Spa. Whirlpool type bath for more than one person, with a heating and filtration system. Frequently installed out side in warmer climates.

Spread. Distance between holes of a bathtub or lavatory faucet.

Surround. The walls encircling a bathtub or shower area (see Figures 9–1 and 9–4).

Urinals. Wall hung vitreous plumbing fixtures used in men's rooms, with a flushometer valve for cleaning purposes (see Figure 9–9).

Vacuum breaker. A device which prevents water from being siphoned back into the potable water system.

Vanity. Layman's term for a prefabricated lavatory and base cabinet.

Water pressure. Measured as so many pounds per square inch. Usually 30 to 50 psi.

Wet wall. The wall in which the water and waste pipes are located.

Wrist control. Long lever handles operated by pressure of the wrist rather than with the fingers.

Manufacturers
and Associations

Some materials such as the stones do not have manufacturers and these materials may only be found through the Yellow Pages. For information on other manufacturers not listed in the Yellow Pages, write to the addresses in Appendix B.

Remember that the names listed are just a few of those manufacturing that particular product. As far as possible, the listed names are nationally distributed items, but there are many local products that may be similar in quality.

Associations and Institutes represent their members in sales promotions and informational services only. They do not sell products, but many can provide a list of suppliers in your area.

CHAPTER 1

*Paints**
Benjamin Moore & Co.
The Glidden Company
Sherwin Williams

*Stains**
Olympic Stain

*Denotes that the local distributor may be found in the Yellow Pages under the particular product, brand name or manufacturer's name.

*Danish Oil**
Watco Dennis Corp.

CHAPTER 2

The Carpet and Rug Institute (CRI) is the trade association representing the dynamic carpet and rug industry.

Carpet Manufacturers*
Mannington Mills, Inc.

Dirt Control Foot Mats and Grating
J. L. Industries
Monsanto Chemical Co.
Nuway Matting Systems, Inc.

CHAPTER 3

Associations and Institutes
American National Standards Institute (ANSI) sets the codes and standards based on consensus of their membership.

American Parquet Association represents some of the parquet manufacturers and prints a brochure listing manufacturers and the types of patterns each company produces.

American Society for Testing and Materials (ASTM) sets the standard for all types of products.

Hardwood Plywood Manufacturers Association (HPMA) with ANSI sets the standards of hardwood and decorative plywood.

Marble Institute of America represents the marble industry. They have a publication, *How to Keep your Marble Lovely*, which is available from the address in Appendix B.

National Oak Flooring Manufacturers Association (NOFMA) sets the standards by which wood flooring should be installed.

National Terrazzo and Mosaic Association, Inc., represents the terrazzo industry.

National Wood Flooring Association represents the wood floor industry.

The Tile Council of America, Inc. publishes *CERAMIC TILE: The Installation Handbook* annually. These specifications cover all types of tile installations and are a guide for the tile industry.

Strip Finished
Bruce Hardwood Floors
Mannington Wood Floors
Robbins Inc.

Plank Unfinished
Bruce Hardwood Floors
Kentucky Wood Floors Inc.
Tarkett

Plank Finished
Bruce Hardwood Floors
Robbins Inc.
Harris-Tarkett

Parquet
Anderson Hardwood Floors
Bruce Hardwood Floors
Kentucky Wood Floors Inc.
Memphis Hardwood Flooring Co.
Oregon Lumber Co.
Harris-Tarkett

Acrylic Impregnated
Gammapar, Applied Radiant Energy Co.,
Hartco

Foam backed Parquet
Hartco.
Robbins Inc.

Prefinished Parquet
Kentucky Wood Floors Inc.
Robbins Hardwood Flooring

Mesquite
Du Bose Architectural Floors

End Grain
Du Bose Architectural Floors
Jennison-Wright Corp.

Inlaid Border
Bangkok Industries
Kentucky Wood Floors Inc.
Tarkett

Laminated Wood Floors
Robbins Inc.
Tarkett

Marble
The Georgia Marble Co.

Marble Veneers
Terrazzo & Marble Supply Co.
The Georgia Marble Co.

Cast Marble
Armstar

Backer Board
Durock®
Hardibacker® from James Hardie Building Products
UTIL-A-CRETE® distributed by American Olean
Wonderboard® Glascrete Inc.

Agglomerate
Terrazzo & Marble Supply Co.

Granite*
Terrazzo & Marble Supply Co.
The Granitech Corp.

Flagstone*

Slate*
Buckingham-Virginia Slate Corp.
Structural Slate Co.

Ceramic Tile*
Buchtal USA
Dal Tile
Florida Tile, Division of Sikes Corp.
Summitville Tile Co.

Ceramic Mosaic Tile*

Pregrouted Ceramic Tile*

Quarry Tile*

Mexican Tile*
U.S.A. Solarq

Glass Block
Pittsburgh Corning Corp.

Monolithic Terrazzo*

Terrazzo
Fritz Chemical Corp.
Wausau Tile Inc.

Brick

Floor Maintenance*
Hillyard

Vinyl Composition
Kentile Floors

Vinyl Tile
Kentile Floors

Conductive Vinyl Tile
Kentile Floors

Vinyl and Rubber Bases
Burke Flooring
Johnson Rubber
Kentile

Rubber Tile and/or Sheet
Endura, Division of Biltrite Corp.
R.C.A. Rubber Co.
Roppe Corporation

Sheet Vinyl
Congoleum
Mannington Mills, Inc.
Custom Designed Vinyl
GMT Floor Tile Inc.

Cork
Dodge-Regupol Inc.
Ipocork

Decorative Laminate
Perma-Kleen, Ralph Wilson Plastics

CHAPTER 4

Associations and Institutes
The Architectural Woodwork Institute (AWI) is a nonprofit organization devoted to the elevation of industry standards, to continuing research into new and better materials and methods, and to the publication of technical data helpful to architects and specification writers in the design and use of architectural woodwork. Write for the price list covering all the books mentioned in this book as well as many others.

The National Association of Mirror Manufacturers promotes the many uses of mirror and produces a compilation of outstanding mirror ideas by leading interior designers.

Granite*
Veneer—Stone Panels Inc.

Marble*
Georgia Marble Co.

Veneer
Stone Panels Inc.

Travertine*

Brick*

Concrete Block*

Glass Block
Pittsburgh Corning Corp.

Plaster*

Gypsum Wallboard
Gold Bond Building Products
SHEETROCK, U.S.G. Interiors Inc.

Vinyl-Surfaced Gypsum Wall Panels
Gold Bond Building Products

Wallpaper
Anaglypta®, Mile Hi Crown.
Katzenbach & Warren
Albert Van Luit & Co.

Paperbacking Fabrics
Custom Laminations, Inc.

Commercial Wallcoverings
Bay View Wallcoverings
Blumenthal Inc.
Koroseal Wallcoverings
Jack Lenor Larsen
MDC Wallcoverings
Numetal Surfaces
Tretford from Eurotex

Tambours
Flexible Materials Inc.
National Products

Redwood*
California Redwood Association

Solid Wood Strips*
Potlatch Corp.

Plywood Paneling*
Consult a member of the Architectural Woodwork
Institute

Prefinished Plywood*

Hardboard*
Masonite

Decorative Laminate
Formica Corp.
Nevamar Corp.
Ralph Wilson Plastics

Duraplex
Triarch Industries

Glass
Restoration Glass™ Bendheim Co.
Taliq Varilite™ Vision Panels

Mirror*

Metal*

Acoustic Panels
Forbo-Vicracoustic Inc.

Cork
Other Materials
Paleo® Forms + Surfaces
Vitricor®, Nevamar Corp.

CHAPTER 5

Plaster Ceiling Tiles
Above View, Inc.

Wood*
Any of the wood flooring manufacturers

Acoustic Ceiling—Residential
Armstrong

Acoustic Ceiling—Commercial
Armstrong
Hunter Douglas, Architectural Products
USG Interiors, Inc.
Forbo-Vicracoustics Inc.

Mirrored Effect
Mitsubishi North America
USG Interiors, Inc.

Banners and Others
Barrisol North America, Inc.
Dome It®, The Original Dome Ceiling, Inc.

Stamped Metal Ceiling
AA Abbingdon Affiliates, Inc.
Chelsea Decorative Metal Co.
W. F. Norman Corp.
Pinecrest
Shanker Industries

Strip Metal Ceilings
Shanker
Alcan Building Products
Hunter Douglas Inc., Architectural Products

CHAPTER 6

The Door and Hardware Institute promotes those two industries.

Mouldings
Driwood Moulding Co.
Focal Point
Old World Moulding

Doors
Customwood
Kentucky Millwork
Pinecrest Inc.

Hinges
Grass America
Hager Hinge Co.
Soss

*Hardware**
Baldwin Hardware

The Broadway Collection
Gainsborough Hardware Industries Inc.
Sargent
Schlage Lock Co.
Stanley Hardware Division
Valli & Colombo (USA) Inc.
Yale Security

Glass Door Hardware
HEWI Inc.
Hiawatha Inc.

*Closers**
Corbin Architectural Hardware, A Black & Decker Co.
LCN Closers
Rixson-Firemark

*Keyless Locks**
InteLock^R

CHAPTER 7

Shelving
Knape & Vogt Manufacturing Co.

CHAPTER 8

Kitchen Cabinets
Allmilmo
Amera Custom Cabinetry
Poggenpohl U.S., Inc.
Quaker Maid
The St. Charles Companies
Siematic Corp.
Wood-Mode Cabinetry

Kitchen Appliances
Amana Refrigeration Inc.
DACOR
Gaggenau US Corp.
KitchenAid
SubZero Freezer Co.
Thermador/Waste King
Traulsen & Co., Inc.

Restaurant Ranges
Russell Range, Inc.
Welbilt Appliance, Inc.

Under counter Refrigerators and Coolers
Marvel-Industries
Up-Line Corp.

Exhaust Fans
Thermador
WCI

Kitchen Sinks
Elkay Manufacturing Co.
Moen Inc.
Kohler
Elkay

Kitchen Faucets
Chicago Faucet
Delta
Elkay Manufacturing Co.
Kroin Inc.
Moen Inc.
Speakman Company

Kitchen Counters
Formica Corp.
Wilsonart

Solid Surface Materials
Corian®, DuPont
Avonite® Avonite, Inc.
Fountainhead®, Nevamar
GIBRALTAR® Ralph Wilson Plastics
Novastone®, Johnstone Industries
Surell®, Formica Corp.

CHAPTER 9

Plumbing Fixture Manufacturers
American Standard
Eljer
Jacuzzi Whirlpool Bath
Kohler
Universal Rundle Corp.

Lavatories
Broadway Collection
Sherle Wagner

Faucets
Chicago Faucet
Delta
Moen Inc.
Speakman Company

Accessories
Broan Mfg. Co. Inc.

Commercial Bathroom Fixtures
Briggs
Eljer

Stall Partitions
Accurate Partitions Corp.
The Georgia Marble Co.

Bathroom Accessories—Commercial
Bobrick Washroom Equipment Inc.
HEWI Inc.
Sanymetal Products

B

Resources

AA Abbingdon Affiliates, Inc.
2149 Utica Avenue
Brooklyn NY 11234

Above View, Inc.
241 East Erie Street
Milwaukee WI 53202

Accurate Partitions Corp.
P.O. Box 287
Lyons IL 60534

Allcan Building Products
9900 Brookford Street
Charlotte NC 28273

Allmillmo Corp.
P.O. Box 629
Fairfield NJ 07006

Amana Refrigeration Inc.
Amana IA 52204

Amera Custom Cabinetry
Adrian MI 49221

American National Standards Institute
1430 Broadway
New York NY 10018

American Olean Tile
Lansdale PA 19446-0271

American Society for Testing and Materials
1916 Rose Street
Philadelphia PA 19103

American Standard Inc.
P.O. Box 6820
Piscataway NJ 08855-6820

Anderson Hardwood Floors
P.O. Box 1155
Clinton SC 29325

Applied Radiant Energy Co.
P.O. Box 289
Forest VA 24521

Architectural Woodwork Institute
13924 Braddock Road
Centreville VA 22020

Armstar
P.O. Box 820
Lenoir City TN 37771

Armstrong World Industries Inc.
P.O. Box 3001
Lancaster PA 17604

Avonite Inc.
1945 Highway 304
Belen NM 87002

Azrock Industries Inc.
P.O. Box 34030
San Antonio TX 78265

Baldwin Hardware Corp.
P.O. Box 15048
Reading PA 19612

Bangkok Industries Inc.
Gillingham & Worth Street
Philadelphia PA 19124

Barrisol North America Inc.
1340 Depot Street, Suite 110
Cleveland OH 44116

Bay View Wallcoverings
41 East Sunrise Hwy.
Lindenhurst NY 11757

S.A. Bendheim Co., Inc.
661 Willett Street
Passaic NJ 07055

Bentley Brothers
918 Baxter Avenue
Louisville KY 40204

Blumenthal Inc.
42-20 12 Street
Long Island City NY 11101

Bobrick Washroom Equipment Inc.
11611 Hart Street
North Hollywood CA 91605

The Broadway Collection
250 N. Troost Street
Olathe KS 66061

Broan Mfg. Co. Inc.
Hartford WI 53027

Bruce Hardwood Floors
16803 Dallas Parkway
Dallas TX 75248

Buckingham-Virginia Slate Corporation
P.O. Box 8
Arvonia VA 23004-0008

Burke Flooring Products a division of Burke
Industries
2250 South Tenth Street
San Jose CA 95112

California Redwood Association
591 Redwood Highway, Suite 3100
Mill Valley CA 94941

Carpet Cushion Council
P.O. Box 546
Riverside CT 06878

Celotex Corporation
P.O. Box 22602
Tampa FL 33622

Chelsea Decorative Metal Co.
9603 Moonlight
Houston TX 77096

Chicago Faucet
2100 South Nuclear Drive
Des Plaines IL 60018-5999

Congoleum Corporation
195 Belgrove Drive
Kearny NJ 07032

Corbin Architectural Hardware
A Black & Decker Co.
225 Episcopal Road
Berlin CT 06037

Custom Laminations Inc.
P.O. Box 2066
Paterson NJ 07509

Customwood
Box 26208
Albuquerque NM 87125

DACOR
950 South Raymond Avenue
Pasadena CA 91109-7202

Dal-Tile Corp.
P.O. Box 17130
Dallas TX 75217

Delta Faucet Co.
P.O. Box 40980
Indianapolis IN 46280

Dodge-Rugupol Inc.
P.O. Box 989
Lancaster PA 17603

Door and Hardware Institute
7711 Old Springhouse Road
McLean VA 22102-3474

Driwood Moulding Company
P.O. Box 1729
Florence SC 29503

Du Bose Architectural Floors
905 San Pedro
San Antonio TX 78212

E. I. DuPont de Nemours & Co. Corian Products
Market Street Room X39196
Wilmington DE 19898

Eljer Plumbingware
901 10th Street
Plano TX 75086

Elkay Manufacturing Co.
2222 Camden Court
Oak Brook IL 60521

Endura, Division of Biltrite Corp.
Two University Office Park
Waltham MA 02254-9045

Eurotex
165 West Ontario Street
Philadelphia PA 19140

Flexible Materials Inc.
11209 Electron Drive
Louisville KY 40299

Florida Tile, Division of Sikes Corp.
P.O. Box 447
Lakeland FL 33802

Focal Point Inc.
P.O. Box 93327
Atlanta GA 30377-0327

Forbo Vicracoustic
135 Lions Drive
Valmont Industrial Park
West Hazelton, PA 18201

Forms + Surfaces
Box 5215
Santa Barbara CA 93150

Formica Corp.
10155 Reading Road
Cincinnati OH 45241

Fritz Chemical Company
P.O. Drawer 17040
Dallas TX 75217

Gaggenau USA Corp.
425 University Avenue
Norwood MA 02062

Gainsborough Hardware Industries Inc.
3640 Windsor Park Drive N.E. Suite 100
Suwanee GA 30174

GE Monogram
GE Appliances
Louisville KY 40225

The Georgia Marble Company
Structural Division
Nelson GA 30151

Glascrete Inc.
13001 Seal Beach Blvd
Seal Beach CA 90740

The Glidden Company
925 Euclid Avenue
Cleveland OH 44115

GMT Floor Tile Inc.
1255 Oak Point Avenue
Bronx NY 10474

Gold Bond Building Products
2001 Rexford Road
Charlotte NC 28211-3498

Granitech Corp.
P.O. Box 1780
Fairfield IA 52556-1780

Grass America Inc
P.O. Box 1019
Kennersville NC 27284

Hager Hinge Co.
139 Victor Street
St. Louis MO 63104

James Hardie Building Products, Inc.
26300 La Alameda, Suite 400
Mission Viejo CA 92691

Hardwood Plywood Manufacturers Association
P.O. Box 2789
Reston VA 22090

Harris-Tarkett
P.O. Box 300
Johnson City TN 37601

Hartco Inc.
P.O. Drawer A
Oneida TN 37841

HEWI Inc.
2851 Old Tree Drive
Lancaster PA 17603

Hiawatha Inc.,
4450 W. 78th Street Circle
Bloomington MN 55435

Hillyard, Inc.
P.O. Box 909
St. Joseph MO 64502-0909

Hunter Douglas Inc. Architectural Products
11455 Lakefield Drive
Duluth GA 30136

J.L. Industries
4450 W. 78th Street Circle
Bloomington MN 55435

Ipocork
1590 N. Roberts Road
Building 100, Suite 104
Kennesaw GA 30144

Jacuzzi Whirlpool Bath
P.O. Drawer J
Walnut Creek CA 94596

Jason Industrial Inc.
340 Kaplan Drive
Fairfield NJ 07006

Jenn-Air Company
3035 Shadeland
Indianapolis IN 46226-0901

Johnson Rubber Co.
16025 Johnson Street
Middlefield OH 44062

Katzenbach & Warren
200 Garden City Plaza
Garden City NY 11530

Kentile Floors
58 Second Avenue
Brooklyn NY 11215

Kentucky Millwork Inc.
4200 Reservoir Avenue
Louisville KY 40213

Kentucky Wood Floors Inc.
P.O. Box 33276
Louisville KY 40232

KitchenAid
701 Main Street
St. Joseph MI 49085

Knape & Vogt Manufacturing Co.
2700 Oak Industrial Drive N.E.
Grand Rapids MI 49505

Kohler Company
Kohler WI 53044

Koroseal Wallcoverings
3875 Embassy Parkway
Fairlawn OH 44333

Kroin Architectural Complements
14 Story Street
Cambridge MA 02138

Jack Lenor Larsen Inc.
41 East 11th Street
New York NY 10003

LCN Closers
P.O. Box 100
Princeton IL 61656

Luck Stone Corp.
P.O. Box 29682
Richmond VA 23229

Mannington Mills Inc.
P.O. Box 30
Salem NJ 08079

Mannington Wood Floors
1327 Lincoln Drive
High Point NC 27260-9945

Marble Institute of America Inc.
33505 State Street
Farmington MI 48025

Marlite
P.O. Box 250
Dover OH 44622

Marvel Industries
P.O. Box 997
Richmond IN 47375-0997

MDC Wallcoverings
1200 Arthur Avenue
Elk Grove IL 60007

Memphis Hardwood Flooring Co.
1551 Thomas Street
Memphis TN 38107

Mile Hi Crown, Inc.
D/B/A/ Crown Corporation. NA
1801 Wynkoop Suite 235
Denver CO 80202

Mitsubishi North America
100 Wade Avenue
South Plainfield NJ 07080

Moen Inc.
377 Woodland Avenue
Elyria OH 44036

Monsanto Chemical Co.
320 Interstate North Parkway
Atlanta GA 30339

Benjamin Moore & Co.
51 Chestnut Ridge Road
Montvale NJ 07645-1862

National Association of Mirror Manufacturers
9005 Congressional Court
Potomac MD 20854

National Oak Flooring Manufacturers' Association
Inc.
P.O. Box 3009
Memphis TN 38173-0009

National Products
900 Baxter Avenue
Louisville KY 40204

National Terrazzo and Mosaic Association
3166 Des Plaines Avenue
Des Plaines IL 60018

National Wood Flooring Association
11046 Manchester Road
St. Louis MO 63122

Nevamar Corp.
8339 Telegraph Road
Odenton MD 21113

W. F. Norman Corporation
P.O. Box 323
Nevada MO 64772

Numetal Surfaces Inc.
235 Pavilion Avenue
Riverside NJ 08075

Nuway Matting Systems Inc.
8 Sagamore Street
Glen Falls NY 12801

Old World Moulding & Finishing Inc.
115 Allen Boulevard
Farmingdale NY 11735

Oregon Lumber Company
P.O. Box 711
Lake Oswego OR 97034

The Original Dome Ceiling, Inc.
2037 J and C Boulevard
Naples FL 33942

Osterman & Scheiwe USA
P.O. Box 669
Spanaway WA 98387

PermaGrain Products Inc.
13 West Third Street
Media PA 19063

Pinecrest Inc.
2118 Blaisdell Avenue
Minneapolis MN 55404

Pittcon Industries Inc.
6409 Rhode Island Avenue
Riverdale MD 20737-1098

Pittsburgh Corning Corp.
800 Presque Isle Drive
Pittsburgh PA 15239

Poggenpohl U.S. Inc.
5905 Johns Road
Tampa FL 33634

Potlatch Corp., Townsend Unit
P.O. Box 916
Stuttgart AR 72160

Quaker Maid
Rt 61
Leesport PA 19533

RCA Rubber Co. an Ohio Corp. of Akron Ohio
1833 E. Market Street
Akron OH 44305

Rixson-Firemark
9100 W. Belmont Avenue
Franklin Park IL 60131

Robbins Hardwood Flooring
P.O. Box 999
Warren AR 71671

Roppe Corp.
1602 N. Union Street
Fostoria OH 44830

Russell Range Inc.
325 South Maple Avenue
South San Francisco CA 94080

The St. Charles Companies
1401 Greenbrier Parkway, Suite 200
Chesapeake VA 23320

The Sanymetal Products Co. Inc.
1705 Urbana Road
Cleveland OH 44112

Sargent, Unit of L. B. Foster Co.
P.O. Box 9725
New Haven CT 06536

Schlage Lock Co.
P.O. Box 193324
San Francisco CA 94119

Shanker Industries Inc.
P.O. Box·3116,
Seacaucus NJ 07096

Sherle Wagner International Inc.
60 East 57th Street
New York NY 10022

Sherwin Williams Co.
101 Prospect Avenue N.W.
Cleveland OH 44115

SieMatic Corporation
One Neshaminy Interplex
Suite 207
Trevose PA 19047

Simplex Security Systems Inc.
P.O. Box 377
Collinsville CT 06022

H. Soss & Co.
P.O. Box 45707
Los Angeles CA 90045

Speakman Company
P.O. Box 191
Wilmington DE 19899-0191

Stanley Hardware Division
Box 1840
New Britain CT 06050

Stone Panels Inc.
1725 Sandy Lake Road
Carrollton TX 75006

The Structural Slate Co.
P.O. Box 187
Pen Argyl PA 18072-01

Stone Panels Inc.
1725 Sandy Lake Road
Carrollton TX 75006

SubZero Freezer Co.
P.O. Box 4130
Madison WI 53711-0130

Summitville Tiles Inc.
Summitville OH 43962

Taliq Corporation
1277 Reamwood Avenue
Sunnyvale CA 94089-2234

Tarkett Inc.
P.O. Box 264
Parsippany NJ 07054

Terrazzo and Marble Supply Co.
5700 South Hamilton Avenue
Chicago IL 60636

Thermador/Waste King
5119 District Boulevard
Los Angeles CA 90040

Tile Council of America Inc.
P.O. Box 326
Princeton NJ 08542-0326

Traulsen & Co., Inc.
P.O. Box 169
College Point NY 11356

Triarch Industries
10605 Stebbens Circle
Houston TX 77043

U-Line Corp.
P.O. Box 23220
Milwaukee WI 53223

U.S.A. Solarq
14560 Woodruff Avenue
Bellflower CA 90706

USG Interiors Inc.
101 South Wacker Drive
Chicago IL 60606-4385

Universal-Rundle Corp.
303 North Street
New Castle PA 16103

Valli & Colombo (USA) Inc.
P.O. Box 245
Duarte CA 91010-0245

Albert Van Luit & Co.
23645 Mercantile Road
Cleveland OH 44122

Watco-Dennis Corp.
19610 Rancho Way
Rancho Dominguez CA 90220

Wausau Tile Inc.
P.O. Box 1520
Wausau WI 54402-1520

Welbilt Appliance, Inc.
P.O. Box 3618
New Hyde Park NY 11042-1287

WCI. White Consolidated Industries
P.O. Box 182056
Columbus OH 43218

Ralph Wilson Plastics Co.
600 General Bruce Drive
Temple TX 76501

Wood-Mode Cabinetry
Kreamer PA 17833

Yale Security Inc.
P.O. Box 25288
Charlotte NC 28229-8010

Index

The index may be used as a dictionary by looking up the word and turning to the page number in parentheses.